Government Procedures and Operations

Insights into Secrecy and Information Policy

Government Procedures and Operations

Additional books and e-books in this series can be found
on Nova's website under the Series tab.

American Political, Economic, and Security Issues

Additional books and e-books in this series can be found
on Nova's website under the Series tab.

GOVERNMENT PROCEDURES AND OPERATIONS

INSIGHTS INTO SECRECY AND INFORMATION POLICY

CLARENCE ARMSTRONG
EDITOR

New York

Library of Congress Cataloging-in-Publication Data

ISBN: 978-1-53615-408-5

Published by Nova Science Publishers, Inc. † New York

CONTENTS

PREFACE

This book is a compilation of government reports from 2018 and 2019 on secrecy and information policies and procedures. The first 49-page report is from January 2019 and begins with an overview of the standards governing – and exceptions applicable to grand jury secrecy. The report examines whether and how the rule of grand jury secrecy and its exceptions apply to Congress. The second report in this book focuses on disclosure requirements that provide transparency so that the electorate, the Senate and employing agencies are aware of potential conflicts of interest that presidential candidates, executive branch nominees and other high-ranking executive officials have. Should Congress consider legislation addressing financial conflicts of interests for executive branch officials, it may revisit disclosure requirements.

The next 3-page report from 2018 revisits the issue of whether courts have inherent authority (and obligation) to release secret grand jury materials. Following this chapter is a discussion on the public release of newly appointed Judge Kavanaugh's records and whether the scope and volume of the records released is similar to previous Supreme Court nominees.

The fifth report provides information on locating military unit histories and individual service records of discharged, retired and deceased military personnel. It also provides information n locating and replacing military awards and medals. Included is contact information for military history centers, websites for additional sources of research and a bibliography of other publications, including related CRS reports. Next, is an exploration of whether executive privilege applies to the communications of a President-Elect. The final chapter in this book is a 76-page analysis of the Resolutions of Inquiry (a simple resolution making a direct request or demand of the President or the head of an executive department to furnish the House with specific factual information in the Administration's possession) and their use in the House from 1947 to 2017.

Chapter 1 - The Fifth Amendment to the U.S. Constitution states that "[n]o person shall be held to answer for a capital, or otherwise infamous crime, unless on a presentment or indictment of a Grand Jury." This provision requires that a federal prosecutor, in order to charge a suspect with a serious federal crime, secure the assent of an independent investigative and deliberative body comprising citizens drawn from the jurisdiction in which the crime would be tried. Federal grand juries serve two primary functions: (1) they aid federal prosecutors in investigating possible crimes by issuing subpoenas for documents, physical evidence, and witness testimony; and (2) they determine whether there is sufficient evidence to charge a criminal suspect with the crime or crimes under investigation.

Traditionally, the grand jury has conducted its work in secret. Secrecy prevents those under scrutiny from fleeing or importuning the grand jurors, encourages full disclosure by witnesses, and protects the innocent from unwarranted prosecution, among other things. The long-established rule of grand jury secrecy is enshrined in Federal Rule of Criminal Procedure 6(e), which provides that government attorneys and the jurors themselves, among others, "must not disclose a matter occurring before the grand jury." Accordingly, as a general matter, persons and entities external to the grand jury process are precluded from obtaining transcripts of grand jury testimony or other documents or information that would reveal what took place in the proceedings, even if the grand jury has concluded its work and even if the information is sought pursuant to otherwise-valid legal processes.

At times, the rule of grand jury secrecy has come into tension with Congress's power of inquiry when an arm of the legislative branch has sought protected materials pursuant to its oversight function. For instance, some courts have determined that the information barrier established in Rule 6(e) extends to congressional inquiries, observing that the Rule contains no reservations for congressional access to grand jury materials that would otherwise remain secret. Nevertheless, the rule of grand jury secrecy is subject to a number of exceptions, both codified and judicially crafted, that permit grand jury information to be disclosed in certain circumstances (usually only with prior judicial authorization). Perhaps the most significant of these for congressional purposes are (1) the exception that allows a court to authorize disclosure of grand jury matters "preliminarily to or in connection with a judicial proceeding," and (2) the exception, recognized by a few courts, that allows a court to authorize disclosure of grand jury matters in special or exceptional circumstances. In turn, some courts have determined that one or both of these exceptions applies to congressional requests for grand jury materials in the context of impeachment proceedings, though there is authority to the contrary.

Additionally, because Rule 6(e) covers only "matters occurring before the grand jury," courts have recognized that documents and information are not independently insulated from disclosure merely because they happen to have been presented to, or considered by, a grand jury. As such, even if Rule 6(e) generally limits congressional access to grand jury information, Congress has a number of tools at its disposal to seek materials connected to a grand jury investigation.

Prior Congresses have considered legislation that would have expressly permitted a court to authorize disclosure of grand jury matters to congressional committees on a showing of substantial need. However, in response to such proposals, the executive branch has voiced concerns that the legislation would raise due-process and separation of-powers issues and potentially undermine the proper functioning of federal grand juries. These concerns may have resulted in Congress declining to alter Rule 6(e). As a result, to the extent Rule 6(e) constrains Congress's ability to conduct oversight, legislation seeking to amend the rules governing grand jury secrecy in a way that would give Congress independent access to grand jury materials may raise additional legal and pragmatic issues for the legislative branch to consider.

Chapter 2 - Recent media reports indicate that the 116th Congress may address government ethics reform, including conflicts of interest among executive branch officials. Federal officials have a basic duty not to allow private gain to influence their government service, which includes "not hold[ing] financial interests that conflict with the conscientious performance of duty." Federal statutes, as well as a code of conduct for executive branch employees, make this principle part of a federal regulatory scheme intended to prevent officials from benefitting personally from their offices. The current federal statutory scheme regulating conflicts between an official's personal financial interests and his or her official duties has three prongs: disclosure, disqualification, and divestiture (i.e., a "3-D system"). This sidebar is the first in a three-part series examining conflicts of interest in the executive branch.

Chapter 3 - This is an edited, reformatted and augmented version of Congressional Research Service Publication No. LSB10201, dated October 5, 2018.

Chapter 4 - This is an edited, reformatted and augmented version of Congressional Research Service Publication No. IN10959, dated August 27, 2018.

Chapter 5 - This guide provides information on locating military unit histories and individual service records of discharged, retired, and deceased military personnel. It also provides information on locating and replacing military awards and medals. Included is contact information for military history centers, websites for additional sources of research, and a bibliography of other publications, including related CRS reports.

Chapter 6 - This is an edited, reformatted and augmented version of Congressional Research Service Publication No. LSB10094, dated March 8, 2018.

Chapter 7 - A resolution of inquiry is a simple resolution making a direct request or demand of the President or the head of an executive department to furnish the House with specific factual information in the

Administration's possession. Under the rules and precedents of the House of Representatives, such resolutions, if properly drafted, are given a privileged parliamentary status. This means that, under certain circumstances, a resolution of inquiry can be brought to the House floor for consideration even if the committee to which it was referred has not reported it and the majority party leadership has not scheduled it for action.

Between 1947 and October 20, 2017, 313 resolutions of inquiry were submitted in the House of Representatives. Two periods in particular, 1971-1975 and 2003-2006, saw the highest levels of activity on resolutions of inquiry during the 70 years studied. Early evidence suggests that the House may be entering another period of heightened activity on resolutions of inquiry: The number of such resolutions submitted thus far in the 115th Congress (2017-2018) already exceeds the number introduced in the previous three Congresses combined.

Although nearly every standing House committee has been referred at least one resolution of inquiry during the post-World War II period, the Committees on Armed Services, Foreign Affairs, and the Judiciary have received the largest share of references because the most commonly sought information has related to matters of defense, foreign relations, and intelligence. Most resolutions of inquiry are directed to the President himself, but other executive branch officials have been the subject of such information requests as well.

Just over half of the resolutions of inquiry introduced between 1947 and October 20, 2017, were reported by the House committee to which they were referred—in most cases adversely, indicating that the committee opposed the resolution. This opposition might be because the resolution had been made moot by the executive branch complying in whole or in part with the request, or because such a request would, in the view of the committee, compromise an ongoing investigation, endanger sensitive information, or seek already-available information. Approximately one-fifth of the resolutions of inquiry introduced during the period studied received House floor action, the last one in 1995.

Although Representatives of both political parties have utilized resolutions of inquiry, in recent Congresses, such resolutions have overwhelmingly become a tool of the minority party in the House. This development has led some to question whether resolutions of inquiry are being used primarily for partisan gain or are unduly increasing the workload of certain House committees. Others have attributed the increase to a frustration among minority party Members over their inability to readily obtain information from the executive branch.

Available data suggest that 28% of the time, a resolution of inquiry has resulted in the production of information to the House. In half of the cases examined here, however, it is simply unknown, unclear, or in dispute whether the resolution of inquiry produced any of the requested information, a fact which might suggest the need for additional investigation of the efficacy of this parliamentary oversight tool by policymakers.

In: Insights into Secrecy and Information Policy ISBN: 978-1-53615-408-5
Editor: Clarence Armstrong

Chapter 1

FEDERAL GRAND JURY SECRECY: LEGAL PRINCIPLES AND IMPLICATIONS FOR CONGRESSIONAL OVERSIGHT*

Michael A. Foster

SUMMARY

The Fifth Amendment to the U.S. Constitution states that "[n]o person shall be held to answer for a capital, or otherwise infamous crime, unless on a presentment or indictment of a Grand Jury." This provision requires that a federal prosecutor, in order to charge a suspect with a serious federal crime, secure the assent of an independent investigative and deliberative body comprising citizens drawn from the jurisdiction in which the crime would be tried. Federal grand juries serve two primary functions: (1) they aid federal prosecutors in investigating possible crimes by issuing subpoenas for documents, physical evidence, and witness testimony; and (2) they determine whether there is sufficient evidence to charge a criminal suspect with the crime or crimes under investigation.

---

* This is an edited, reformatted and augmented version of Congressional Research Service Publication No. R45456, dated January 10, 2019.

Traditionally, the grand jury has conducted its work in secret. Secrecy prevents those under scrutiny from fleeing or importuning the grand jurors, encourages full disclosure by witnesses, and protects the innocent from unwarranted prosecution, among other things. The long-established rule of grand jury secrecy is enshrined in Federal Rule of Criminal Procedure 6(e), which provides that government attorneys and the jurors themselves, among others, "must not disclose a matter occurring before the grand jury." Accordingly, as a general matter, persons and entities external to the grand jury process are precluded from obtaining transcripts of grand jury testimony or other documents or information that would reveal what took place in the proceedings, even if the grand jury has concluded its work and even if the information is sought pursuant to otherwise-valid legal processes.

At times, the rule of grand jury secrecy has come into tension with Congress's power of inquiry when an arm of the legislative branch has sought protected materials pursuant to its oversight function. For instance, some courts have determined that the information barrier established in Rule 6(e) extends to congressional inquiries, observing that the Rule contains no reservations for congressional access to grand jury materials that would otherwise remain secret. Nevertheless, the rule of grand jury secrecy is subject to a number of exceptions, both codified and judicially crafted, that permit grand jury information to be disclosed in certain circumstances (usually only with prior judicial authorization). Perhaps the most significant of these for congressional purposes are (1) the exception that allows a court to authorize disclosure of grand jury matters "preliminarily to or in connection with a judicial proceeding," and (2) the exception, recognized by a few courts, that allows a court to authorize disclosure of grand jury matters in special or exceptional circumstances. In turn, some courts have determined that one or both of these exceptions applies to congressional requests for grand jury materials in the context of impeachment proceedings, though there is authority to the contrary.

Additionally, because Rule 6(e) covers only "matters occurring before the grand jury," courts have recognized that documents and information are not independently insulated from disclosure merely because they happen to have been presented to, or considered by, a grand jury. As such, even if Rule 6(e) generally limits congressional access to grand jury information, Congress has a number of tools at its disposal to seek materials connected to a grand jury investigation.

Prior Congresses have considered legislation that would have expressly permitted a court to authorize disclosure of grand jury matters to congressional committees on a showing of substantial need. However, in response to such proposals, the executive branch has voiced concerns that the legislation would raise due-process and separation of-powers issues and potentially undermine the proper functioning of federal grand juries. These concerns may have resulted in Congress declining to alter Rule 6(e). As a result, to the extent Rule 6(e) constrains Congress's ability to conduct oversight, legislation seeking to amend the rules governing grand jury secrecy in a way that would give Congress independent access to grand jury materials may raise additional legal and pragmatic issues for the legislative branch to consider.

INTRODUCTION

The Fifth Amendment to the U.S. Constitution provides that "[n]o person shall be held to answer for a capital, or otherwise infamous crime, unless on a presentment or indictment of a Grand Jury."[1] This provision requires that a federal prosecutor,[2] in order to charge a suspect with a serious[3] federal crime, secure the assent of an independent investigative and deliberative body comprising citizens drawn from the jurisdiction in which the crime would be tried.[4] Federal grand juries serve two primary functions: (1) they aid federal prosecutors in investigating possible crimes by issuing subpoenas for documents, physical evidence, and witness testimony; and (2) they determine whether there is sufficient evidence to charge a criminal suspect with the crime or crimes under investigation.[5]

---

[1] U.S. CONST. amend. V. Exception is made for "cases arising in the land or naval forces, or in the Militia, when in actual service in time of War or public danger." *Id.*

[2] The grand jury requirement of the Fifth Amendment is one of the few provisions in the U.S. Constitution's Bill of Rights that has not been applied to the states through the Fourteenth Amendment. Hurtado v. California, 110 U.S. 516, 534-35 (1884); McDonald v. City of Chicago, 561 U.S. 742, 765 n.13 (2010). Thus, although some states have developed their own constitutional provisions calling for grand jury indictment in felony cases or cases punishable by death or life imprisonment, *see, e.g.*, ALASKA CONST. art. I, § 8; FLA. CONST. art. I, § 15 (capital cases), the U.S. Constitution requires indictment only with respect to certain federal criminal prosecutions.

[3] *See* Fed. R. Crim. P. 7(a) (providing that felony offenses punishable by death or imprisonment for more than one year must be prosecuted by indictment).

[4] *See* 28 U.S.C. § 1861.

[5] *See* United States v. Williston, 862 F.3d 1023, 1031 (10th Cir. 2017) ("The grand jury functions as both a shield and a sword."); 1 Wright & Leipold, *Federal Practice & Procedure: Criminal* § 101 (2008 & 2018 Supp.) (describing dual grand jury functions).

Traditionally, the grand jury has done its work in secret.[6] Secrecy prevents those under scrutiny from fleeing or importuning the grand jurors, encourages full disclosure by witnesses, and protects the innocent from unwarranted prosecution, among other things. The long-established rule of grand jury secrecy is enshrined in Federal Rule of Criminal Procedure 6(e), which provides that government attorneys and the jurors themselves, among others, "must not disclose a matter occurring before the grand jury." Accordingly, as a general matter, persons and entities external to the grand jury process are precluded from obtaining transcripts of grand jury testimony or other documents or information that would reveal "what took place" in the proceedings,[7] even if the grand jury has concluded its work and even if the information is sought pursuant to otherwise-valid legal processes.

At times, the rule of grand jury secrecy has come into tension with Congress's power of inquiry when an arm of the legislative branch has sought protected materials pursuant to its oversight function.[8] For example, some courts have determined that the information barrier established in Rule 6(e) extends to congressional inquiries, noting that the Rule "contains no reservations in favor of . . . congressional access to grand jury materials" that would otherwise remain secret.[9]

Nevertheless, the rule of grand jury secrecy is subject to a number of exceptions, both codified and judicially crafted, that permit grand jury information to be disclosed in certain circumstances (usually only with

---

[6] *See* United States v. Procter & Gamble Co., 356 U.S. 677, 681 (1958) ("[W]e start with a long-established policy that maintains the secrecy of the grand jury proceedings in the federal courts.").

[7] SEC v. Dresser Indus., Inc., 628 F.2d 1368, 1383 (D.C. Cir. 1980).

[8] In one high-profile example, the House Judiciary Committee, in connection with the House's consideration of whether to impeach President Nixon, sought to obtain a report prepared by the Watergate grand jury. *See In re* Report and Recommendation of June 5, 1972 Grand Jury Concerning Transmission of Evidence to House of Representatives, 370 F. Supp. 1219, 1230 (D.D.C. 1974), *mandamus denied sub nom.* Haldeman v. Sirica, 501 F.2d 714 (D.C. Cir. 1974).

[9] *In re* Grand Jury Investigation of Uranium Industry, 1979-2 Trade Cas. 78,639, 78,642 (D.D.C. 1979). As discussed more fully *infra*, a few courts have found in Congress a "constitutionally independent legal right to" secret grand jury information in furtherance of "legitimate legislative activity," notwithstanding the restrictions of Rule 6.

prior judicial authorization).[10] And because Rule 6(e) covers only "matters occurring before the grand jury," courts have recognized that documents and information are not independently insulated from disclosure merely because they happen to have been presented to, or considered by, a grand jury.[11] As such, even if Rule 6(e) generally limits congressional access to grand jury information, Congress has a number of tools at its disposal to seek materials connected to a grand jury investigation.

This chapter begins with an overview of the standards governing— and exceptions applicable to— grand jury secrecy under Federal Rule of Criminal Procedure 6(e). The report also addresses whether and how the rule of grand jury secrecy and its exceptions apply to Congress, including the circumstances under which Congress may obtain grand jury information and what restrictions apply to further disclosures. Concluding this chapter is a discussion of past legislative efforts to amend Rule 6(e) in order to provide congressional committees with access to grand jury materials.

BRIEF OVERVIEW OF THE FEDERAL GRAND JURY[12]

Federal law requires the various United States District Courts to order one or more grand juries to be summoned when the public interest requires.[13] Grand jurors must be "selected at random from a fair cross section of the community in the district or division wherein the court

[10] *See infra* § Exceptions to Grand Jury Secrecy.

[11] *E.g.*, Senate of Commonwealth of P.R. v. Dep't of Justice, 823 F.2d 574, 582 (D.C. Cir. 1987) ("There is no *per se* rule against disclosure of any and all information which has reached the grand jury chambers."); *cf. In re* Grand Jury Proceedings, 851 F.2d 860, 866 (6th Cir. 1988) ("The general rule . . . must be that confidential documentary information not otherwise public obtained by the grand jury by coercive means is [rebuttably] presumed to be 'matters occurring before the grand jury.'").

[12] This section is largely drawn from CRS Report 95-1135, *The Federal Grand Jury*, by Charles Doyle.

[13] FED. R. CRIM. P. 6(a).

convenes,"[14] among other things. Grand jury panels consist of 16 to 23 members.[15]

After selection, the court swears in members of the grand jury;[16] names a "foreperson and deputy foreperson";[17] and instructs the panel.[18] Federal grand juries sit until discharged by the court, but generally for no longer than 18 months, with the possibility of one six-month extension.[19]

The authority of a federal grand jury is sweeping, but it is limited to the investigation of possible violations of federal criminal law triable in the district in which it is sitting.[20] The grand jury may begin its examination even in the absence of probable cause or any other level of suspicion that a crime has been committed within its reach.[21]

The grand jury does not conduct its business in open court, nor does a federal judge preside over its proceedings.[22] The grand jury meets behind closed doors, with only the jurors, attorney for the government, witnesses, someone to record testimony, and possibly an interpreter present.[23]

The grand jury acts on the basis of evidence presented by witnesses called for that purpose. The attorney for the government will ordinarily arrange for the appearance of witnesses before the grand jury, will suggest the order in which they should be called, and will take part in questioning

---

[14] 28 U.S.C. § 1861.

[15] FED. R. CRIM. P. 6(a), (f).

[16] Sara Sun Beale, et al., *Grand Jury Law and Practice*, § 4:3 (2008 & 2017 Supp.).

[17] FED. R. CRIM. P. 6(c).

[18] BEALE, *supra* note 16, § 4:5.

[19] FED. R. CRIM. P. 6(g).

[20] Brown v. United States, 245 F.2d 549, 554-55 (8th Cir. 1957); United States v. Brown, 49 F.3d 1162, 1168 (6th Cir. 1995).

[21] *See* United States v. Williams, 504 U.S. 36, 48 (1992) (recognizing that the grand jury may "investigate merely on suspicion that the law is being violated, or even just because it wants assurance that it is not" (citations omitted)).

[22] *See* United States v. Navarro, 608 F.3d 529, 536 (9th Cir. 2010) ("All the judge does, unless a motion comes to him, is swear in and charge the grand jury before it begins its work, and days, weeks, or months later, receive the indictments it hands down. A district judge does not preside in or even enter the grand jury room. The only contact the grand jurors have with the court is the charge the judge gives before they begin, and the use of a room in the courthouse.").

[23] FED. R. CRIM. P. 6(d).

them.[24] The grand jury most often turns to the prosecutor for legal advice and to draft most of the indictments, which the grand jury returns.[25]

Grand jury witnesses usually appear before the grand jury under subpoena.[26] Subpoenas may be issued and served at the request of the panel itself,[27] although the attorney for the government usually arranges the case to be presented to the grand jury.[28] Unjustified failure to comply with a grand jury subpoena may result in a witness being held in contempt.[29] A witness who lies to a grand jury may be prosecuted for perjury or for making false declarations to the grand jury.[30]

Neither a potential defendant nor a grand jury target nor any of their counsel has any right to appear before the grand jury unless invited or subpoenaed.[31] Nor does a potential defendant, a grand jury target, or their counsel have any right to present exculpatory evidence or substantive objection to the grand jury.[32]

There are four possible outcomes of convening a grand jury—(1) indictment;[33] (2) a vote not to indict;[34] (3) discharge or expiration without

---

[24] United States v. Merrill, 685 F.3d 1002, 1013 (11th Cir. 2012); United States v. Wadlington, 233 F.3d 1067, 1075 (8th Cir. 2000).

[25] United States v. Sigma Intern, Inc., 196 F.3d 1314, 1323 (11th Cir. 1999) ("A prosecutor's job is to present evidence of criminal activity to a grand jury. In so doing, the prosecutor may explain why a piece of evidence is legally significant . . ."); *see generally* BEALE, *supra* note 16, § 4:15.

[26] A subpoena is an order of the court demanding that an individual appear at one of its proceedings and produce evidence on a matter then under consideration. There are two kinds of subpoenas—subpoenas ad testificandum and subpoenas duces tecum. The first is simply a command to appear and testify; the second not only demands the witness's presence at a certain time and place but also requires him to bring certain evidence with him. Federal law with regard to subpoenas in criminal cases is governed in large measure by Rule 17 of the Federal Rules of Criminal Procedure.

[27] *See* United States v. Calandra, 414 U.S. 338, 343 (1974) (noting that "[t]he grand jury may compel the production of evidence or the testimony of witnesses as it considers appropriate").

[28] Lopez v. Dep't of Justice, 393 F.3d 1345, 1349 (D.C. Cir. 2005) (commenting that "the term 'grand jury subpoena' is in some respects a misnomer, because the grand jury itself does not decide whether to issue the subpoena; the prosecuting attorney does").

[29] *See* 28 U.S.C. § 1826(a) (governing civil contempt); 18 U.S.C. § 401 (governing criminal contempt).

[30] 18 U.S.C. § 1621 (governing perjury); 18 U.S.C. § 1623 (governing false declarations before grand jury).

[31] United States v. Williams, 504 U.S. 36, 51-54 (1992).

[32] *Id.*

[33] FED. R. CRIM. P. 7(c)(1).

[34] Vasquez v. Hillery, 474 U.S. 254, 263 (1986).

any action;[35] or (4) submission of a report to the court under certain circumstances.[36] A grand jury indictment may issue upon the vote of 12 of its members that probable cause exists to believe the accused committed the crime charged.[37]

OVERVIEW OF GRAND JURY SECRECY

Historical Underpinnings

"Since the 17th Century, grand jury proceedings have been closed to the public, and records of such proceedings have been kept from the public eye."[38] An early justification for maintaining the secrecy of grand jury proceedings in England was to prevent suspected criminals from learning of an inquest and absconding.[39] By the late 17th century, legal scholars had begun to recognize the need for secrecy in most matters pertaining to grand jury inquiries—including the identities of subjects and witnesses, the evidence collected, and the plans and deliberations of the jury—in order to realize the additional aims of preserving juror independence, sussing out witness bias and mendacity, and allowing evidence to be fully developed.[40]

When the right to grand jury indictment crossed the Atlantic Ocean from England to the American colonies, the rule of grand jury secrecy came with

---

35 FED. R. CRIM. P. 6(g).

36 United States v. Christian, 660 F.2d 892, 902 (3d Cir. 1981).

37 United States v. Calandra, 414 U.S. 338, 343 (1974). For more information on grand jury outcomes, as well as the law governing federal grand juries more generally, see CRS Report 95-1135, *The Federal Grand Jury*, by Charles Doyle.

38 Douglas Oil Co. v. Petrol Stops Nw., 441 U.S. 211, 218 n.9 (1979) (citing Richard M. Calkins, *Grand Jury Secrecy*, 63 MICH. L. REV. 455, 457 (1965)).

39 *See* Mark Kadish, *Behind the Locked Door of an American Grand Jury: Its History, Its Secrecy, and Its Process*, 24 FLA. ST. U. L. REV. 1, 13 (1996) (tracing grand jury secrecy from pre-colonial England through early American jurisprudence).

40 *Id.* at 15 (citing John Sommers, *The Security Of Inglish-Mens Lives, Or The Trust, Power, And Duty Of The Grand Jurys Of England* 46-54 (London, Benjamin Alsop 1682)); *see also* Earl of Shaftesbury's Trial, 8 How. St. Tr. 759, 771-74 (1681) ("[I]t is the opinion of the jury, that they ought to examine the witnesses in private, and it hath been the constant practice of our ancestors and predecessors to do it.").

it.[41] Prior to the adoption of the Federal Rules of Criminal Procedure, the federal courts developed a fairly robust, though not unyielding, conception of grand jury secrecy at common law. Secrecy challenges most often arose in the context of criminal defendants' motions to dismiss their indictments on the grounds that the evidence considered by the grand jury could not justify the charges or that some type of misconduct had occurred.[42] Recognizing that these motions called for inspecting records of the proceedings before the grand jury, courts typically acknowledged that they had the discretionary power to permit such inspection "in the furtherance of justice" but found that the power should be "sparingly exercised" in light of the traditional rule of secrecy.[43] Thus, although a number of courts identified a theoretical imperative for "removing the veil of secrecy whenever evidence of what has transpired before [the jury] becomes necessary to protect public or private rights,"[44] courts often declined to

---

[41] Costello v. United States, 350 U.S. 359, 362 (1956). Some commentators have suggested that the grand jury right protected by the Fifth Amendment to the U.S. Constitution implicitly encapsulates grand jury secrecy. *See* Kadish, *supra* note 39, at 16. In dictum, the Supreme Court has appeared to agree with this view. *See* Midland Asphalt Corp. v. United States, 489 U.S. 794, 802 (1989) ("Undoubtedly the common-law protections traditionally associated with the grand jury attach to the grand jury required by [the Fifth Amendment]—including the requisite secrecy of grand jury proceedings."); *but see Costello*, 350 U.S. at 363 ("An indictment returned by a legally constituted and unbiased grand jury . . . if valid on its face, is enough to call for trial of the charge on the merits. The Fifth Amendment requires nothing more."). However, the Court has not squarely addressed the extent to which secrecy is constitutionally required, and indeed, courts have often recognized Congress's power to modify or limit the scope of secrecy protections without mentioning any theoretical constitutional limits. *E.g.*, United States v. Sells Engineering, Inc., 463 U.S. 418, 424 (1983) (acknowledging that a "breach" of grand jury secrecy may be "authorized" through "a clear indication in a statute or Rule"); *see also* Bank of Nova Scotia v. United States, 487 U.S. 250, 258-59 (1988) (recognizing violations of Rule 6(e) but separately noting that "no constitutional error occurred"); *cf.* United States v. Amazon Indus. Chem. Corp., 55 F.2d 254, 261 (D. Md. 1931) ("[N]one of the reasons for [secrecy] are founded upon an inherent right in the individual who is being investigated to the same constitutional safeguards that are unquestionably his when he is brought to trial for a given crime."); 18 U.S.C. § 3331-33 (providing for empaneling of "special grand jury" under certain circumstances and authorizing public release of special grand jury report when specific conditions are met).

[42] *E.g.*, United States v. Am. Med. Ass'n, 26 F. Supp. 429 (D.D.C. 1939). Some decisions also addressed government attempts to use grand jury testimony in litigation. *E.g.*, *In re* Grand Jury Proceedings, 4 F. Supp. 283, 283-85 (E.D. Pa. 1933).

[43] United States v. Perlman, 247 F. 158, 161 (S.D.N.Y. 1917); *see also* United States v. Socony-Vacuum Oil Co., 310 U.S. 150, 234 (1940) (finding disclosure "wholly proper where the ends of justice require it").

[44] United States v. Farrington, 5 F. 343, 346 (N.D.N.Y. 1881).

engage in such unveiling based merely on a defendant's "general allegations" or a potential "fishing expedition."[45]

Nevertheless, when deemed "essential" to "the purposes of justice," some courts would consider evidence of what occurred before a grand jury to determine whether an indictment against a criminal defendant should be dismissed.[46] This unveiling apparently reflected an understanding that grand juries served not only an investigative function in furtherance of the governmental interest in law enforcement, but also as a "protector of citizens against arbitrary and oppressive governmental action."[47] Thus, as these decisions suggested, disclosure could be appropriate when continuing secrecy would be inconsistent with the citizen-protective function.

Federal Rule of Criminal Procedure 6(e)

Background and Overview

"[T]he federal courts' modern version" of the traditional rule of grand jury secrecy is established by Federal Rule of Criminal Procedure 6(e), in

---

[45] *See* Cox v. Vaught, 52 F.2d 562, 563-64 (10th Cir. 1931); United States v. Terry, 39 F. 355, 358 (N.D. Cal. 1889) ("[A]n exception to the general rules of law, which forbid . . . a grand juror to disclose the proceedings of the jury, or to impeach its findings, will only be allowed in rare and extraordinary cases."); *see also Perlman*, 247 F. at 161; *American Medical Association*, 26 F. Supp. at 431; United States v. Violon, 173 F. 501, 502 (S.D.N.Y. 1909). Courts divided on the question of whether and to what extent grand jury information should remain secret after a grand jury's work had ended. Some courts viewed disclosure of grand jury materials as permissible once the grand jury concluded its proceedings and dissolved, *see* Atwell v. United States, 162 F. 97, 100 (4th Cir. 1908), a view that the Supreme Court appeared to agree with (at least when necessary to prevent injustice). *Socony-Vacuum*, 310 U.S. at 234 ("Grand jury testimony is ordinarily confidential. . . . But after the grand jury's functions are ended, disclosure is wholly proper where the ends of justice require it."). However, other courts took the view that information about what occurred before the grand jury should remain secret indefinitely. *E.g.*, *In re* April 1956 Term Grand Jury, 239 F.2d 263, 272 (7th Cir. 1956) (distinguishing *Atwell* and concluding that "the safeguard of secrecy, in the interest of the public, continues even after the grand jury has completed its efforts").

[46] .*g.*, *Farrington*, 5 F. at 347, and cases cited therein (recognizing the "justice" of "free disclosure" where it was "patent that the grand jury permitted themselves" to be improperly influenced).

[47] United States v. Calandra, 414 U.S. 338, 343 (1974); *see also* Butterworth v. Smith, 494 U.S. 624, 629 (1990) (noting the "equally important function" of "safeguard[ing] citizens against an overreaching [State] and unfounded accusations").

effect since 1946 and amended numerous times over the following 60 years.[48] The Supreme Court has recognized that Rule 6(e) simply "codifie[d]" the pre-existing common law requirement "that grand jury activities generally be kept secret," an "integral part of [the United States] criminal justice system."[49] An Advisory Committee Note reflects this understanding, making clear that the Rule "continues the traditional practice of secrecy . . . except when the court permits a disclosure."[50]

Courts have identified five principal justifications underlying Rule 6(e)'s secrecy requirement:

1. to prevent the escape of those whose indictment may be contemplated;
2. to insure the utmost freedom to the grand jury in its deliberations, and to prevent persons subject to indictment or their friends from importuning the grand jurors;
3. to prevent subornation of perjury or tampering with the witnesses who may testify before [the] grand jury and later appear at the trial of those indicted by it;
4. to encourage free and untrammeled disclosures by persons who have information with respect to the commission of crimes;
5. to protect [the] innocent accused who is exonerated from disclosure of the fact that he has been under investigation, and from the expense of standing trial where there was no probability of guilt.[51]

---

48 *In re* Grand Jury Subpoenas, 454 F.3d 511, 521 (6th Cir. 2006). Creation of the Rules was authorized by Act of June 29, 1940, ch. 445, 54 Stat. 688, which gave the Supreme Court the power to prescribe general rules of criminal procedure prior to and including verdict or plea in criminal proceedings. The Attorney General was required to report the Rules to Congress before they could take effect. Pursuant to this authority, the Court established an "Advisory Committee" of practitioners that developed draft Rules for the Court's consideration. The Court's Rules were finalized and adopted in 1944, submitted to Congress in 1945, and became effective in 1946. *See* Staff Of H.R. Comm. On The Judiciary, 114th Cong., Federal Rules Of Criminal Procedure VII (Comm. Print 2016).

49 Douglas Oil Co. v. Petrol Stops Nw., 441 U.S. 211, 218 n.9 (1979).

50 FED. R. CRIM. P. 6(e) advisory committee's note to 1944 adoption.

51 United States v. Procter & Gamble Co., 356 U.S. 677, 681 n.6 (1958) (quoting United States v. Rose, 215 F.2d 617, 628-29 (3d Cir. 1954)). The genesis of these oft-repeated justifications appears to have been a pre-Rules district court opinion. *See* United States v. Amazon Indus.

At the time of its adoption, Rule 6(e) ensured the secrecy of grand jury proceedings by authorizing "[d]isclosure of matters occurring before the grand jury" in only limited circumstances. First, such matters "other than [the jury's] deliberations and the vote of any juror" automatically could be disclosed to "the attorneys for the government for use in the performance of their duties."[52] Beyond this, "a juror, attorney, interpreter or stenographer"[53] could disclose matters occurring before the grand jury only with court authorization (1) "preliminarily to or in connection with a judicial proceeding," or (2) "at the request of the defendant upon a showing that grounds may exist for a motion to dismiss the indictment because of matters occurring before the grand jury."[54]

Chem. Corp., 55 F.2d 254, 261 (D. Md. 1931). In other cases, the Supreme Court has framed the justifications slightly differently:

First, if preindictment proceedings were made public, many prospective witnesses would be hesitant to come forward voluntarily, knowing that those against whom they testify would be aware of that testimony. Moreover, witnesses who appeared before the grand jury would be less likely to testify fully and frankly, as they would be open to retribution as well as to inducements. There also would be the risk that those about to be indicted would flee, or would try to influence individual grand jurors to vote against indictment. Finally, by preserving the secrecy of the proceedings, we assure that persons who are accused but exonerated by the grand jury will not be held up to public ridicule.

Douglas Oil, 441 U.S. at 219. Not all of the identified justifications apply in every case; in particular, once a grand jury's work has concluded, there is "no longer a need" to prevent the escape of targets or the importuning of grand jurors. *Butterworth*, 494 U.S. at 632-33. As described in more detail *infra*, the status of a grand jury proceeding may be relevant to whether a party seeking disclosure of otherwise-secret grand jury materials may obtain them under an exception to Rule 6(e) in a particular case. *See Douglas Oil*, 441 U.S. at 223 ("[A]s the considerations justifying secrecy become less relevant, a party asserting a need for grand jury transcripts will have a lesser burden in showing justification.").

[52] FED. R. CRIM. P. 6(e) (1946).

[53] The original version of Federal Rule of Criminal Procedure 6(d) established that only government attorneys, the witness under examination, "interpreters when needed," and a stenographer could be present during grand jury sessions. FED. R. CRIM. P. 6(d) (1946). Only the jurors themselves could be present during grand jury deliberations or voting. *Id.* The current Rule 6(d) preserves these limitations largely without change, though it replaces "stenographer" with the more-modern "court reporter or an operator of a recording device" and clarifies that interpreters may also be present during deliberations or voting "to assist a hearing-impaired or speech-impaired juror." FED. R. CRIM. P. 6(d)(1)- (2).

[54] FED. R. CRIM. P. 6(e) (1946). As discussed *infra*, the majority view is and has been that grand jury witnesses are not obligated to maintain secrecy with respect to their testimony under Rule 6. *See id.* (providing that "[n]o obligation of secrecy may be imposed upon any person except in accordance with this rule").

Amendments to Rule 6(e) from 1966 to 2014 have sought, among other things, to align the Rule's text with court-developed exceptions and clarifications that have sometimes extended beyond the literal terms of the version of the Rule in force at a given point in time.[55] The current iteration of Rule 6(e) establishes a general rule of secrecy by setting out a list of persons, including grand jurors and attorneys for the government, who "must not disclose a matter occurring before the grand jury" unless the Federal Rules of Criminal Procedure "provide otherwise."[56] Rule 6(e) then "provide[s] otherwise" by listing complex exceptions to the prohibition. The exceptions generally fall into two categories: (1) disclosures permitted without judicial authorization, and (2) disclosures permitted with judicial authorization.[57]

In the first category, persons prohibited by the Rule from disclosing matters occurring before the grand jury may nevertheless disclose such matters (other than grand jury deliberations or grand juror votes) to an attorney for the government "for use in performing that attorney's duty" and to non-attorney "government personnel" who are needed to help a government attorney enforce federal criminal law.[58] Government attorneys may also disclose such matters (1) to another federal grand jury; (2) to federal law enforcement, intelligence, protective, immigration, national defense, or national security officials *only* with respect to matters involving foreign intelligence or counterintelligence; and (3) to "any appropriate . . . government official" *only* with respect to matters involving threats of attack or intelligence gathering by foreign powers or threats of sabotage or terrorism.[59]

In the second category of exceptions, the court under whose auspices the grand jury was empaneled may authorize disclosure of a grand jury matter (1) preliminarily to or in connection with a judicial proceeding; (2) to a defendant who shows grounds may exist to dismiss the indictment

---

[55] *See In re* Petition to Inspect and Copy Grand Jury Materials, 735 F.2d 1261, 1268 (11th Cir. 1984) ("Rule 6(e) has been repeatedly amended to incorporate subsequent developments wrought in decisions of the federal courts.").

[56] FED. R. CRIM. P. 6(e)(2)(B).

[57] FED. R. CRIM. P. 6(e)(3).

[58] FED. R. CRIM. P. 6(e)(3)(A)(i)-(ii).

[59] FED. R. CRIM. P. 6(e)(3)(C)-(D).

because of something that occurred before the grand jury; or (3) at the request of the government, to a foreign court or prosecutor or to an "appropriate" state, state-subdivision, Indian tribal, military, or foreign government official for the purpose of enforcing or investigating a violation of the respective jurisdiction's criminal law.[60]

Beyond the express terms of Rule 6(e), three circuits[61] and a number of district courts[62] have held that courts have inherent authority to disclose grand jury materials in situations where an enumerated Rule 6(e) exception is not otherwise applicable, though the authority may be exercised only in rare or special cases. Additional Rules and statutes also permit disclosure in particular circumstances.[63]

When a court-authorized disclosure is at issue, the person or entity seeking grand jury information must make a "strong showing of particularized need" that "outweighs the public interest in secrecy."[64] If that showing is made, the court may authorize disclosure "at a time, in a manner, and subject to any other conditions that it directs."[65]

The following sections of this chapter provide more detail on the various provisions of Rule 6(e).

Persons Subject to Rule 6(e)

Rule 6(e)(2)(B) lists eight categories of persons who "must not disclose a matter occurring before the grand jury" unless an exception applies:

---

[60] FED. R. CRIM. P. 6(e)(3)(E)(i)-(v).

[61] *See* Carlson v. United States, 837 F.3d 753, 756 (7th Cir. 2016); *In re* Craig, 131 F.3d 99, 103 (2d Cir. 1997); *In re* Petition to Inspect and Copy Grand Jury Materials, 735 F.2d 1261, 1268-69 (11th Cir. 1984).

[62] *E.g.*, *In re* Nichter, 253 F. Supp. 3d 160, 165 (D.D.C. 2017).

[63] For example, Rule 6(e)(3)A)(iii) cross-references 18 U.S.C. § 3322, which (1) permits government attorneys and personnel to disclose grand jury information to other government attorneys for use in enforcing the civil penalty provision of the Financial Institutions Reform, Recovery, and Enforcement Act (FIRREA) or other civil forfeiture provisions of federal law, and (2) permits court-authorized disclosure of grand jury information to certain regulatory personnel in connection with investigations of banking law violations on a showing of "substantial need." 18 U.S.C. § 3322(a)-(b).

[64] United States v. Sells Eng'g, 463 U.S. 418, 443 (1983); Douglas Oil Co. v. Petrol Stops Nw., 441 U.S. 211, 223 (1979).

[65] FED. R. CRIM. P. 6(e)(3)(E).

1. grand jurors;
2. interpreters;
3. court reporters;
4. operators of recording devices;[66]
5. persons who transcribe recorded testimony;
6. attorneys for the government;
7. government personnel needed to assist attorneys for the government;
8. persons authorized to receive grand jury materials under 18 U.S.C. § 3322.[67]

In other words, the Rule generally imposes an obligation of secrecy on each person permitted to be present while the grand jury is in session, as well as certain persons given access to grand jury information.[68] Yet there is a notable exception to this general imperative: though a "witness being questioned" is authorized by Rule 6(d) to be present during grand jury proceedings (for obvious reasons), grand jury witnesses are not included on the list of persons precluded from disclosing grand jury matters. Viewed in conjunction with Rule 6(e)(2)(A)'s admonition that "[n]o obligation of secrecy may be imposed on any person except in accordance with Rule 6(e)(2)(B),"[69] the Rule by its plain terms does not obligate grand jury witnesses to maintain the secrecy of the proceedings or their testimony. An Advisory Committee note to the original adoption of Rule 6(e) supports this reading, stating that "[t]he rule does not impose any obligation of secrecy on witnesses."[70] According to the note, such an obligation would

---

[66] Rule 6(e)(1) requires that all grand jury proceedings other than deliberations and voting be "recorded by a court reporter or by a suitable recording device," though unintentional failure to make a recording will not affect the validity of a prosecution. FED. R. CRIM. P. 6(e)(1). Recordings, court reporter notes, and transcripts prepared from the notes are retained by an attorney for the government unless the court orders otherwise. *Id.*

[67] FED. R. CRIM. P. 6(e)(2)(B). For a description of the persons authorized to receive grand jury materials under 18 U.S.C. § 3322, See *supra* note 63.

[68] Rule 6(d) provides that "attorneys for the government, the witness being questioned, interpreters when needed, and a court reporter or an operator of a recording device" may be present "while the grand jury is in session," though only the jurors and any necessary interpreters may be present during deliberations and voting. FED. R. CRIM. P. 6(d)(1)-(2)

[69] FED. R. CRIM. P. 6(e)(2)(A).

[70] FED. R. CRIM. P. 6(e) advisory committee's note to 1944 adoption.

constitute "an unnecessary hardship [that] may lead to injustice if a witness is not permitted to make a disclosure to counsel or to an associate."[71] Court decisions generally have been in accord,[72] although a handful of courts have taken the position that an order requiring a witness to refrain from discussing grand jury matters may be entered in rare circumstances when justified by a compelling need.[73] Courts taking this position have relied on "inherent judicial power" to "protect the integrity of the grand jury process," which the adoption of Rule 6(e) ostensibly did not undermine.[74]

Though a witness is ordinarily free to disclose grand jury information of which he is aware, witnesses cannot be *compelled* to disclose such information to investigation targets or in separate proceedings.[75] Relatedly, courts have recognized that federal prosecutors may *request* (but not

---

[71] *Id.* The reference to "injustice" in the note may signal a recognition of First Amendment limitations on restricting a private person's ability to "make a truthful statement of information he acquired on his own." *See* Butterworth v. Smith, 494 U.S. 624, 636 (1990).

[72] United States v. Sells Engineering, Inc., 463 U.S. 418, 425 (1983) ("Witnesses are not under the prohibition unless they also happen to fit into one of the enumerated classes."); *see also In re* Grand Jury Proceedings, 814 F.2d 61, 69 (1st Cir. 1987) ("[A]n obligation of secrecy on witnesses was forbidden in these circumstances under all interpretations of the rule."); *In re* Grand Jury Investigation, 610 F.2d 202, 217 (5th Cir. 1980) ("Rule 6(e) does not prevent disclosures by a witness who testifies before the grand jury."); Bast v. United States, 542 F.2d 893, 896 (4th Cir. 1976) ("[W]e recognize that [Rule] 6 imposes no condition of secrecy on the witness.").

[73] *In re* Grand Jury Proceedings, 417 F.3d 18, 26 (1st Cir. 2005) ("[T]he rule's phrasing can, and should, accommodate rare exceptions . . . ."); *In re* Subpoena to Testify Before Grand Jury Directed to Custodian of Records, 864 F.2d 1559, 1564 (11th Cir. 1989) (affirming authority to enter order based on compelling necessity); *In re* Grand Jury Subpoena Duces Tecum, 797 F.2d 676, 680-81 (8th Cir. 1986) (recognizing that policy of non-secrecy as to grand jury witnesses may be set aside based on "need for secrecy" that "outweighs the countervailing policy" and is shown with particularity); *In re* Grand Jury Proceedings, 17 F. Supp. 3d 1033, 1035-36 (S.D. Cal. 2013) ("Rule 6(e)(2)(A) does not preclude an order imposing nondisclosure in appropriate circumstances.").

[74] *Grand Jury Proceedings*, 417 F.3d at 26; *Subpoena to Testify*, 864 F.2d at 1563. Relatedly, several courts have relied on their inherent "supervisory authority" over grand jury proceedings to conclude that they may *authorize* disclosure of grand jury materials in circumstances not addressed by Rule 6(e). *E.g.*, Carlson v. United States, 837 F.3d 753, 756 (7th Cir. 2016). These decisions are discussed in more detail *infra*.

[75] United States v. Bryant, 655 F.3d 232, 239 (3d Cir. 2011) (quoting Kines v. Butterworth, 669 F.2d 6, 9 (1st Cir. 1981)) ("[A] witness may of his own free will refuse to be interviewed by either the prosecution or the defense."); SEC v. Oakford Corp., 141 F. Supp. 2d 435, 437 (S.D.N.Y. 2001) (stating that a witness "may not be compelled to testify whether or not he has appeared and testified before a grand jury as to a particular matter" or disclose the substance of that testimony "absent a court order to do so").

demand) that witnesses refrain from disclosing the existence of a subpoena or their testimony.[76]

Because Rule 6(e)'s language suggests that the list of persons prohibited from disclosing grand jury matters is exclusive,[77] unlisted third parties who obtain grand jury information—even from persons obligated to maintain grand jury secrecy—are also generally not required to keep the information secret.[78] That said, a court authorizing a disclosure under a Rule 6(e) exception may impose a condition that further disclosures not be made,[79] subject to First Amendment limitations.[80]

---

[76] *Bryant*, 655 F.3d at 238-39 (concluding that witness subpoenas "requesting nondisclosure and discretion on the part of witnesses" did not impermissibly "impose[] an obligation of secrecy"); *In re* Grand Jury Proceedings, 558 F. Supp. 532, 535 (W.D. Va. 1983) ("[T]he government may indicate to witnesses that it would prefer that they not discuss their testimony with third parties (apart from their own attorneys), although they may do so if they choose."); *cf. In re* Grand Jury Proceedings, 814 F.2d at 70 (finding letter advising that disclosure "could seriously impede the investigation being conducted" imposed an impermissible obligation of secrecy). Conversely, witnesses have been permitted to receive, or at least review, transcripts of their own testimony after it is given, though they may be required to establish some degree of need. *E.g.*, *In re* Grand Jury, 490 F.3d 978, 990 (D.C. Cir. 2007) (concluding witness may access transcript); *In re* Grand Jury, 566 F.3d 12, 18 (1st Cir. 2009) (holding witness must show particularized need to obtain transcript but less demanding standard applies to access and review).

[77] *See* FED. R. CRIM. P. 6(e)(2)(A) (indicating that "[n]o obligation of secrecy may be imposed on any person except in accordance with Rule 6(e)(2)(B)").

[78] *See, e.g.*, Dassault Sys., SA v. Childress, 663 F.3d 832, 847 (6th Cir. 2011) ("The rule imposes no obligation of secrecy on persons or entities that are not included on [the] list."); Fund for Constitutional Gov't v. Nat'l Archives & Records Serv., 656 F.2d 856, 870 n.33 (D.C. Cir. 1981) ("Rule 6(e)'s prohibition on disclosure applies only to individuals who have had access to that information by virtue of their relationship to the grand jury investigation or under another provision of the rule."); *In re* Polypropylene Carpet Antitrust Litig., 181 F.R.D. 680, 693 (N.D. Ga. 1998) ("Rule 6(e)(2), however, does not create a privilege to be invoked or waived by the Government, a defendant, or any other party when information makes its way into the hands of private citizens."). One exception is that, by statute, financial institutions served with subpoenas for customer records in the course of grand jury investigations into certain crimes may not notify the customers of the subpoenas or any information furnished in response. *See* 12 U.S.C. §§ 3413(i), 3420(b).

[79] *See* FED. R. CRIM. P. 6(e)(3)(E) (stating that court may authorize disclosure "at a time, in a manner, and subject to any other conditions that it directs"). It is also possible that, depending on the circumstances, a third party who obtains and further discloses grand jury materials could be prosecuted for obstruction of justice or another federal crime. United States v. Forman, 71 F.3d 1214, 1220 (6th Cir. 1995) ("[O]ne who divulges grand jury materials but is not subject to Rule 6(e)(2) is still liable to prosecution under 18 U.S.C. § 1503 for obstruction of justice."); United States v. Jeter, 775 F.2d 670 (6th Cir. 1985) (affirming convictions of theft of federal property and obstruction of justice); *Polypropylene Carpet*, 181 F.R.D. at 693 n.9 ("[I]t is true that, if a private party schemes to come into

At least one court has observed that courts themselves are not included on the list of those who must refrain from "disclos[ing] a matter occurring before the grand jury" under Rule 6(e)(2)(B), interpreting this omission to mean that courts have inherent authority to release grand jury materials regardless of whether a textual exception to grand jury secrecy in Rule 6(e) otherwise applies.[81] This judicial "inherent authority" exception, which the Supreme Court has never endorsed, is discussed in more detail *infra* in the section addressing exceptions to grand jury secrecy.

Disclosure of Matters Occurring Before the Grand Jury

Rule 6(e) prohibits only "disclosure of matters occurring before the grand jury." Accordingly, the Rule is not contravened unless something is "disclos[ed]," meaning that a person "with information about the workings of the grand jury . . . [has] reveal[ed] such information to other persons who are not authorized to have access to it under the Rule."[82] Thus, mere *use* of grand jury information by a person who has already been legitimately exposed to it does not constitute "disclosure" within the meaning of Rule 6(e).[83]

A more difficult issue is determining what types of information or materials fall within the meaning of "matters occurring before the grand jury." Though not defined in Rule 6(e), courts have tended to view the phrase as broadly encompassing anything that might reveal what took place in the grand jury room.[84] Clear examples include transcripts of proceedings and witness testimony, as well as written "summaries" or "discussions" of

---

possession of grand jury documents surreptitiously for purposes that foil law enforcement efforts, the private party may be subject to prosecution for obstruction of justice.").

[80] *Cf.* Bartnicki v. Vopper, 532 U.S. 514, 535 (2001) (holding that application of federal Wiretap Act to respondents' disclosure of truthful information of public concern that had been illegally intercepted by a third party violated First Amendment).

[81] *See In re* Application to Unseal Dockets Re: Indep. Counsel's 1998 Investigation of President Clinton, 308 F. Supp. 3d 314, 324-25 (D.D.C. 2018) ("The district court is notably absent from this list of the persons bound by Rule 6(e)'s prohibition on disclosure.").

[82] United States v. John Doe, Inc. I, 481 U.S. 102, 108 (1987).

[83] *Id.* at 107-11 (concluding that attorney who was involved in grand jury investigation could review information from investigation for purposes of filing subsequent civil complaint).

[84] *In re* Special Grand Jury 89-2, 450 F.3d 1159, 1176 (10th Cir. 2006); United States v. Smith, 123 F.3d 140, 148 (3d Cir. 1997); United States v. Dynavac, Inc., 6 F.3d 1407, 1411 (9th Cir. 1993); *In re* Grand Jury Subpoena, 920 F.2d 235, 241 (4th Cir. 1990).

the proceedings or evidence presented.[85] Information about the composition and focus of the grand jury—including the identities of witnesses and jurors,[86] the targets and subjects of the investigation,[87] and even the dates and times a grand jury is in session[88]—are also covered by the Rule.

Particular challenges arise in the context of documents such as business records that have been subpoenaed or considered by the grand jury but do not on their face relate to the grand jury itself. In general, "[t]here is no *per se* rule against disclosure of any and all information which has reached the grand jury chambers,"[89] and thus "[t]he mere fact that information [or documents have] been presented to the grand jury" does not bar independent disclosure in other proceedings.[90] For example, an agency or litigant may seek corporate records directly from a company, and the company has no basis to claim that the records are insulated from disclosure simply because a federal grand jury separately has subpoenaed them.[91]

---

[85] United States v. Index Newspapers LLC, 766 F.3d 1072, 1085 (9th Cir. 2014); United States v. E. Air Lines, 923 F.2d 241, 244 (2d Cir. 1991).

[86] *E.g.*, Hodge v. FBI, 703 F.3d 575, 580 (D.C. Cir. 2013).

[87] *In re* Subpoena to Testify Before Grand Jury Directed to Custodian of Records, 864 F.2d 1559, 1564 (11th Cir. 1989); *see also In re* Sealed Case No. 99-3091, 192 F.3d 995, 1004 (D.C. Cir. 1999) (recognizing that matters include "what is likely to occur" before the grand jury, including "the strategy or direction of the investigation"); *In re* Grand Jury Investigation, 610 F.2d 202, 217 (5th Cir. 1980) (holding that Rule 6(e) applies to "disclosures of matters which will occur, such as statements which reveal the identity of persons who will be called to testify or which report when the grand jury will return an indictment").

[88] Murphy v. Exec. Office for U.S. Attorneys, 789 F.3d 204, 211 (D.C. Cir. 2015); *see also* Peltier v. FBI, 218 F. App'x 30, 32 (2d Cir. 2007) (addressing dates of grand jury testimony).

[89] Senate of Commonwealth of P.R. v. Dep't of Justice, 823 F.2d 574, 582 (D.C. Cir. 1987).

[90] Labow v. Dep't of Justice, 831 F.3d 523, 529 (D.C. Cir. 2016); *see also In re* Grand Jury Proceedings Relative to Perl, 838 F.2d 304, 306 (8th Cir. 1988) ("Courts have consistently distinguished the request for documents generated independent of the grand jury investigation from the requests for grand jury minutes or witness transcripts."); United States v. Interstate Dress Carriers, Inc., 280 F.2d 52, 54 (2d Cir. 1960). This general rule also means that "information produced by criminal investigations paralleling grand jury investigations does not constitute matters 'occurring before the grand jury' if the parallel investigation was truly independent of the grand jury proceedings," regardless of whether the grand jury gains access to the same information. *In re* Grand Jury Subpoena, 920 F.2d 235, 242 (4th Cir. 1990); Anaya v. United States, 815 F.2d 1373, 1380 (10th Cir. 1987) ("[R]evelation of information learned by other governmental agencies in a parallel investigation without disclosure of what had been submitted to the grand jury was not improper.").

[91] *E.g.*, SEC v. Dresser Indus., Inc., 628 F.2d 1368, 1383 (D.C. Cir. 1980); United States v. Eastern Air Lines, Inc., 923 F.2d 241, 244 (2d Cir. 1991). For the same reason, information

However, utilizing various (and sometimes conflicting) tests,[92] courts have acknowledged that independently generated documents presented to a grand jury may sometimes constitute "matters occurring before the grand jury" in a particular case if the context of a *request* would make production revelatory of the substance of the grand jury's investigation. For instance, a request for "documents subpoenaed by the grand jury" might impermissibly call for disclosure of grand jury matters, as production "would reveal to the requester that [the documents] had been subpoenaed" and potentially suggest the focus of the grand jury's investigation.[93] By contrast, a request for documents presented to a grand jury, when coupled with broader requests for "all evidence" or documents related to a factual matter, would not necessarily call for disclosure of grand jury matters if production would leave the requester unable to "determine *which* documents," if any, "had been submitted to the grand jury."[94] The framing of a particular request for documents, and the context in which the request

regarding witness interviews conducted by law enforcement agents does not necessarily constitute "matters occurring before the grand jury" even if the witnesses later testify before the grand jury. *See* Dassault Sys., S.A. v. Childress, No. 09-10534, 2012 WL 3109423, at *3 (E.D. Mich. July 31, 2012).

[92] *See In re* Doe, 537 F. Supp. 1038, 1043 (D.R.I. 1982) (identifying four approaches). Several courts have looked to the effect that disclosure of particular documents would have, asking whether disclosure would "tend to reveal some secret aspect of the grand jury's investigation." *E.g.*, *In re* Special Grand Jury 89-2, 450 F.3d 1159, 1177 (10th Cir. 2006); *Senate of P.R.*, 823 F.2d at 583; *In re* Grand Jury Subpoena (United States v. Under Seal), 920 F.2d 235, 241 (4th Cir. 1990). A few other courts have focused on the purpose of the request at issue, deeming a document not subject to the Rule if it is "sought for its own sake-for its intrinsic value in furtherance of a lawful investigation-rather than to learn what took place before the grand jury." DiLeo v. CIR, 959 F.2d 16, 19 (2d Cir. 1992) (quoting *In re* Special March 1981 Grand Jury, 753 F.2d 575, 578 (7th Cir. 1985)). It is not always clear whether or to what extent these approaches are distinct. United States v. Dynavac, Inc., 6 F.3d 1407, 1413 (9th Cir. 1993) (characterizing court decisions under both approaches as utilizing an "'effect' test"); *see also In re* Optical Disk Drive Antitrust Litig., 801 F.3d 1072, 1077 (9th Cir. 2015) (comparing the "effect test" to the "pre-existing documents exception" and finding that they share "at least one characteristic"); *but see In re* Grand Jury Proceedings, 851 F.2d 860, 863 (6th Cir. 1988) (referring to purpose test as a "virtually *per se* rule" that almost always permits disclosure).

[93] *Labow*, 831 F.3d at 529; *see also Anaya*, 815 F.2d at 1379 ("[I]t is not the information itself, but the fact that the grand jury was considering that information which is protected by Rule 6(e).").

[94] *Senate of P.R.*, 823 F.2d at 583; *see also* Optical Disk Drive, 801 F.3d at 1077 ("Production of all material responsive to the subpoena . . . would not establish that any or all of those materials were ever presented to the grand jury, much less shed light on its inner workings.").

is made, will thus impact whether documents presented to or obtained by a grand jury are considered "matters occurring before" it within the meaning of Rule 6(e).

One court has addressed the difficulty inherent in parsing when and to what extent documents subpoenaed or reviewed by a grand jury constitute grand jury "matters" by applying a presumption that "confidential documentary information not otherwise public obtained by the grand jury by coercive means" is covered by the Rule.[95] A party seeking disclosure may rebut the presumption, however, "by showing that the information is public or was not obtained through coercive means or that disclosure would be otherwise available by civil discovery and would not reveal the nature, scope, or direction of the grand jury inquiry."[96] In practice, then, the showing required to rebut the presumption may result in an inquiry similar to that employed by other courts.[97]

In addition to the substance of grand jury matters themselves (e.g., transcripts of testimony), Rule 6(e) protects against the indirect revelation of grand jury matters in ancillary proceedings and filings, such as hearings or orders addressing claims of privilege or efforts to quash a subpoena. The Rule provides that the court must "close any hearing" and keep "[r]ecords, orders, and subpoenas relating to grand-jury proceedings" under seal "to the extent and as long as necessary" to prevent unauthorized disclosure of a grand jury matter.[98] Arguing that the public ordinarily has a First Amendment or common law right of access to criminal proceedings, members of the media have sometimes sought to obtain sealed records and

---

[95] *In re* Grand Jury Subpoenas, 454 F.3d 511, 522 (6th Cir. 2006) (quoting *In re* Grand Jury Proceedings, 851 F.2d 860, 866-67 (6th Cir. 1988)).

[96] Id.

[97] Compare id. (permitting access to a subset of business records subpoenaed by a grand jury because "[t]he marginal increase in the risk that appellants could divine or reverse-engineer the grand jury's investigative purpose . . . seems to us to be minimal at best"), with Labow, 831 F.3d at 529 ("The mere fact th[at] documents were subpoenaed fails to justify withholding under Rule 6(e)," as "the 'touchstone' is whether the information sought would reveal something about the grand jury's identity, investigation, or deliberation.").

[98] FED. R. CRIM. P. 6(e)(5)-(6).

orders notwithstanding these provisions, but multiple circuits have rejected such efforts.[99]

The prohibition on disclosure of matters occurring before a grand jury is indefinite—in other words, the veil of secrecy is not lifted merely because a grand jury has completed its investigation and either issued an indictment or declined to do so.[100] That said, because some of the "interests" underlying the rule of secrecy are "reduced" once a grand jury's work is completed, the passage of time may be relevant to whether a court will authorize disclosure pursuant to a Rule 6(e) exception in a particular case.[101]

Exceptions to Grand Jury Secrecy

Federal Rule of Criminal Procedure 6(e)(3) contains a series of "[e]xceptions" to the general rule of grand jury secrecy that permit disclosure of grand jury matters to specified persons or in certain situations. The exceptions fall into two general categories: (1) disclosures that may be made without judicial authorization[102] (though notice must in

---

[99] *See, e.g.*, United States v. Index Newspapers LLC, 766 F.3d 1072, 1088 (9th Cir. 2014) ("[T]here is no First Amendment public right of access to the filings and transcripts related to a motion to quash a grand jury subpoena while the grand jury investigation is ongoing."); *In re* Grand Jury Subpoena, Judith Miller, 493 F.3d 152, 154 (D.C. Cir. 2007) ("First Amendment protections [do not] extend to ancillary materials dealing with grand jury matters[.]"); United States v. Smith, 123 F.3d 140, 150 (3d Cir. 1997) ("[T]here is no presumptive First Amendment right of access if the hearing, and related papers must be sealed under Rule 6(e)(5) and 6(e)(6)[.]"). As Rule 6(e)(5) recognizes, portions of a contempt proceeding that do not reveal substantive grand jury matters may be required to be made public. *See* FED. R. CRIM. P. 6(e)(5) (making Rule "[s]ubject to any right to an open hearing in a contempt proceeding"); *Index Newspapers*, 766 F.3d at 1091 (collecting cases).

[100] *See, e.g.*, Douglas Oil Co. v. Petrol Stops Nw., 441 U.S. 211, 222 (1979) ("[T]he interests in grand jury secrecy . . . are not eliminated merely because the grand jury has ended its activities."); Murphy v. Exec. Office for U.S. Attorneys, 789 F.3d 204, 211 (D.C. Cir. 2015) ("[T]here is no time limit on the secrecy of grand jury proceedings.").

[101] *Douglas Oil*, 441 U.S. at 222-23. As explained *infra*, a person seeking court authorization for disclosure of grand jury materials must make a showing of need for the materials that "outweighs the public interest in secrecy." *Id.* at 223.

[102] FED. R. CRIM. P. 6(e)(3)(A)-(D). Though these disclosures may, by definition, occur without court intervention, the scope of the exceptions in this first category has most often been the subject of court decisions where (1) a government attorney desires to make a disclosure in a marginal case and seeks judicial guidance on whether he may do so, *e.g.*, United States v.

some cases be provided), and (2) disclosures that may be made only upon order of the court.[103] Certain statutes and Federal Rules of Criminal Procedure beyond Rule 6(e) also permit disclosure of grand jury information in particular circumstances.

Disclosures Without Judicial Authorization

Disclosure to a Government Attorney

Rule 6(e)(3)(A)(i) provides that disclosure of a grand jury matter "other than the grand jury's deliberations or any grand juror's vote" may be made without court authorization to "an attorney for the government for use in performing that attorney's duty."[104] The term "attorney for the government" is defined elsewhere in the Federal Rules of Criminal Procedure as, in relevant part, (1) the Attorney General "or an authorized assistant"; (2) a United States attorney or an authorized assistant; or (3) "any other attorney authorized by law to conduct proceedings under these rules as a prosecutor."[105] Thus, an "attorney for the government" under Rule 6(e)(3)(A)(i) encompasses attorneys within the United States Department of Justice, as well as local or federal agency attorneys that have been appointed to act as federal prosecutors.[106] Attorneys outside the

---

Sells Eng'g, Inc., 463 U.S. 418, 421-22 (1983), or (2) a criminal defendant moves to dismiss his indictment on the grounds that improper disclosures of grand jury matters have been made, *e.g.*, United States v. Tager, 638 F.2d 167, 168 (10th Cir. 1980).

[103] FED. R. CRIM. P. 6(e)(3)(E).

[104] FED. R. CRIM. P. 6(e)(3)(A)(i).

[105] FED. R. CRIM. P. 1(b)(1). The Rule also includes in its definition the Guam Attorney General or another person who Guam law authorizes to act in cases arising under Guam law. *Id.*

[106] *See Sells Eng'g*, 463 U.S. at 426 ("'Attorney for the government' is defined . . . in such broad terms as potentially to include virtually every attorney in the Department of Justice."); United States v. Smith, 324 F.3d 922 (7th Cir. 2003) (recognizing that state prosecutor who was duly appointed as an unpaid Special Assistant United States Attorney was "authorized" and thus within meaning of "attorney for the government"); United States v. Reece, 614 F.2d 1259, 1263 (10th Cir. 1980) (recognizing that Department of Agriculture attorney was authorized to appear before grand jury due to appointment as Special Assistant United States Attorney). The D.C. Circuit has held that a duly appointed independent counsel is an attorney for the government under Rule 6(e), meaning that he is subject to the obligation of secrecy. *See In re* Cisneros, 426 F.3d 409, 412 (D.C. Cir. 2005) ("As the independent counsel is an attorney for the government, any release of grand jury material by him, including his final report, falls within the protective provisions of Rule 6(e).").

Department of Justice who have not been so appointed, however, are excluded.[107]

Concerning the Rule's limitation that disclosure to a government attorney be "for use in performing that attorney's duty," an Advisory Committee note states that attorneys are entitled to disclosure "inasmuch as they may be present in the grand jury room during the presentation of evidence."[108] The Supreme Court accordingly has determined that disclosure under the Rule "is limited to use by those attorneys who conduct the criminal matters to which the materials pertain."[109] Accordingly, "every attorney (including a supervisor) who is working on a [particular] prosecution," but not a related civil matter, "may have access to grand jury materials" underlying that prosecution.[110] And at least one court has taken a more expansive view, reading the Rule as permitting disclosure to "government attorneys conducting other criminal matters to which the materials disclosed are relevant," even if such attorneys are located in a different jurisdiction than the empaneled grand jury.[111]

---

[107] Illinois v. Abbott & Assoc., Inc., 460 U.S. 557, 567 (1983) ("Plainly Rule 6(e) does not permit the Attorney General of the United States to disclose any grand jury proceedings to a State attorney general unless he is directed to do so by a court."); United States v. Bates, 627 F.2d 349, 351 (D.C. Cir. 1980) ("If it had been intended that the attorneys for the administrative agencies were to have free access to matters occurring before a grand jury, the rule would have so provided."); Bradley v. Fairfax, 634 F.2d 1126, 1131 (8th Cir. 1980) ("Case law suggests that a hearing officer employed by the Parole Commission is an attorney for the agency, not an attorney for the government within the meaning of [Rule] 6."); *In re* Perlin, 589 F.2d 260, 267 (7th Cir. 1978) (collecting cases); Special February 1971 Grand Jury v. Conlisk, 490 F.2d 894, 896 (7th Cir. 1973) ("[T]his phrase has been construed to include only attorneys for the United States government and not municipal, county or state attorneys."). As *Perlin* reflects, other attorneys may be considered "government personnel" entitled to disclosure depending on the circumstances. 589 F.2d at 267. The "government personnel" exception is discussed *infra*.

[108] FED. R. CRIM. P. 6(e) advisory committee's note to 1944 adoption.

[109] *Sells Eng'g*, 463 U.S. at 427.

[110] *Id.* at 429 n.11 (emphasis omitted).

[111] Impounded, 277 F.3d 407, 413 (3d Cir. 2002). The "attorney for the government" exception appears to extend at least this far, given that a separate exception in the Rule (discussed *infra*) permits automatic disclosure by an "attorney for the government" to "another federal grand jury." FED. R. CRIM. P. 6(e)(3)(C). As the court in *Impounded* pointed out, it would be anomalous if an attorney involved in one grand jury investigation could disclose grand jury matters to another grand jury but not to the attorneys appearing before the second grand jury. 277 F.3d at 414-15; *cf. Sells Eng'g*, 463 U.S. at 428 (rejecting proposition that "any Justice Department attorney is free to rummage through the records of any grand jury in the country, simply by right of office").

Once an attorney for the government has access to grand jury materials, he may use the materials as needed for the continued investigation and prosecution of the violations of federal criminal law to which they pertain, including in preparation for trial or during the examination of witnesses.[112] Disclosures not connected to such violations of federal criminal law, however, are prohibited.[113]

Disclosure to Government Personnel

Under Rule 6(e)(3)(A)(ii), disclosure of a grand jury matter, excluding grand jury deliberations and votes, may be made to "any government personnel—including those of a state, state subdivision, Indian tribe, or foreign government—that an attorney for the government considers necessary to assist in performing that attorney's duty to enforce federal criminal law."[114] This provision was added to Rule 6(e) in 1977[115] to address the need of Justice Department attorneys "for active assistance from outside personnel" in the course of grand jury investigations, including "investigators from the F[ederal Bureau of Investigation], I[nternal Revenue Service], and other law enforcement agencies[,]" without the "time-consuming requirement of prior judicial interposition."[116]

The term "government personnel" has been interpreted to extend to non-attorney government employees such as law enforcement agents and

---

[112] *E.g.*, United States v. Garcia, 420 F.2d 309, 311 (2d Cir. 1970) ("There has never been any question of the right of government attorneys to use grand jury minutes, without prior court approval, in preparation for trial and even to make them public at trial to the extent of referring to such minutes during the examination of witnesses."). One prominent treatise has noted that "use in performing [an] attorney's duty" can include certain disclosures that "are directly incidental to the preparation and presentation of the criminal case" in situations not otherwise contemplated by Rule 6(e). *See* BEALE, *supra* note 16, § 5:8.

[113] *Sells Eng'g*, 463 U.S. at 427.

[114] FED. R. CRIM. P. 6(e)(3)(A)(ii).

[115] The 1977 amendment did not specify whether the term "government personnel" extended beyond *federal* government personnel; the language was amended again in 1985 to make clear that it does. *See* FED. R. CRIM. P. 6(e) advisory committee's note to 1985 amendments.

[116] *Sells Eng'g*, 463 U.S. at 436, 441 (quoting S. REP. NO. 95-354, at 8 (1977), *reprinted in* 1977 U.S.C.C.A.N. 527, 531); *see also In re* Grand Jury Proceedings, 158 F. Supp. 2d 96, 107-15 (D. Mass. 2001) (examining legislative history in detail).

subject-matter experts,[117] as well as agency attorneys outside the Department of Justice who, because they have not been authorized to act as federal prosecutors, would not be entitled to disclosure under Rule 6(e)(3)(A)(i).[118] One question that has arisen is the extent to which employees of private entities that are controlled by or connected to the government may be considered "government personnel." The few cases addressing this question have tended to find that purely private entities and contractors are excluded from the Rule,[119] though a "quasi-governmental entity" that has both public and private attributes may not be, "depending on the facts of the situation."[120]

As the text of the Rule indicates, government personnel to whom disclosure of information is made may use that information only to assist government attorneys in enforcing federal criminal law.[121] Resultantly, disclosure to government personnel is constrained to an equal degree as

---

[117] *E.g.*, United States v. Jones, 766 F.2d 994, 1000 (6th Cir. 1985) (involving ATF agent); *In re* Grand Jury Subpoenas, 581 F.2d 1103, 1109 (4th Cir. 1978) (involving IRS agents); SEC v. Everest Mgmt. Corp., 87 F.R.D. 100, 106 (S.D.N.Y. 1980) (involving an SEC representative).

[118] *Sells*, 463 U.S. at 436 n.21 ("[T]he provisions of (A)(ii) apply as well to attorneys for government agencies outside the Justice Department, unless they are specially retained [by the department to act as prosecutors]."); *In re* Perlin, 589 F.2d 260, 267 (7th Cir. 1978) (concluding that Rule evinces "Congressional support for interagency cooperation and the active participation of agency personnel, including agency attorneys, in grand jury proceedings").

[119] *See, e.g.*, United States v. Tager, 638 F.2d 167, 168 (10th Cir. 1980) (concluding that employees of investigative entity voluntarily funded and controlled by private insurance companies were not "government personnel"); *Grand Jury Proceedings*, 158 F. Supp. 2d at 115 (reading Rule as "excluding disclosure to private individuals regardless of whether the private individual's use of the grand jury information is limited to assisting in the criminal investigation"); United States v. Pac. Gas & Elec. Co., No. 14-CR-175, 2016 WL 3255069, at *2 (N.D. Cal. June 14, 2016) (finding that retained consultants were not "government personnel" where it was "undisputed that both individuals are private consultants who do not work for government or quasi-governmental entities, who were not exclusively working for the government on this case, and whose access to data was not controlled by the government").

[120] *See* United States v. Pimental, 380 F.3d 575, 592, 594, 596 (1st Cir. 2004) (involving state insurance fraud board authorized by statute, partially governed by public officials, and funded by associations of private insurance carriers); United States v. Lartey, 716 F.2d 955, 964 (2d Cir. 1983) (involving former IRS agent who was de facto temporary government employee); *In re* Disclosure of Matters Occurring Before a Grand Jury to the Litig. Tech. Serv. Ctr., No. 11-163, 2011 WL 3837277, at *3-*4 (D. Haw. Aug. 25, 2011) (involving litigation support facility owned by government but operated by private contractor).

[121] FED. R. CRIM. P. 6(e)(3)(B).

disclosure to government attorneys under Rule 6(e)(3)(A)(i), that is, for use in the investigation and prosecution of criminal law violations—but not related civil matters—to which the information pertains.[122]

To balance the benefit of disclosure to government personnel as needed against the risk that secrecy will thereby be compromised, Rule 6(e)(3)(B) requires prosecuting attorneys to "promptly" provide the court that impaneled the grand jury with the names of all government personnel to whom a disclosure is made under Rule 6(e)(3)(A)(ii).[123] Though the text of this provision suggests that the names need only be provided *after* disclosure, the legislative history and an Advisory Committee note "contemplate[] that the names of such personnel will generally be furnished to the court before disclosure is made to them."[124]

The attorney who provides the court with the names of government personnel to whom disclosure has been made must also "certify" that he has "advised" those personnel "of their obligation of secrecy" under Rule 6(e).[125] Added in 1985, this requirement stemmed from concern that, particularly with respect to state and local government personnel who "otherwise would likely be unaware of th[e] obligation[,]" disclosure could result in "inadvertent breach[es] of grand jury secrecy" if personnel were not expressly advised to keep the information secret.[126]

---

122 *See Sells*, 463 U.S. at 442 (reading the "'criminal-use' limitation" as applying equally to government attorneys and personnel); United States v. Bazzano, 570 F.2d 1120, 1125 (3d Cir. 1977) ("[T]he F.B.I. agent cannot use the disclosed material in a manner which is not permissible for the Government attorney."); *cf. In re* Grand Jury Subpoenas, 472 F.3d 990, 999 (8th Cir. 2007) (concluding criminal investigator properly made privy to grand jury information does not violate grand jury secrecy by being involved in concurrent civil investigation absent "evidence that the knowledge of matters before the grand jury held by the investigator has been put to use in some way other than to further the criminal investigation").

123 FED. R. CRIM. P. 6(e)(3)(B).

124 FED. R. CRIM. P. 6(e) advisory committee's note to 1977 enactment; S. REP. NO. 95-354, at 8 (1977), *reprinted in* 1977 U.S.C.C.A.N. 527, 531; *see also* United States v. Hogan, 489 F. Supp. 1035, 1038 (W.D. Wash. 1980) ("The disclosure of the names of the Government personnel to whom grand jury testimony is to be released should ordinarily be made prior to the time of disclosure.").

125 FED. R. CRIM. P. 6(e)(3)(B).

126 FED. R. CRIM. P. 6(e) advisory committee's note to 1985 amendments.

Disclosure to Another Grand Jury

Rule 6(e)(3)(C) permits an attorney for the government to disclose "any grand jury-matter to another federal grand jury" without court authorization.[127] The Advisory Committee note to the Rule's 1983 addition reflects practical reasons for the exception: courts already "permitted such disclosure in some circumstances" despite the absence of a specific provision to that effect, and secrecy would "be protected almost as well by the safeguards at the second grand jury proceeding . . . as by judicial supervision of the disclosure of such materials."[128] In other words, when materials from one grand jury are disclosed to a second grand jury, "secrecy is not thereby compromised, since the second grand jury is equally under Rule 6's requirement of secrecy."[129]

Courts have held that the exception allows grand jury materials to be transferred not only to "successor"[130] grand juries within the same judicial district, but to grand juries in other jurisdictions pursuing separate investigations as well.[131]

Disclosure of Intelligence and National Security Information

Two of the most recent, and unique, exceptions to grand jury secrecy in Rule 6(e) permit disclosure of certain information to specified government officials based on the *subject matter* of that information.[132]

---

[127] FED. R. CRIM. P. 6(e)(3)(C).

[128] FED. R. CRIM. P. 6(e) advisory committee's note to 1983 amendments (quoting United States v. Malatesta, 583 F.2d 748, 753 (5th Cir. 1978)).

[129] United States v. Sells Eng'g, Inc., 463 U.S. 418, 425 n.7 (1983).

[130] The Rule facilitates the practice of seeking an indictment from a successive grand jury if the prosecutor cannot secure an indictment from the original grand jury during its term. *See* FED. R. CRIM. P. 6(g) (providing for 18-month term with possibility of a six-month extension); United States v. Contenti, 735 F.2d 628, 630 (1st Cir. 1984); United States v. Plaskett, No. 07-60, 2008 WL 444552, at *4 (D.V.I. Feb. 4, 2008).

[131] *In re* Grand Jury Subpoenas Duces Tecum, Aug. 1986, 658 F. Supp. 474, 480 (D. Md. 1987); *see also* Impounded, 277 F.3d 407, 414 (3d Cir. 2002) (noting that the provision reflects a "desire to expedite and facilitate the use of one grand jury's information by other grand juries investigating other crimes," without geographical limitation). Prior to adoption of the amendment, there was at least some authority disapproving of transfers between grand juries in different districts without court authorization. *See In re* Grand Jury Investigation of Banana Indus., 214 F. Supp. 856, 858-59 (D. Md. 1963).

[132] *See* FED. R. CRIM. P. 6(e)(3)(D).

First, as part of the USA PATRIOT Act of 2001,[133] Congress amended Rule 6(e) to allow an attorney for the government to disclose any grand jury matter involving *foreign intelligence*, *counterintelligence*, or *foreign intelligence information* to "any federal law enforcement, intelligence, protective, immigration, national defense, or national security official to assist the official receiving the information in the performance of that official's duties."[134] The terms "*foreign intelligence*" and "*counter-intelligence*" are respectively defined in a separate statute as

> information relating to the capabilities, intentions, or activities of foreign governments or elements thereof, foreign organizations, or foreign persons, or international terrorist activities," and "information gathered, and activities conducted, to protect against espionage, other intelligence activities, sabotage, or assassinations conducted by or on behalf of foreign governments or elements thereof, foreign organizations, or foreign persons, or international terrorist activities.[135]

The Rule itself defines the term "*foreign intelligence information*" as

(a) information, whether or not it concerns a United States person, that relates to the ability of the United States to protect against—

- actual or potential attack or other grave hostile acts of a foreign power or its agent;
- sabotage or international terrorism by a foreign power or its agent; or
- clandestine intelligence activities by an intelligence service or network of a foreign power or by its agent; or

(b) information, whether or not it concerns a United States person, with respect to a foreign power or foreign territory that relates to—

- the national defense or the security of the United States; or

---

[133] Pub. L. No. 107-56, 115 Stat. 272 (2001).
[134] FED. R. CRIM. P. 6(e)(3)(D).
[135] 50 U.S.C. § 3003.

- the conduct of the foreign affairs of the United States.[136]

The Intelligence Reform and Terrorism Prevention Act of 2004[137] added another exception, allowing an attorney for the government to disclose any grand jury matter "involving, within the United States or elsewhere, a threat of attack or other grave hostile acts of a foreign power or its agent, a threat of domestic or international sabotage or terrorism, or clandestine intelligence gathering activities by an intelligence service or network of a foreign power or by its agent" to "any appropriate federal, state, state subdivision, Indian tribal, or foreign government official, for the purpose of preventing or responding to such threat or activities."[138]

As commentators have noted, these contemporary exceptions are fairly expansive in that they allow prosecutors to unilaterally disclose grand jury materials to persons not involved in the prosecution of federal crimes based on definitions that could arguably encompass a "broad range of information."[139] In this sense, the exceptions appear to be a significant departure from the traditional practice of strictly limiting dissemination of grand jury materials.[140] In recognition of the potentially expansive application of the new exceptions, the Rule stipulates that any official to whom a disclosure is made "may use the information only as necessary in the conduct of that person's official duties subject to any limitations on the unauthorized disclosure of such information."[141] Additionally, with respect to state, local, Indian tribal, and foreign government officials, Rule 6(e)

---

[136] FED. R. CRIM. P. 6(e)(3)(D)(iii).

[137] Pub. L. No. 108-458 § 6501, 118 Stat. 3638 (2004).

[138] FED. R. CRIM. P. 6(e)(3)(D).

[139] Lori E. Shaw, *The USA Patriot Act of 2001, the Intelligence Reform and Terrorism Prevention Act of 2004, and the False Dichotomy Between Protecting National Security and Preserving Grand Jury Secrecy*, 35 SETON HALL L. REV. 495, 511 (2005).

[140] *Id.*

[141] FED. R. CRIM. P. 6(e)(3)(D)(i). Though the "limitations" on unauthorized disclosure are unclear from the text of the Rule, one commentator has noted that the provision "appears to impose . . . the same secrecy obligations that apply to the government attorney who disclosed it to the official." 2 David S. Kris & J. Douglas Wilson, *National Security Investigations and Prosecutions* § 22:3 (2d ed. 2012 & 2016 Supp.); *but see* 2 Susan W. Brenner & Lori E. Shaw, *Federal Grand Jury: A Guide To Law And Practice* § 17:8 (2d ed. 2006 & 2017 Supp.) (viewing the reference as "hav[ing] little meaning" because there are no "limitations within Rule 6(e) that would apply to federal officials receiving information pursuant to Rule 6(e)(3)(D)").

provides that they may "use the information only in a manner consistent with any guidelines issued by the Attorney General and the Director of National Intelligence."[142] Finally, within a "reasonable time after" any disclosure is made under Rule 6(e)(3)(D), an attorney for the federal government must file a sealed notice with the court indicating that "such information was disclosed" and identifying "the departments, agencies, or entities to which the disclosure was made."[143]

Despite the facial breadth of the recently added exceptions, it does not appear that they have yet been subject to substantial judicial scrutiny or interpretation.[144] At least one commentator, however, has anticipated that a constitutional challenge is inevitable, given the degree to which the exceptions impact grand jury secrecy (and thus potentially undermine the Fifth Amendment's grand jury requirement).[145]

Disclosures with Judicial Authorization

Disclosure Related to a Judicial Proceeding

Federal Rule of Criminal Procedure 6(e)(3)(E)(i) permits a court to authorize disclosure of a grand jury matter "preliminarily to or in

---

[142] FED. R. CRIM. P. 6(e)(3)(D)(i). The Attorney General has issued guidelines requiring, among other things, that grand jury information identifying U.S. persons be labeled as such. *See* Memorandum from the Attorney Gen. to Heads of Dept. Components, Guidelines for Disclosure of Grand Jury and Electronic, Wire, and Oral Interception Information Identifying United States Persons 2 (Sept. 23, 2002), https://www.dni.gov/index.php/ic-legal-reference-book/guidelines-for-disclosure-of-grand-jury-and-electronic-wire-and-oral-interception-information-identifying-united-states-persons. And although the language in Rule 6(e) is permissive, separate guidelines make disclosure mandatory (subject to the possibility of some use limitations imposed by the disclosing attorney for the government). *See* Memorandum from the Attorney Gen. to Heads of Dept. of Just. Components & Heads of Fed. Depts' & Agencies with L. Enforcement Resps., Guidelines Regarding Disclosure to the Director of Central Intelligence and Homeland Security Officials of Foreign Intelligence Acquired in the Course of a Criminal Investigation 2 (Sept. 23, 2002), https://www.dni.gov/index.php/ic-legal-reference-book/guidelines-regarding-disclosure-to-the-director-of-centralintelligence-and-homeland-security-officials-of-foreign-intelligence-acquired-in-the-course-of-a-criminal-investigation.

[143] FED. R. CRIM. P. 6(e)(3)(D)(ii).

[144] *See* BRENNER & SHAW, *supra* note 141, §§ 17:8-9 (noting that the exceptions have "yet to be tested in the courts").

[145] Shaw, *supra* note 139, at 496 ("Constitutional challenges are almost certain."). As explained in note 41, *supra*, it is unclear whether grand jury secrecy is encapsulated in the Fifth Amendment's grand jury requirement.

connection with a judicial proceeding."[146] This exception, which has been part of the Rule since its inception in 1946, is one of the most frequently litigated.

An oft-cited definition of the term "judicial proceeding" comes from an early U.S. Court of Appeals for the Second Circuit[147] opinion: "[A]ny proceeding determinable by a court, having for its object the compliance of any person, subject to judicial control, with standards imposed upon his conduct in the public interest, even though such compliance is enforced without the procedure applicable to the punishment of crime."[148] Criminal and civil litigation qualify as judicial proceedings,[149] but so too may quasi-judicial matters such as impeachment proceedings and certain disciplinary hearings.[150] Purely administrative or nonjudicial investigations or hearings, on the other hand, typically do not qualify.[151]

One question that has arisen is whether the grand jury investigation itself is a "judicial proceeding" such that a court may permit materials generated by the investigation to be disclosed for use in connection with those proceedings. Answering this question in the affirmative would, for

---

146 FED. R. CRIM. P. 6(e)(3)(E)(i).

147 This report references a significant number of decisions by federal appellate courts of various regional circuits. For purposes of brevity, references to a particular circuit in the body of this report (e.g., the Second Circuit) refer to the U.S. Court of Appeals for that particular circuit.

148 Doe v. Rosenberry, 255 F.2d 118, 120 (2d Cir. 1958); *see In re* Grand Jury 89-4-72, 932 F.2d 481, 484 (6th Cir. 1991) (referring to the definition from *Rosenberry* as "[t]he most commonly relied upon" and collecting cases).

149 *E.g., In re* Grand Jury Proceedings, 654 F.2d 268, 271-72 (3d Cir. 1981) (involving state criminal trial).

150 *See In re* Request for Access to Grand Jury Materials Grand Jury No. 81-1, Miami, 833 F.2d 1438, 1440 (11th Cir. 1987) (noting lower court ruling and party agreement that "within the meaning of the rule a Senate impeachment trial qualifies as a 'judicial proceeding[.]'"); *In re* Barker, 741 F.2d 250, 254 (9th Cir. 1984) (involving quasi-judicial disciplinary proceedings); *In re* Report and Recommendation of June 5, 1972 Grand Jury Concerning Transmission of Evidence to House of Representatives, 370 F. Supp. 1219, 1230 (D.D.C. 1974), *mandamus denied sub nom.* Haldeman v. Sirica, 501 F.2d 714 (D.C. Cir. 1974) (involving impeachment proceedings).

151 *See* Bradley v. Fairfax, 634 F.2d 1126, 1129 (8th Cir. 1980) (determining that parole revocation hearings are not judicial proceedings); *In re* Grand Jury 89-4-72, 932 F.2d 481, 485 (6th Cir. 1991) (concluding that bar disciplinary proceedings do not qualify where authority to discipline attorneys is completely delegated to a privately funded board of laypersons and attorneys); *In re* Grand Jury Proceedings, 309 F.2d 440, 444 (3d Cir. 1962) (holding that ex parte administrative proceeding related to Federal Trade Commission cease and desist order is not a judicial proceeding).

example, allow an expert witness to review grand jury material prior to testifying before the grand jury. Some courts have concluded either that a grand jury investigation is a judicial proceeding for these purposes or that it is "preliminary" to a judicial proceeding—the criminal trial that would follow indictment.[152] Consistent with this approach, said criminal trial generally has been viewed as a judicial proceeding permitting disclosure of materials from the underlying grand jury,[153] though there is authority to the contrary.[154] Conversely, courts have rejected the argument that a proceeding instituted primarily or solely to *obtain* grand jury materials can itself be considered the "judicial proceeding" needed to justify disclosure, recognizing that such a reading of the exception would be circular and "rule-swallowing."[155]

---

[152] *E.g.*, *In re* Grand Jury, 490 F.3d 978, 986 (D.C. Cir. 2007) (noting it "makes sense" that a grand jury investigation is a judicial proceeding "given that the district court itself convenes and supervises the grand jury proceedings," and it also "may be considered 'preliminary' to a judicial proceeding—namely, preliminary to a possible criminal trial."); United States v. Mayes, 670 F.2d 126, 129 (9th Cir. 1982) ("[I]t seems clear that grand jury proceedings are at least preliminary to a judicial proceeding."). Courts have not been unanimous in this view, however. *See, e.g.*, United States v. Tager, 638 F.2d 167, 171 (10th Cir. 1980) ("The grand jury proceedings themselves from which information is sought to be revealed are not the 'judicial proceeding' contemplated by" the Rule.); *In re* Nov. 1992 Special Grand Jury, 836 F. Supp. 615, 618 (N.D. Ind. 1993) (same).

[153] *Mayes*, 670 F.2d at 129; United States v. Rodriguez, 380 F. Supp. 2d 1041, 1058 (D.N.D. 2005).

[154] One court has noted that applying the "judicial proceeding" exception to the criminal trial authorized by the grand jury's indictment would render superfluous the separate Rule 6(e) exception for a defendant seeking to dismiss the indictment, "as the first exception would always encompass the second." United States v. Loc Tien Nguyen, 314 F. Supp. 2d 612, 616 (E.D. Va. 2004); *see also* United States v. Bunty, 617 F. Supp. 2d 359, 372 (E.D. Pa. 2008) (agreeing with *Nguyen*). There is also some tension between the view that a court may authorize disclosure in this context and the Jencks Act provision that transcripts of witness testimony not be released until after the witness has testified on direct examination. *See* United States v. Diaz, No., 2006 WL 1806161, at *3 (N.D. Cal. June 29, 2006) (suggesting view that disclosure may be authorized under "judicial proceeding" exception "does not come to grips with the express prohibition in the Jencks Act"); *but see* United States v. Ferguson, 844 F. Supp. 2d 810, 828 (E.D. Mich. 2012) (alluding to Sixth Circuit view that Jencks Act prohibition does not apply to grand jury testimony).

[155] Am. Friends Serv. Comm. v. Webster, 720 F.2d 29, 72 (D.C. Cir. 1983); *see also* McDonnell v. United States, 4 F.3d 1227, 1248 (3d Cir. 1993); *In re* Applications for Orders Directing the Review or Release of Certain Grand Jury Testimony of Mario Biaggi, 478 F.2d 489, 492 (2d Cir. 1973); *cf. In re* Cisneros, 426 F.3d 409, 413 (D.C. Cir. 2005) (recognizing court function in determining whether to release independent counsel report is a "judicial proceeding").

With respect to the "preliminarily to or in connection with" requirement, the Supreme Court has said that the relevant inquiry is the *use* for which the grand jury information is being requested: "the Rule contemplates only uses related fairly directly to some identifiable litigation, pending or anticipated."[156] Thus, "it is not enough to show that some litigation may emerge from the matter in which the material is to be used, or even that litigation is . . . likely to emerge . . . . If the primary purpose of disclosure is not to assist in preparation or conduct of a judicial proceeding, disclosure . . . is not permitted."[157] What this limitation on the exception means is that a request for grand jury materials pursuant to a preliminary inquiry or investigation does not come within the scope of the exception where the prospect of a judicial proceeding stemming from the investigation is merely speculative.[158] That said, an administrative or other investigative inquiry may be considered "preliminar[y]" to a judicial proceeding if "a clear pathway exists" between that process "and the judicial process and the ultimate judicial role is a very substantial one."[159]

Disclosure to Defendant on Showing of Ground to Dismiss Indictment

Rule 6(e)(3)(E)(ii) permits a court to order disclosure "at the request of a defendant who shows that a ground may exist to dismiss the indictment because of a matter that occurred before the grand jury."[160] Along with the "judicial proceeding" exception, this exception is the only other

---

[156] United States v. Baggot, 463 U.S. 476, 480 (1983).

[157] *Id.*

[158] *See id.* (concluding Internal Revenue Service investigation to determine civil tax liability was not "preliminar[y] to or in connection with" judicial proceeding "because the purpose of the audit is not to prepare for or conduct litigation, but to assess the amount of tax liability through administrative channels"); *Grand Jury 89-4-72*, 932 F.2d at 485 (determining that possibility of eventual, discretionary court review did not make nonjudicial disciplinary process "preliminary to" a judicial proceeding).

[159] *In re* Dec. 1988 Term Grand Jury Investigation, 714 F. Supp. 782, 784 (W.D.N.C. 1989) (collecting cases); *see also Grand Jury No. 81-1*, 833 F.2d at 1440 (noting lower court ruling and party agreement that "a House impeachment inquiry is 'preliminary to'" judicial proceeding in the form of "the Senate trial"); *Mayes*, 670 F.2d at 129 (finding it clear that grand jury proceedings are preliminary to the judicial proceeding that is the criminal trial); *cf. Bradley*, 634 F.2d at 1129 (expressing reluctance to include determinations of agencies merely because their "decisions are subject to judicial review").

[160] FED. R. CRIM. P. 6(e)(3)(E)(ii).

mechanism for seeking court authorization to disclose grand jury materials that has been in the Rule since its inception in 1946.[161]

There is a strong "presumption of regularity" in grand jury proceedings,[162] and thus a defendant requesting court authorization for disclosure under this exception carries a heavy burden in seeking to make the requisite showing. First, dismissal of an indictment itself is a remedy only for misconduct before the grand jury that "amounts to a violation of one of those 'few, clear rules which were carefully drafted and approved by [the Supreme] Court and by Congress to ensure the integrity of the grand jury's functions'"—such as violations of Rule 6 or certain statutory provisions establishing prosecutorial standards of conduct.[163] For example, indictment dismissal may be warranted where the prosecutor secures the indictment by actively misleading the grand jury about key evidence,[164] but mere failure to present evidence favorable to the defendant will not justify dismissal.[165]

Second, to make the requisite showing that one of the above-mentioned grounds exists, the defendant must do more than make "conclusory or speculative allegations of misconduct."[166] Rather, the defendant must

---

[161] *See* FED. R. CRIM. P. 6(e) (1946).

[162] Hamling v. United States, 418 U.S. 87, 139 n.23 (1974) (quoting United States v. Hamling, 481 F.2d 307, 313 (9th Cir. 1973)).

[163] United States v. Williams, 504 U.S. 36, 46 & n.6 (1992) (quoting United States v. Mechanik, 475 U.S. 66, 74 (1986) (O'Connor, J., concurring in judgment)); *see* United States v. Skelos, No. 15-CR-317, 2018 WL 2849712, at *1-*2 (S.D.N.Y. June 8, 2018) (noting that "the ability of courts to dismiss grand jury indictments" is "severely limited"). A defendant must also show that he was actually prejudiced by a non-constitutional error in a grand jury proceeding. Bank of Nova Scotia v. United States, 487 U.S. 250, 254 (1988).

[164] *See* United States v. Naegele, 474 F. Supp. 2d 9, 12 (D.D.C. 2007) (recognizing that case was "exceedingly rare" example of adequate showing that indictment dismissal could be warranted, where prosecutor procured testimony that a statement of financial affairs had been signed under oath and filed with court while knowing there was no signature page on file).

[165] *See, e.g.*, United States v. Finn, 919 F. Supp. 1305, 1327 (D. Minn. 1995) ("The rule is well-settled that a defendant may not challenge an Indictment on the ground that evidence favorable to a defendant had not been presented to the Grand Jury.").

[166] *Naegele*, 474 F. Supp. 2d at 10; *see also* United States v. Leung, 40 F.3d 577, 582 (2d Cir. 1994) (rejecting "speculations about possible irregularities" as "insufficient"); United States v. Warren, 16 F.3d 247, 253 (8th Cir. 1994) (agreeing that "a bare allegation that the records are necessary to determine if there may be a defect in the grand jury process" is insufficient); United States v. Lisinski, 728 F.2d 887, 894 (7th Cir. 1984) (rejecting "unsupported speculation"); United States v. George, 839 F. Supp. 2d 430, 437 (D. Mass.

identify a factual basis for inferring that misconduct warranting indictment dismissal has occurred.[167] At least one court has described this as an "exceedingly high burden."[168] For this reason, courts rarely grant requests by defendants under Rule 6(e)(3)(E)(ii), as "a defendant often can make the necessary showing only with the aid of the [very] materials he seeks to discover."[169] Defendants have, at times, pointed out this conundrum, but courts have not been particularly sympathetic.[170]

Disclosure to a Foreign Court or Prosecutor

Under Rule 6(e)(3)(E)(iii), a court "at the request of the government" may authorize disclosure of a grand jury matter "when sought by a foreign court or prosecutor for use in an official criminal investigation."[171] This provision was added to the Rule as part of the Intelligence Reform and Terrorism Prevention Act of 2004,[172] and appears to have been intended to address uncertainty as to whether a foreign criminal investigation could be considered "preliminar[y] to . . . a judicial proceeding" within the meaning of that separate exception.[173] With the 2004 addition, the Rule now expressly recognizes that government attorneys may seek court

---

2012) (noting that provision is "not an invitation to engage in 'fishing expeditions' for misconduct in grand jury proceedings").

[167] *See Leung*, 40 F.3d at 582 (requiring "concrete allegations of Government misconduct"); United States v. Bruno, 159 F. Supp. 3d 311, 322-23 (E.D.N.Y. 2016) (rejecting request for *in camera* review where defendant lacked "solid and specific evidentiary basis" for misconduct); *see also* United States v. Sitzmann, 74 F. Supp. 3d 128, 138 (D.D.C. 2014); United States v. Bunty, 617 F. Supp. 2d 359, 372 (E.D. Pa. 2008).

[168] 168 United States v. Tajideen, 319 F. Supp, 3d 445, 473 (D.D.C. 2018), *appeal docketed*, No. 18-3059 (D.C. Cir. Aug. 27, 2018).

[169] United States v. Mechanik, 475 U.S. 66, 80 (1986) (Marshall, J., dissenting).

[170] *E.g.*, United States v. Bennett, 702 F.2d 833, 836 (9th Cir. 1983) (dismissing defendant's "assertion that he has no way of knowing whether prosecutorial misconduct occurred" absent discovery of grand jury transcripts); United States v. McElroy, 392 F. Supp. 2d 115, 117 (D. Mass. 2005) (rejecting argument that "there is no way [defendants] can test whether the government acted properly unless they are provided with the discovery sought," because "[t]he rule clearly puts the burden on the defendant to make a preliminary showing").

[171] FED. R. CRIM. P. 6(e)(3)(E)(iii).

[172] Pub. L. No. 108-458 § 6501, 118 Stat. 3638 (2004).

[173] *See In re* Baird, 668 F.2d 432, 434 n.3 (8th Cir. 1982) (assuming without deciding "that the phrase 'judicial proceeding' includes a criminal trial conducted in a foreign country"); *see also In re* Grand Jury Subpoena of Flanagan, 691 F.2d 116, 123-24 (2d Cir. 1982); Shaw, *supra* note 139, at 522 n.167 (noting that the addition "clarified that at least some foreign proceedings qualify as 'judicial proceedings' under Rule 6").

authorization to disclose materials for use in the course of a foreign criminal investigation, rather than having to separately subpoena the same documents in order to provide them to foreign prosecuting authorities.[174]

Disclosure for State, Foreign, or Military Law Enforcement

Closely related to the exception for court-authorized disclosures to foreign courts and prosecutors, Rule 6(e)(3)(E)(iv) permits a court, "at the request of the government" and upon a showing by the government that a grand jury matter "may disclose a violation of State, Indian tribal, or foreign criminal law," to order disclosure of a grand jury matter "to an appropriate state, state-subdivision, Indian tribal, or foreign government official for the purpose of enforcing that law."[175] Rule 6(e)(3)(E)(v) extends the same exception to "an appropriate military official" for enforcement of "military criminal law under the Uniform Code of Military Justice."[176]

Before these exceptions were adopted in 1985,[177] non-federal law enforcement officials could obtain federal grand jury materials for purposes other than federal law enforcement only with court authorization pursuant to the exception permitting disclosure "preliminarily to or in connection with a judicial proceeding."[178] The judicial proceeding exception proved to be "of limited practical value" in such circumstances,[179] however, given the requirement that there be some "identifiable litigation"[180] to which the disclosure related; where state or

---

[174] *See* H.R. Rep. No. 107-534, at 11-12 (2002) (noting that although existing legal mechanisms allow foreign prosecutors and investigating courts to seek evidence in the United States, and U.S. prosecutors actively assist them, "the rule as currently written does not expressly authorize courts to order disclosure" even "when the Government makes an appropriate showing to the court (i.e., a showing similar to that required for disclosure of grand jury material in a domestic proceeding)").

[175] FED. R. CRIM. P. 6(e)(3)(E)(iv).

[176] FED. R. CRIM. P. 6(e)(3)(E)(v).

[177] The 1985 amendment was limited to state and local officials, with subsequent amendments extending the exceptions to foreign, Indian tribal, and military officials for enforcement of their respective jurisdictions' criminal laws. *See* FED. R. CRIM. P. 6(e) advisory committee's note to 2002 amendments.

[178] FED. R. CRIM. P. 6(e)(3)(E)(i).

[179] BEALE, *supra* note 16, § 5:11.

[180] United States v. Baggot, 463 U.S. 476, 480 (1983).

other non-federal officials were not already aware of the facts tending to show a violation of the relevant jurisdiction's criminal law, there would likely be no "pending or anticipated"[181] judicial proceeding prior to disclosure that would justify such disclosure under the "judicial proceeding" exception.[182]

According to an Advisory Committee note, "[t]his inability lawfully to disclose evidence of a [non-federal] criminal violation—evidence legitimately obtained by the grand jury"—was perceived as "an unreasonable barrier to the effective enforcement" of criminal law across jurisdictions.[183] Thus, pursuant to the exceptions, courts may now permit disclosure to a nonfederal official "when an attorney for the government so requests and makes the requisite showing."[184] Department of Justice guidelines require that federal prosecutors request and receive internal authorization to apply for a court order under these exceptions before doing so.[185]

With respect to which officials are "appropriate" within the meaning of the Rule, the Department of Justice takes the position that the term "shall be interpreted to mean any official whose official duties include enforcement of the . . . criminal law whose violation is indicated in the

---

[181] *Id.*

[182] As recognized in the Advisory Committee note to the 1985 amendments, another perceived barrier to information-sharing between law enforcement officials across jurisdictions was the "particularized need" requirement read into the Rule by the Supreme Court. *See* Illinois v. Abbott & Assoc., 460 U.S. 557 (1983). The stringency of the Supreme Court's standard prompted the inclusion in the 1985 amendment of the requirement that the government attorney seeking court authorization for disclosure show only that the grand jury information at issue "may disclose a violation of State, Indian tribal, or foreign criminal law." *See* FED. R. CRIM. P. 6(e) advisory committee's note to 1985 amendments (indicating that evidence tending to show a violation of state law often "cannot be communicated to the appropriate state officials for further investigation" because, among other things, "state officials who might seek this information must show particularized need"). The "particularized need" requirement is discussed in more detail *infra*.

[183] FED. R. CRIM. P. 6(e) advisory committee's note to 1985 amendments.

[184] *Id.*

[185] Assistant United States Attorneys must seek prior authorization from the United States Attorney or a delegated supervisor, and prosecutors within a litigating division of the Department of Justice must seek prior authorization from the Assistant Attorney General of that division or a delegate. U.S. DEP'T OF JUSTICE, JUSTICE MANUAL § 9-11.260 (2018), https://www.justice.gov/jm/jm-9-11000-grand-jury#9-11.260.

matters for which disclosure authorization is sought."[186] The few court decisions construing the term appear to take a similar view.[187]

Courts' Inherent Authority to Order Disclosure

The Supreme Court has said that where a statute "explicitly enumerates certain exceptions to a general prohibition, additional exceptions are not to be implied, in the absence of evidence of a contrary legislative intent."[188] As discussed above, Rule 6(e) provides that a matter occurring before a grand jury must not be disclosed "[u]nless these rules provide otherwise."[189] Rule 6(e) then explicitly "provide[s] otherwise" by granting authority to courts to order disclosure of grand jury matters in particular, enumerated circumstances.[190] Thus, based solely on Rule 6(e)'s text and general principles of statutory construction, it would seem that courts can authorize disclosure of grand jury matters only if one of the express exceptions in Rule 6(e) applies. Some courts have appeared to agree with this proposition, at least in the abstract.[191]

Nevertheless, a number of federal courts have determined that the list of court-authorized exceptions in Rule 6(e) is not exclusive, and that courts have "inherent authority" to permit disclosure of grand jury information and materials in circumstances not expressly provided for in the Rule.[192]

---

186 Id.

187 See United States v. Velez, 344 F. Supp. 2d 329, 331 (D.P.R. 2004) (holding that recipient is "appropriate" where he "ha[s] the authority to investigate and prosecute criminal cases against individuals or entities implicated in the grand jury materials").

188 Andrus v. Glover Const. Co., 446 U.S. 608, 616-17 (1980).

189 FED. R. CRIM. P. 6(e)(2)(B).

190 See generally FED. R. CRIM. P. 6(e)(3)(E).

191 See United States v. McDougal, 559 F.3d 837, 841 (8th Cir. 2009) (suggesting that disclosure would not be permitted "[a]bsent a contention that [a] request fell under one of the enumerated exceptions to the grand jury secrecy requirement").

192 Carlson v. United States, 837 F.3d 753, 766-67 (7th Cir. 2016); *In re* Craig, 131 F.3d 99, 102 (2d Cir. 1997) (citing *In re* Biaggi, 478 F.2d 489, 494 (2d Cir. 1973)); *In re* Petition to Inspect and Copy Grand Jury Materials, 735 F.2d 1261, 1268 (11th Cir. 1984); *In re* Nichter, 253 F. Supp. 3d 160, 165 (D.D.C. 2017); *see also In re* Special Grand Jury 89-2, 450 F.3d 1159, 1178 (10th Cir. 2006) (positing that relief "may be proper under the court's inherent authority" but declining to rule on the issue). Two other Circuits have appeared to take inconsistent views on the issue without squarely ruling on it. *Compare McDougal*, 559 F.3d at 840 ("[C]ourts will not order disclosure absent a recognized exception to Rule 6(e)[.]") *and In re* Sealed Case, 250 F.3d 764, 768 (D.C. Cir. 2001) (indicating that disclosure is "prohibited" absent an express exception in Rule 6(e)), *with In re* Grand Jury

Courts in this camp have pointed to various justifications for recognizing such extra-textual judicial authority to breach grand jury secrecy, including that

- courts have always had supervisory authority over the grand juries that they impanel, which historically included the discretion to determine when grand jury materials should be released;[193]
- the advent of the Federal Rules of Criminal Procedure did not eliminate a court's supervisory authority as a general matter, meaning that courts may still take certain actions that are consistent with, though not explicitly authorized by, the Rules;[194]
- Rule 6(e)(2)(B)'s list of persons who are prohibited from disclosing a matter occurring before the grand jury does not include the court itself;[195]
- Rule 6(e)(3)(E)'s list of circumstances in which a court "may" authorize disclosure does not indicate that those circumstances are exclusive, and the presence of limiting language elsewhere in Rule 6 suggests its absence in (e)(3)(E) was intentional;[196] and
- the history of the Rules and Advisory Committee notes indicates that Rule 6(e) was meant to be responsive to and reflective of

---

Subpoena Duces Tecum, 797 F.2d 676, 680 (8th Cir. 1986) (recognizing inherent authority of court to impose disclosure limitations on witness "in an appropriate case" despite lack of authority in Rule 6(e)) *and* Haldeman v. Sirica, 501 F.2d 714, 715 (D.C. Cir. 1974) (expressing "general agreement" with lower court ruling that, among other things, court had inherent authority to permit release of grand jury materials). A case currently before the D.C. Circuit may resolve the legal ambiguity in that circuit. *See* McKeever v. Sessions, No. 17-5149 (D.C. Cir. June 26, 2017) (oral argument held Sept. 21, 2018); CRS Legal Sidebar LSB10201, *Do Courts Have Inherent Authority to Release Secret Grand Jury Materials?*, by Michael A. Foster.

[193] *E.g.*, *Carlson*, 837 F.3d at 762.

[194] *E.g.*, *id.* at 763; *Grand Jury Materials*, 735 F.2d at 1268 ("[T]he rule is not the true source of the district court's power with respect to grand jury records but rather is a codification of standards pertaining to the scope of the power entrusted to the discretion of the district court[.]").

[195] *In re* Petition to Unseal Dockets Related to Indep. Counsel's 1998 Investigation of President Clinton, 308 F. Supp. 3d 314, 324-25 (D.D.C. 2018), *appeal docketed*, No. 18-5142 (D.C. Cir. May 17, 2018).

[196] *E.g.*, *id.* at 325.

common exceptions that courts developed of their own volition over time.[197]

Fearing that an exception to grand jury secrecy not textually constrained could undermine secrecy writ large, courts recognizing their "inherent authority" to release grand jury materials in situations not governed by Rule 6(e) have generally cabined the exercise of such authority to "special" or "exceptional" circumstances.[198] Though a determination that such circumstances exist is "highly discretionary and fact sensitive," factors that courts have considered include

- the identity of the party seeking disclosure;
- whether the defendant to the grand jury proceeding or the government opposes the disclosure;
- why disclosure is being sought in the particular case;
- what specific information is being sought for disclosure;
- how long ago the grand jury proceedings took place;
- the current status of the principals of the grand jury proceedings and that of their families;
- the extent to which the desired material—either permissibly or impermissibly— has been previously made public;
- whether witnesses to the grand jury proceedings who might be affected by disclosure are still alive; and

---

[197] *E.g.*, *Craig*, 131 F.3d at 102 (noting that "the origins of Rule 6(e)" indicate that it "reflects rather than creates the relationship between federal courts and grand juries"); *see also* Pittsburgh Plate Glass Co. v. United States, 360 U.S. 395, 399 (1959) (indicating that Rule 6(e) is "but declaratory" of the principle that "disclosure [is] committed to the discretion of the trial judge").

[198] *See Craig*, 131 F.3d at 102 ("Rule 6(e) governs almost all requests for the release of grand jury records," but "there are certain 'special circumstances' in which release of grand jury records is appropriate even outside of the boundaries of the rule."); *Carlson*, 837 F.3d at 766 (acknowledging that supervisory authority may only be employed "as needed to ensure the proper functioning of a grand jury"); *Grand Jury Materials*, 735 F.2d at 1269 ("[C]ourts must adhere to Rule 6(e) in 'garden variety' petitions for grand jury disclosure. The rule was intended to provide a reliable statement of the law in this area, and would be rendered meaningless if departures were freely sanctioned. We assume that courts are not empowered to act outside Rule 6(e) in other than exceptional circumstances consonant with the rule's policy and spirit.").

- the additional need for maintaining secrecy in the particular case in question.[199]

The circumstances in which courts have most often ordered disclosure of grand jury materials using their inherent authority have involved matters of significant public or historical interest related to grand jury proceedings that have long since concluded.[200] For instance, one district court in the District of Columbia recently unsealed certain dockets associated with the 1998 investigation into the relationship between former President Clinton and a White House intern, citing the length of time that had elapsed and the substantial public interest in the information.[201]

Although the trend appears to be in favor of recognizing a court's extra-textual inherent authority to release grand jury materials, at least in exceptional circumstances, there is some reason to question whether the Supreme Court would agree that this authority exists if faced squarely with the question. Setting aside the text of Rule 6(e) and the general principles discussed above, the Supreme Court in recent years has expressed

---

[199] *Craig*, 131 F.3d at 106; *see also President Clinton*, 308 F. Supp. 3d at 326 (relying on *Craig* factors). Other courts have simply applied the "particularized need" balancing test, described *infra*, which includes consideration of factors that substantially overlap with those listed in *Craig*. *See Grand Jury Materials*, 735 F.2d at 1272-73.

[200] *E.g.*, *President Clinton*, 308 F. Supp. 3d at 327 (concluding that, because grand jury proceedings "took place two decades ago" and disclosure would "satisfy the substantial public interest in learning more about" impeachment proceedings, factors weighed "heavily in favor of disclosure"); *In re* Kutler, 800 F. Supp. 2d 42, 50 (D.D.C. 2011) (finding that "undisputed historical interest in the requested records" related to Watergate scandal far outweighed the need to maintain secrecy); *In re* Am. Historical Ass'n, 49 F. Supp. 2d 274, 295-97 (S.D.N.Y. 1999) (permitting disclosure of decades-old grand jury materials based on "sustained and widespread historical interest" in the case); *but see Grand Jury Materials*, 735 F.2d at 1272 (authorizing disclosure to committee of materials from grand jury that recently indicted a judge because a statute expressly authorized the committee to investigate judicial misconduct). A related but distinct principle recognized by some courts is that although there is generally no time limit on grand jury secrecy, *see, e.g.*, Douglas Oil Co. v. Petrol Stops Nw., 441 U.S. 211, 222 (1979), the passage of time and the steady drip of grand jury information into the public domain can at some point cause such information to lose the protection of Rule 6(e). *E.g.*, *In re* Grand Jury Subpoena, Judith Miller, 438 F.3d 1138, 1140 (D.C. Cir. 2006). This principle does not appear to be expressly reliant on a court's "inherent authority" to disclose grand jury materials, but rather recognizes the "common-sense proposition that secrecy is no longer 'necessary'" within the meaning of Rule 6(e) "when the contents of grand jury matters have become public." *Id.* (quoting FED. R. CRIM. P. 6(e)(6)).

[201] *President Clinton*, 308 F. Supp. 3d at 327.

"reluctan[ce] to invoke the judicial supervisory power as a basis for prescribing modes of grand jury procedure," as the grand jury's status as an independent constitutional fixture "suggest[s] that any power federal courts may have to fashion" such procedures "is a very limited one[.]"[202] These statements have led one treatise to refer to the existence of judicial inherent authority to release grand jury materials beyond the terms of Rule 6(e) as "exceedingly doubtful."[203]

Showings Required for Court Authorization to Disclose Grand Jury Matters

Although Rule 6(e) enumerates the contexts in which a court is *authorized* to order disclosure of grand jury matters, courts have had to grapple with determining what standard governs the exercise of a court's discretion to order disclosure in a particular case—that is, the showing a requester must make in order for a court to agree that releasing grand jury material is warranted under one of the exceptions for court-authorized disclosure in Rule 6(e).

The Supreme Court has said that "disclosure is appropriate only in those cases where the need for it outweighs the public interest in secrecy," and "the burden of demonstrating this balance" rests on the party seeking disclosure.[204] Put differently, the secrecy of grand jury proceedings "must not be broken except where there is a compelling necessity," and the

---

[202] United States v. Williams, 504 U.S. 36, 50 (1992); *see also* Carlisle v. United States, 517 U.S. 416, 425-26 (1996) (holding that court may not use inherent supervisory power to fashion rules that circumvent or conflict with Federal Rules of Criminal Procedure); United States v. Baggot, 463 U.S. 476, 479 (1983) (referring to Rule 6(e) exception as "an affirmative limitation on the availability of court-ordered disclosure of grand jury materials"). It is notable that the trial court in *Baggot* had authorized disclosure pursuant to its inherent authority, but the Supreme Court affirmed the Court of Appeals' ruling that disclosure was improper because the circumstances did not meet Rule 6(e)'s "judicial proceeding" exception. *See id.* Thus, although the Supreme Court did not address the court's inherent authority to order release of grand jury materials in *Baggot*, at least one court has viewed *Baggot* as "impl[ying] that the exceptions in Rule 6(e) are the only authority for disclosure of grand jury materials and that disclosure is improper where not explicitly authorized by Rule 6(e)." *In re* Elec. Surveillance, 596 F. Supp. 991, 1001 (E.D. Mich. 1984), *abrogated by In re* Grand Jury 89-4-72, 932 F.2d 481 (6th Cir. 1991).

[203] BRENNER & SHAW, *supra* note 141, § 18:2.

[204] Douglas Oil Co. v. Petrol Stops Nw., 441 U.S. 211, 223 (1979).

"instances when that need will outweigh the countervailing policy" of secrecy "must be shown with particularity" by the requester.[205]

From these general principles has emerged the standard that Rule 6(e) "require[s] a strong showing of particularized need for grand jury materials before any disclosure will be permitted."[206] The Supreme Court announced the contours of this so-called "particularized need" standard in the context of the "judicial proceeding" exception to Rule 6(e), explaining that "[p]arties seeking grand jury transcripts under Rule 6(e) must show that the material they seek is needed to avoid a possible injustice in another judicial proceeding, that the need for disclosure is greater than the need for continued secrecy, and that their request is structured to cover only material so needed."[207]

When the cases describing the "particularized need" standard were decided, the only Rule 6(e) exceptions permitting a court to authorize disclosure of grand jury matters were (1) the "judicial proceeding" exception, and (2) the exception for a defendant upon showing grounds to dismiss the indictment. As the number of Rule 6(e) exceptions permitting court-authorized disclosure has grown over time, however, one question that has arisen is whether and how the Supreme Court's "particularized need" standard applies outside of the "judicial proceeding" context in which it was announced. Courts have typically recognized that the general requirement imposed on a requester to show a need for the grand jury materials at issue extends to *any* exception authorizing court-ordered disclosure.[208] This requirement, whether given the appellation

---

[205] United States v. Procter & Gamble Co., 356 U.S. 677, 682 (1958).

[206] United States v. Sells Eng'g, Inc., 463 U.S. 418, 443 (1983).

[207] *Douglas Oil*, 441 U.S. at 222.

[208] *See, e.g.*, United States v. McDougal, 559 F.3d 837, 840-41 (8th Cir. 2009) (describing Rule 6(e) exceptions and pronouncing that "[a] request for disclosure that falls under one of these specified exceptions must also contain a 'showing of particularized need for grand jury materials' before disclosure becomes appropriate"); *In re* Craig, 131 F.3d 99, 104 n.5 (2d Cir. 1997) (noting that although "the *Douglas Oil* test cannot be carried over directly to 'special circumstances' cases" because "the *Douglas Oil* test's first prong presumes use of the grand jury material in a subsequent judicial proceeding[], it serves as a useful aid to guide [the] inquiry" into whether circumstances beyond those contemplated in Rule 6(e) warrant court-ordered disclosure); *In re* Grand Jury Testimony, 832 F.2d 60, 62 (5th Cir. 1987) ("Rule 6(e) provides certain exceptions, and case law has established that a district court may properly order release of grand jury materials where a party demonstrates with

"particularized need" or not, will obligate a person seeking court authorization for disclosure to show some factual exigency outweighing the interest in secrecy, which will vary depending on the precise exception being invoked. Thus, for example and as discussed above, a defendant seeking an order authorizing disclosure under Rule 6(e)(3)(E)(ii) must be able to present a factual basis for inferring that misconduct that would warrant dismissal of the indictment has occurred, and a government attorney seeking authorization under Rule 6(e)(3)(E)(iv) must show that the grand jury matter for which disclosure is sought may disclose a violation of State, Indian tribal, or foreign criminal law.[209] Likewise, courts

---

particularity a 'compelling necessity' for the materials."); *In re* Am. Historical Ass'n, 49 F. Supp. 2d 274, 283 (S.D.N.Y. 1999); *but see* BRENNER & SHAW, *supra* note 141, § 18:7 (asserting that "[p]articularized need only controls disclosure under Rule 6(e)(3)(E)(i)" but noting the "similarity between" that standard and the standard for disclosure under Rule 6(e)(3)(E)(ii)).

[209] With respect to this and the other exceptions contained in Rules 6(e)(3)(E)(iii) and (v) permitting a court to authorize disclosure for state, local, and foreign law enforcement purposes, there is some indication from the Advisory Committee that the exceptions were needed because the Supreme Court's "particularized need" requirement was stymieing useful information-sharing for law enforcement purposes across jurisdictions. *See* FED. R. CRIM. P. 6(e) advisory committee's note to 1985 amendments (indicating that evidence tending to show a violation of state law often "cannot be communicated to the appropriate state officials for further investigation" because, among other things, "state officials who might seek this information must show particularized need"). This justification for the newer exceptions has prompted some commentators, as well as the Department of Justice, to take the position that the requisite showing for the exceptions is less stringent. *See* BRENNER & SHAW, *supra* note 141, § 18:8 (citing U.S. DEP'T OF JUSTICE, FEDERAL GRAND JURY PRACTICE 197 (1993)) (asserting that it is "not necessary" to show particularized need, but a "substantial need," such as the need to prosecute or investigate felony offenses, is required by Department policy). To the extent this position recognizes that the government need not show "possible injustice in another judicial proceeding" to obtain a disclosure order pursuant to the exceptions for grand jury matters that may disclose a violation of another jurisdiction's criminal law, the position is likely correct (though the showing that the material may disclose such a violation, whether framed as a "particularized need" or not, must still be made). *But see* 15 U.S.C. § 6204 (establishing that a foreign antitrust authority "with respect to which a particularized need" for antitrust evidence is shown "shall be considered to be an appropriate official" within meaning of Rule 6(e)(3)(E)(iv)). This position seems more tenuous with respect to the exception for disclosure to a foreign court or prosecutor "for use in an official criminal investigation" under Rule 6(e)(3)(E)(iii), however, as that exception appears to establish only that such foreign investigations are to be considered preliminary to judicial proceedings (making disclosure appropriate for the same reasons, and subject to the same showing, as the "judicial proceeding" exception). *See* H.R. Rep. No. 107-534, at 11-12 (2002) (noting that the exception was intended to remedy the fact that "the rule as currently written does not expressly authorize courts to order disclosure" even "when the Government

addressing whether to authorize release of grand jury materials pursuant to their inherent authority engage in "a nuanced and fact-intensive assessment" of whether the need for the materials is greater than the need to maintain secrecy.[210]

Courts considering whether a "particularized need" exists in a given case have emphasized that although the standard is "highly flexible,"[211] a showing of "mere relevance, economy, and efficiency will not suffice" to meet it.[212] Thus, the inquiry often focuses on the contemplated use of the materials at issue and whether alternative channels exist to obtain them.[213] In the context of judicial proceedings, the need to impeach or refresh the recollection of a witness is a well-recognized and valid need, so long as the need is "real" and not merely a "bald assertion[.]"[214] Other needs that courts have found valid include (1) to substantiate malicious prosecution allegations based on prosecutorial and witness misconduct;[215] (2) to rehabilitate a witness at trial after he has been impeached on cross-examination;[216] and (3) to avoid stymieing an investigation of official improprieties.[217] On the other hand, the mere desire to discover what evidence the grand jury considered has been held to be insufficient.[218]

---

makes an appropriate showing to the court (i.e., a showing similar to that required for disclosure of grand jury material in a domestic proceeding)").

[210] *See, e.g.*, *In re* Kutler, 800 F. Supp. 2d 42, 47-48 (D.D.C. 2011); *see supra* § Courts' Inherent Authority to Order Disclosure.

[211] *Sells Eng'g*, 463 U.S. at 445.

[212] *E.g.*, Pizzuti v. United States, 809 F. Supp. 2d 164, 194 (S.D.N.Y. 2011).

[213] *See, e.g.*, *In re* Request for Access to Grand Jury Materials Grand Jury No. 81-1, Miami, 833 F.2d 1438, 1442 (11th Cir. 1987) (recognizing particularized need to "conduct[] a full and fair impeachment inquiry"); *In re* Grand Jury Proceedings Relative to Perl, 838 F.2d 304, 308 (8th Cir. 1988) (noting that requested documents were "unavailable through any other channel of discovery"); Lucas v. Turner, 725 F.2d 1095, 1102 (7th Cir. 1984) (plaintiffs failed to demonstrate that "the information contained therein could not have been obtained through normal discovery channels").

[214] *In re* Grand Jury Testimony, 832 F.2d 60, 63 (5th Cir. 1987); *see Douglas Oil*, 441 U.S. at 222 n.12 (recognizing that "the typical showing of particularized need arises" when a litigant seeks to impeach, test the credibility of, or refresh the recollection of a witness).

[215] Anilao v. Spota, 918 F. Supp. 2d 157, 177 (E.D.N.Y. 2013).

[216] United States v. McMahon, 938 F.2d 1501, 1505 (1st Cir. 1991).

[217] Application of U.S. for Order Pursuant to Provisions of Rule 6(e), Fed. Rules of Criminal Procedure, 505 F. Supp. 25, 27 (W.D. Pa. 1980).

[218] *See* United States v. Haire, 103 F.3d 697, 699 (8th Cir. 1996) (concluding that where defendant received transcripts of grand jury testimony of witnesses who testified at trial,

Consistent with the flexible and fact-dependent nature of the "particularized need" inquiry, the Supreme Court has said that "as the considerations justifying secrecy become less relevant, a party asserting a need for grand jury transcripts will have a lesser burden in showing justification."[219] Thus, factors courts consider in weighing need against the interest in secrecy may include (1) the nature of the materials sought;[220] (2) whether the requester is a government official or a private party;[221] (3) the time that has elapsed between the grand jury proceedings and the request for disclosure;[222] and (4) whether, in the case of witness testimony or documents, the witness objects to disclosure.[223]

Disclosures Authorized by Another Statute or Rule

Despite the general presumption of grand jury secrecy established by Federal Rule of Criminal Procedure 6(e), other federal statutes and procedural rules sometimes permit (or even mandate) disclosure of grand jury information in particular circumstances. These statutes and rules are explicit in their limited retraction of grand jury secrecy, as they must be, for the Supreme Court has made clear that it "will not infer" that Congress has exercised its power to modify the secrecy requirement unless Congress has "affirmatively express[ed] its intent to do so."[224]

---

desire to discover substance of statements of other "potential witnesses" was not a particularized need).

219 *Douglas Oil*, 441 U.S. at 223.

220 *In re* Grand Jury Proceedings Relative to Perl, 838 F.2d 304, 306 (8th Cir. 1988) ("Courts have consistently distinguished the request for documents generated independent of the grand jury investigation from the request for grand jury minutes or witness transcripts[.]").

221 United States v. Sells Eng'g, Inc., 463 U.S. 418, 445 (1983) (recognizing that although particularized need standard applies to government officials, "the standard itself accommodates any relevant considerations, peculiar to government movants, that weigh for or against disclosure in a given case. For example, a district court might reasonably consider that disclosure to Justice Department attorneys poses less risk of further leakage or improper use than would disclosure to private parties or the general public").

222 Anilao v. Spota, 918 F. Supp. 2d 157, 179 (E.D.N.Y. 2013) (noting that "the passage of time erodes many of the justifications for continued secrecy" (quoting *In re* Craig, 131 F.3d 99, 107 (2d Cir. 1997))); United States v. Ferguson, 844 F. Supp. 2d 810, 829 (E.D. Mich. 2012) ("Th[e] need for secrecy is reduced when a grand jury's functions are ended.").

223 *In re* Exec. Sec. Corp., 702 F.2d 406, 409 (2d Cir. 1983) (finding it "highly significant" that witness agreed to the release of his testimony).

224 Illinois v. Abbott & Assoc., Inc., 460 U.S. 557, 572-73 (1983). Thus, statutes such as the Clayton Act, which requires the Attorney General "to the extent permitted by law" to

First, Rule 6(e) itself explicitly cross-references 18 U.S.C. § 3322,[225] part of the Financial Institutions Reform, Recovery, and Enforcement Act (FIRREA), which authorizes government attorneys and personnel who are privy to grand jury information to disclose that information, without a court order, to any other government attorney for use in enforcing the civil penalty provisions of FIRREA or "in connection with any civil forfeiture provision of Federal law."[226] In other words, in the specified circumstances, Section 3322 acts as a statutory exception to the rule that government attorneys and personnel may not disclose grand jury matters for use in separate civil proceedings without a court order.[227] The statute also establishes other specific circumstances in which a court may order disclosure of grand jury matters: during an investigation of a "banking law violation,"[228] a court may direct disclosure "to identified personnel of a Federal or State financial institution regulatory agency" for use "in relation to any matter within the jurisdiction of such regulatory agency" or "to assist an attorney for the government to whom matters have been disclosed" under the statute.

In addition, Federal Rule of Criminal Procedure 16 requires that a criminal defendant be given access to any grand jury testimony he has

---

provide a state attorney general with "any investigative files or other materials" that may be relevant to state enforcement of the antitrust laws, do not create further exceptions to Rule 6(e). *See id.*; 15 U.S.C. § 15f(b). Similarly, the Freedom of Information Act (FOIA), which generally requires government agencies to make their records available to the public on request unless disclosure is "specifically exempted" by statute (among other things), does not override grand jury secrecy, as Rule 6(e) is treated as a statute that "specifically exempt[s]" grand jury materials from disclosure. *See* 5 U.S.C. § 552(a)(3)(A), (b)(3); Labow v. Dep't of Justice, 831 F.3d 523, 529 (D.C. Cir. 2016) (Rule 6(e) "is a qualifying statute under Exemption 3"); Rugiero v. Dep't of Justice, 257 F.3d 534, 549 (6th Cir. 2001) ("[C]ourts have unanimously held that Rule 6(e) . . . constitutes a statute under section 552(b)(3) of the FOIA so that an agency may withhold grand jury materials.").

225 *See* FED. R. CRIM. P. 6(e)(3)(A)(iii) (providing that disclosure of a grand jury matter may be made to "a person authorized by 18 U.S.C. § 3322").

226 18 U.S.C. § 3322(a).

227 *Id.* § 3322(b)(1). And although, as discussed *infra*, court-ordered disclosure of grand jury information ordinarily requires a strong showing of particularized need for the information, FIRREA allows a court to authorize these banking-law-related disclosures on a showing of "substantial need." *Id.* § 3322(b)(2).

228 A "banking law violation" is defined as "a violation of, or a conspiracy to violate" sections 215, 656, 657, 1005, 1006, 1007, 1014, 1344, 1956, 1957, or 1341 or 1343 (affecting a financial institution) of title 18 of the U.S. Code, or "any provision of subchapter II of chapter 53 of title 31" of the U.S. Code. *Id.* § 3322(d)(1).

given relating to the charged offense.[229] With respect to the grand jury testimony of other witnesses, Federal Rule of Criminal Procedure 26.2 and the Jencks Act require that such testimony be provided to the defendant only *after* the witness in question has testified on direct examination at trial.[230] Disclosure is limited to grand jury testimony that "relate[s] to the subject matter of the [trial] testimony of the witness."[231] The purpose of these limitations is to balance a defendant's right to confront his accusers using information that may impeach their testimony with the need to protect government files "from unnecessary and vexatious fishing expeditions by defendants."[232]

Disclosure Mechanics and Review

Federal Rules of Criminal Procedure 6(e)(3)(F) and (G) address the procedures for seeking court-authorized disclosure of grand jury materials for use in connection with another judicial proceeding.[233] A party seeking disclosure must file a petition in the district "where the grand jury convened."[234] If the petition is filed by "the government,"[235] the court

---

[229] FED. R. CRIM. P. 16(a)(1)(B)(iii). This requirement extends as well to organizational defendants where the government contends that the person giving grand jury testimony was legally able to bind the organization. *See* FED. R. CRIM. P. 16(a)(1)(C).

[230] *See* 18 U.S.C. § 3500(a)-(b), (e)(3); FED. R. CRIM. P. 26.2(a), (f)(3). The same requirement applies to suppression and certain other hearings. FED. R. CRIM. P. 12(h), 26.2(g). As originally enacted, it was unclear whether the Jencks Act applied to grand jury testimony, leading the Supreme Court to conclude that disclosure of witness testimony to a defendant for use at trial was governed by the ordinary requirements of Rule 6(e). *See* Dennis v. United States, 384 U.S. 855, 872 (1966); Pittsburgh Plate Glass Co. v. United States, 360 U.S. 395, 399 (1959). Partially in response, Congress amended the statute in 1970 to make clear that a defendant is entitled to the relevant grand jury testimony of witnesses against him once they have testified at trial, but not before. *See* United States v. Liuzzo, 739 F.2d 541, 544 (11th Cir. 1984); *cf.* United States v. Short, 671 F.2d 178, 185-86 (6th Cir. 1982).

[231] 18 U.S.C. § 3500(b).

[232] United States v. Carter, 613 F.2d 256, 261 (10th Cir. 1979) (internal quotation marks omitted).

[233] FED. R. CRIM. P. 6(e)(3)(F)-(G). Where grand jury materials are sought by the criminal defendant that was the target of the grand jury's inquiry, a motion in the criminal case may be made. *See In re* Grand Jury Proceedings, 785 F.2d 593, 593-94 (8th Cir. 1985).

[234] FED. R. CRIM. P. 6(e)(3)(F). The purpose of this filing requirement is to secure the participation of "the grand jury's supervisory court" in "reviewing such requests, as it is in

may—but is not required to—hear the matter *ex parte*.[236] Otherwise, the petitioner must provide notice of the petition to (1) an attorney for the government, (2) the parties to the judicial proceeding for which disclosure of the grand jury materials is sought, and (3) "any other person whom the court may designate."[237] The court must "afford a reasonable opportunity" to these persons "to appear and be heard."[238]

Challenges arise when the judicial proceeding for which grand jury materials are sought is pending in a different judicial district than the district where the grand jury convened, as the latter court may be ill-suited to decide the disclosure question. The Supreme Court addressed this

---

the best position to determine the continuing need for secrecy." FED. R. CRIM. P. 6(e) advisory committee's note to 1983 amendments.

[235] It is unclear whether "the government" is limited to an "attorney for the government" within the meaning of other provisions of Rule 6(e)—that is, a prosecuting attorney within the Department of Justice—or whether it extends more broadly to governmental petitioners such as legislative committees. *See In re* Request for Access to Grand Jury Materials Grand Jury No. 81-1, Miami, 833 F.2d 1438, 1447 (11th Cir. 1987) (Guy, J., concurring in part and dissenting in part) (arguing that "government" refers only to Department of Justice attorneys and that the court erred by proceeding *ex parte* when the requester was a congressional committee). The legislative history indicates that the purpose of allowing *ex parte* government petitions is to "preserve, to the maximum extent possible, grand jury secrecy," S. REP. NO. 95-354, at 8 (1977), *reprinted in* 1977 U.S.C.C.A.N. 527, 532, suggesting the narrower interpretation.

[236] An *ex parte* proceeding is one in which the adverse party is not given notice or an opportunity to be heard on the matter at hand. *Ex Parte*, BLACK'S LAW DICTIONARY (10th ed. 2014). The Advisory Committee note contemplates that a court should be able to decide whether to proceed *ex parte* "based upon the circumstances of the particular case," pointing out that an *ex parte* proceeding "is much less likely to be appropriate if the government acts as petitioner as an accommodation to, e.g., a state agency." FED. R. CRIM. P. 6(e) advisory committee's note to 1983 amendments. At least one court has held that when the government files a petition for disclosure on behalf of a private litigant, it must give the requisite notice unless it "makes a specific showing of the need to make the disclosure *ex parte*." United States v. Nix, 21 F.3d 347, 352 (9th Cir. 1994); *see also In re* Grand Jury Proceedings (Roe), 153 F. Supp. 2d 403, 407 (S.D.N.Y 2001) (recognizing that where another party is "the real party in interest, he should be the Petitioner, in which case the Petition would be required to be made on notice").

[237] FED. R. CRIM. P. 6(e)(3)(F).

[238] FED. R. CRIM. P. 6(e)(3)(F). The attorney for the government in the district where the grand jury convened is included so that he may represent "the public interest in secrecy." FED. R. CRIM. P. 6(e) advisory committee's note to 1983 amendments. Inclusion of parties to the other judicial proceeding recognizes that "release of the transcripts to their civil adversaries could result in substantial injury to them." *Id.* Finally, the catch-all allowance for "any other" court-designated person recognizes that those who provided the information to the grand jury that is the subject of the petition and those who were investigated by the grand jury, among others, may have an interest in the matter. *Id.*

situation in *Douglas Oil Co. v. Petrol Stops Northwest*,[239] and the Court's conclusions have essentially been adopted in Rule 6(e)(3)(G). The Rule provides that unless the court in which the petition is filed—that is, the court in the district where the grand jury convened—"can reasonably determine whether disclosure is proper," it must transfer the matter to the district where the separate judicial proceeding is pending for determination.[240] This provision reflects "a preference for having the disclosure issue decided by the grand jury court," while recognizing that that court may be unable to reach a decision because it "will have no first-hand knowledge of the litigation in which the transcripts allegedly are needed, and no practical means by which such knowledge can be obtained."[241]

To facilitate resolution by the transferee court, the grand jury court must transmit to the transferee court "the material sought to be disclosed, if feasible, and a written evaluation of the need for continued grand jury secrecy."[242] The first requirement "facilitate[s] timely disclosure if it is thereafter ordered" and assists the transferee court "in deciding how great the need for disclosure actually is."[243] The Rule does not require transmittal of the grand jury material if it is impracticable to do so, as, for example if the material is "exceedingly voluminous."[244] The requirement of a written evaluation of the need for continuing secrecy recognizes that the grand jury court "is in the best position to assess the interest in continued grand jury secrecy in the particular instance," and it is thus "important that the court

---

[239] 441 U.S. 211 (1979).

[240] FED. R. CRIM. P. 6(e)(3)(G). Transfer may be initiated *sua sponte* or at the request of any party to the disclosure proceeding. FED. R. CRIM. P. 6(e) advisory committee's note to 1983 amendments.

[241] FED. R. CRIM. P. 6(e) advisory committee's note to 1983 amendments (quoting *Douglas Oil*, 441 U.S. at 226). Thus, when the court where the petition is filed has "sufficient knowledge to determine whether disclosure" is proper, it need not transfer the matter to the court where the judicial proceeding is pending. *See, e.g.*, *In re* Grand Jury Investigation, 55 F.3d 350, 356 (8th Cir. 1995).

[242] FED. R. CRIM. P. 6(e)(3)(G).

[243] FED. R. CRIM. P. 6(e) advisory committee's note to 1983 amendments. Consistent with this requirement, the court may view the materials in camera in making the disclosure determination. *E.g.*, United States v. Gatto, 746 F. Supp. 432, 481-82 (D.N.J. 1990).

[244] FED. R. CRIM. P. 6(e) advisory committee's note to 1983 amendments (quoting *In re* 1975-2 Grand Jury Investigation, 566 F.2d 1293 (5th Cir. 1978))

which will now have to balance that interest against the need for disclosure receive the benefit of the [grand jury] court's assessment."[245]

Upon transfer, the same persons specified in Rule 6(e)(3)(F) must be given a reasonable opportunity to appear and be heard.[246] The transferee court then makes the ultimate decision whether to disclose "based on its own determination of the need for disclosure and the transferring court's evaluation of the competing need for continued secrecy."[247]

Generally, a court's order regarding disclosure under Rule 6(e) is immediately appealable.[248] Because the determination of whether "particularized need" exists to justify disclosure in a given case is highly

---

[245] FED. R. CRIM. P. 6(e) advisory committee's note to 1983 amendments.

[246] FED. R. CRIM. P. 6(e)(3)(G). The requirement applies even if the interested parties specified in the rule were previously heard before the court that ordered transfer. FED. R. CRIM. P. 6(e) advisory committee's note to 1983 amendments.

[247] *In re* Moore, 776 F.2d 136, 137 (7th Cir. 1985). As discussed elsewhere in this report, any hearing and filings must be closed and sealed to the extent necessary to protect grand jury secrecy. *See supra* § Disclosure of Matters Occurring Before the Grand Jury; FED. R. CRIM. P. 6(e)(4)-(5). If the court determines that disclosure is warranted, it may impose restrictions or limitations on such disclosure. *See* FED. R. CRIM. P. 6(e)(3)(E) (providing that court may authorize disclosure "at a time, in a manner, and subject to any other conditions that it directs").

[248] *See* 28 U.S.C. § 1291 (providing that courts of appeals have jurisdiction over appeals from "all final decisions of the district courts of the United States); United States v. Campbell, 294 F.3d 824, 827 (7th Cir. 2002) (collecting cases); *In re* Barker, 741 F.2d 250, 252 (9th Cir. 1984) (recognizing order granting disclosure was appealable because it conclusively resolved the only issue in an independent judicial proceeding). Appeals of Rule 6(e) disclosure orders may not be immediately appealable when the defendant seeks disclosure in the criminal proceeding following grand jury indictment, as some courts have treated a disclosure order in this context as an interlocutory order respecting discovery that may be appealed only after final judgment. *See In re* 1985 Grand Jury Proceedings, 785 F.2d 593, 595 (8th Cir. 1985) (indicating that order on motion filed by targets of grand jury investigation was "clearly not a final judgment on the merits of the litigation"); State of Illinois v. F.E. Moran, Inc., 740 F.2d 533, 535 (7th Cir. 1984), *superseded by rule on other grounds as stated in In re* United States, 398 F.3d 615 (7th Cir. 2005) ("If the petition is filed in the federal criminal proceeding that follows indictment by the grand jury, the order granting or denying the petition is an interlocutory order respecting discovery and cannot be appealed under 28 U.S.C. § 1291[.]"). In any event, a writ of mandamus—an extraordinary remedy through which a superior court directly impels a lower court to take or refrain from taking some action—may still be available. *See* FDIC v. Ernst & Whinney, 921 F.2d 83, 85 (6th Cir. 1990) (concluding discovery order regarding disclosure of grand jury matters was interlocutory but recognizing availability of mandamus).

fact-specific and discretionary,[249] an appellate court's review will be under the deferential "abuse of discretion" standard.[250]

Establishing and Remedying Violations of Grand Jury Secrecy

A knowing violation of Rule 6, including the obligation of secrecy, "may be punished as a contempt of court."[251] Though not explicit in the Rule, courts have held that both criminal and civil contempt may be imposed, meaning that the remedy may include imprisonment, monetary sanctions, or equitable relief.[252] In limited circumstances, an indictment may also be dismissed[253] or evidence suppressed.[254] For example, where the government unilaterally disclosed a defendant's grand jury testimony in a separate civil forfeiture proceeding to establish probable cause for

---

[249] Douglas Oil Co. v. Petrol Stops Nw., 441 U.S. 211, 223 (1979) ("[A] court called upon to determine whether grand jury transcripts should be released necessarily is infused with substantial discretion.").

[250] United States v. Index Newspapers LLC, 766 F.3d 1072, 1081 (9th Cir. 2014).

[251] FED. R. CRIM. P. 6(e)(7). Violation of any guidelines jointly issued by the Attorney General and the Director of National Intelligence is punishable as a contempt of court to the same extent. *Id.*

[252] Finn v. Schiller, 72 F.3d 1182, 1188 (4th Cir. 1996); Barry v. United States, 865 F.2d 1317, 1321-23 (D.C. Cir. 1989); *see* 18 U.S.C. § 401 (delineating circumstances in which criminal contempt may be utilized); *cf.* Blalock v. United States, 844 F.2d 1546, 1553 (11th Cir. 1988) (Tjoflat, J., specially concurring) (expressing view that Rule 6 contempt provision simply applies criminal contempt statute to wrongful disclosure of grand jury matters); *In re* Grand Jury Investigation (90-3-2), 748 F. Supp. 1188, 1202 (E.D. Mich. 1990) (reading provision as permitting only criminal contempt remedy). Improper disclosure of grand jury matters may also subject the discloser to prosecution for obstruction of justice in certain circumstances. *E.g.*, United States v. Brenson, 104. F.3d 1267, 1275-80 (11th Cir. 1997) (involving grand juror who disclosed confidential information to target of investigation).

[253] United States v. Williams, 504 U.S. 36, 46 (1992) ("[T]he supervisory power can be used to dismiss an indictment because of misconduct before the grand jury, at least where that misconduct amounts to a violation of one of those few, clear rules which were carefully drafted and approved by this Court and by Congress to ensure the integrity of the grand jury's functions[.]" (internal quotation marks omitted)); United States v. Friedman, 854 F.2d 535, 584 (2d Cir. 1988) ("A betrayal of grand jury secrecy . . . jeopardizes the defendant's right to a fair trial before a petit jury."). A breach of grand jury secrecy will not warrant dismissal of the indictment unless the defendant was actually prejudiced by the breach. *See* Bank of Nova Scotia v. United States, 487 U.S. 250, 253-54 (1988).

[254] United States v. Thomas, 736 F.3d 54, 66 (1st Cir. 2013) (recognizing theoretical availability of suppression of evidence in "severe cases"); United States v. Coughlan, 842 F.2d 737, 740 (4th Cir. 1988).

seizure of the defendant's car, one court suggested that suppression of the testimony could be necessary to "protect the integrity of the grand jury system."[255]

Courts disagree on whether the contempt provision of Rule 6 establishes a private right of action based on an alleged violation of grand jury secrecy.[256]

A party seeking one of the remedies noted above will be required to establish a *prima facie* case that a violation of grand jury secrecy has occurred.[257] This showing will ordinarily require some basis to infer that the source of any leaked grand jury information was one prohibited under Rule 6(e), and the court may consider evidence submitted to rebut the allegation of wrongdoing.[258] If a *prima facie* case is established, the court will hold an evidentiary hearing in which the alleged source of the unauthorized disclosure (typically the government) will bear the burden of "attempt[ing] to explain its actions."[259] For instance, the movants in one case made a *prima facie* showing that an independent counsel breached grand jury secrecy by submitting to the court "various news articles indicating that information relating to grand jury proceedings or witnesses was obtained from sources associated with the" independent counsel's office.[260] The court thus recognized that the independent counsel would be called upon to attempt to rebut the inferences drawn from the news articles by submitting evidence (potentially including affidavits, documents, or live testimony) to

---

[255] *Coughlan*, 842 F.2d at 740.

[256] *See In re* Sealed Case No. 98-3077, 151 F.3d 1059, 1069 (D.C. Cir. 1998) (recognizing that proceeding to enforce Rule 6(e) "is civil in nature and may be initiated by a private plaintiff"); *Blalock*, 844 F.2d at 1551 (recognizing binding authority that "a target may bring suit for injunctive relief against the individuals subject to Rule 6(e)(2)"); *In re* Grand Jury Investigation, 610 F.2d 202, 214 (5th Cir. 1980) (addressing requisite showing to support private party's petition for contempt sanctions); *but see Finn*, 72 F.3d at 1189 (holding that although contempt may be criminal or civil, Rule creates no private cause of action); *Grand Jury Investigation (90-3-2)*, 748 F. Supp. at 1203 ("By its terms, the rule grants no private rights to any identifiable class of persons.").

[257] *Sealed Case No. 98-3077*, 151 F.3d at 1067; United States v. Rioux, 97 F.3d 648, 662 (2d Cir. 1996); *Barry*, 865 F.2d at 1321.

[258] *Rioux*, 97 F.3d at 662; *Blalock*, 844 F.2d at 1551; *see Sealed Case No. 98-3077*, 151 F.3d at 1068 n.7 ("The articles submitted need only be susceptible to an interpretation that the information reported was furnished by an attorney or agent of the government.").

[259] *Sealed Case No. 98-3077*, 151 F.3d at 1068.

[260] *Id.*

show either that the information disclosed to the media did not constitute "matters occurring before the grand jury" or that the source of the information was not the government.[261]

An order denying a defendant's motion to dismiss the indictment based on a violation of Rule 6(e) is not immediately appealable,[262] and any error may be considered harmless if the defendant is subsequently convicted.[263]

GRAND JURY SECRECY AND CONGRESSIONAL OVERSIGHT

As the discussion of grand jury secrecy and Federal Rule of Criminal Procedure 6(e) above reflects, no exception to the general rule of secrecy explicitly authorizes disclosure of grand jury matters to Congress, either by agreement or pursuant to a congressional subpoena. Nevertheless, a few courts have addressed the applicability of Rule 6(e) and its exceptions to congressional requests for information, including in the course of committee investigations and preliminary to impeachment proceedings. At a minimum, these decisions indicate that Congress may be able to obtain grand jury materials by invoking a Rule 6(e) exception before a court under certain circumstances. Congress has also previously considered legislation that would have expressly permitted a court to authorize disclosure of grand jury matters to congressional committees, though the congressional-access provision ultimately did not become law.

This section of the report addresses the circumstances in which Congress may obtain and disseminate grand jury materials under Rule 6(e) as it is presently construed;[264] it then addresses legal issues to consider if

---

[261] *Id.* at 1075. The court suggested such evidence might include information reflecting what actually occurred before the grand jury, the identities of any employees with access to the disclosed information, and/or evidence reflecting general policies concerning press contacts, among other things. *Id.*

[262] Midland Asphalt Corp. v. United States, 489 U.S. 794, 799 (1989).

[263] *See* United States v. Wilkes, 662 F.3d 524, 537 (9th Cir. 2011) ("[G]rand jury leaks are the kind of non-structural errors that are rendered harmless by the trial jury's verdict.").

[264] A discussion of executive privilege and other potential independent limitations on the investigative or law enforcement materials that Congress may obtain in certain situations is

Congress seeks to create a new Rule 6(e) exception for congressional committees.

Congressional Investigative Authority

Congress generally has broad authority to obtain information for oversight and investigative purposes. The power of Congress to conduct investigations is "inherent in the legislative process,"[265] and such power is "as penetrating and far-reaching as the potential power to enact and appropriate under the Constitution."[266] As a corollary, the "[i]ssuance of subpoenas . . . has long been held to be a legitimate use by Congress of its power to investigate."[267] Beyond subpoenas, Congress has exercised its power of inquiry through less formal means, such as by submitting letter requests for information.[268]

Congressional inquiries are broadly protected from judicial scrutiny. Provided that a committee's investigation is authorized and conducted pursuant to a valid legislative purpose, the Speech or Debate Clause[269] of Article I of the Constitution creates "an absolute bar to [judicial] interference."[270]

Application of Grand Jury Secrecy to Congressional Disclosures

Pursuant to its broad authority to investigate, Congress has on several occasions sought grand jury information based on legislative interest in

---

beyond the scope of this report. For more information, see Roberto Iraola, *Congressional Oversight, Executive Privilege, and Requests for Information Relating to Federal Criminal Investigations and Prosecutions*, 87 IOWA L. REV. 1559 (2002).

265 Watkins v. United States, 354 U.S. 178, 187 (1957).

266 Eastland v. United States Servicemen's Fund, 421 U.S. 491, 504 n.15 (1975) (quoting Barenblatt v. United States, 360 U.S. 109, 111 (1959)).

267 *Id.* at 504.

268 *E.g.*, *In re* Request for Access to Grand Jury Materials Grand Jury No. 81-1, Miami, 833 F.2d 1438, 1445 (11th Cir. 1987) ("Although in the instant case the Committee requested rather than subpoenaed records, this Court should grant such access to the House as will not violate our privileges or constitutional powers.").

269 U.S. CONST. art. I, §6, cl. 1.

270 *Eastland*, 421 U.S. at 503.

particular executive branch activities, either through letters or subpoenas to executive branch officials[271] or through petitions filed with the court.[272] Faced with these legislative efforts to obtain otherwise-secret grand jury materials, courts have reached conflicting conclusions as to whether the rule of grand jury secrecy enshrined in Rule 6(e) applies to disclosures to Congress at all.

Relying on an apparently novel conception of the "authority of Congress under the Speech or Debate Clause," two courts have held that Congress has a "constitutionally independent legal right" to obtain documents in furtherance of "legitimate legislative activity" regardless of whether the documents disclose matters occurring before a grand jury.[273] First, in *In re Grand Jury Investigation of Ven-Fuel*, the chairman of the Subcommittee on Oversight and Investigations of the House of Representatives' Committee on Interstate and Foreign Commerce petitioned a district court for an order authorizing disclosure of documents presented to a federal grand jury in Florida in the course of its investigation of possible criminal conduct by a company called VenFuel, Inc.[274] The court recognized that the subcommittee's request implicated "the powers and operations of the coequal, but interdependent, branches of the federal government . . . over theoretical fault lines," but concluded there was no "direct conflict" because the subcommittee's legitimate legislative purpose in seeking the documents meant that it was "entitled to disclosure" regardless of grand jury secrecy rules.[275]

Ten years after the decision in *Ven-Fuel*, the issue of congressional access to grand jury materials came before a different court in connection

---

[271] *See In re* Grand Jury Impanelled Oct. 2, 1978 (79-2), 510 F. Supp. 112, 113-14 (D.D.C. 1981).

[272] *In re* Grand Jury Investigation of Ven-Fuel, 441 F. Supp. 1299, 1300 (M.D. Fla. 1977).

[273] *Ven-Fuel*, 441 F. Supp. at 1307; *see also In re* Grand Jury Proceedings of Grand Jury No. 81-1 (Miami), 669 F. Supp. 1072, 1075 (S.D. Fla. 1987), *aff'd*, 833 F.2d 1438 (11th Cir. 1987); *cf. In re* Report and Recommendation of June 5, 1972 Grand Jury Concerning Transmission of Evidence to House of Representatives, 370 F. Supp. 1219, 1226 (D.D.C. 1974), *mandamus denied sub nom.* Haldeman v. Sirica, 501 F.2d 714 (D.C. Cir. 1974) (concluding that delivery of grand jury report to House committee considering impeachment was "eminently proper, and indeed, obligatory" where the report was "a proper concern" of the committee and need was "not disputed").

[274] 441 F. Supp. at 1302.

[275] *Id.* at 1307.

with the potential impeachment of a federal judge.[276] The judge had been indicted for conspiring to solicit a bribe to influence a judicial decision, causing the House of Representatives to introduce a resolution calling for his impeachment.[277] The resolution was referred to the House Committee on the Judiciary, which subsequently requested that the district court deliver all records of the grand jury that had indicted the judge.[278] The judge objected, but the district court concluded that the committee was entitled to the records for several reasons, one of which was that, in accordance with *Ven-Fuel*, a "congressional investigation relating to the impeachment of a federal judge" falls within the authorized legislative activities "embraced" by the Speech or Debate Clause.[279]

Criticizing the decision in *Ven-Fuel*, other courts have sharply disagreed with the conclusion that the Speech or Debate Clause provides a basis to ignore grand jury secrecy when Congress is the requester. In *In re Grand Jury Investigation of Uranium Industry*,[280] for instance, the Senate Judiciary Committee petitioned a court for an order authorizing disclosure of documents in the possession of the Department of Justice related to its investigation of the uranium industry.[281] The committee's interest in the documents apparently stemmed from the fact that an expansive grand jury investigation conducted by the department's Antitrust Division had yielded

---

[276] *See Grand Jury No. 81-1 (Miami)*, 669 F. Supp. at 1073.

[277] *Id.* at 1073-74.

[278] *Id.*

[279] *Id.* at 1075. The court also determined, among other things, that disclosure was proper pursuant to "the power of impeachment that the Constitution vests in the House of Representatives," which includes "the power to obtain evidence" through means contemplated by the Constitution's Necessary and Proper Clause. *Id.* at 1074-75. It does not appear that any other courts have expressly relied on the impeachment power as an independent basis to disregard Rule 6(e) and the rule of grand jury secrecy. *Cf. June 5, 1972 Grand Jury*, 370 F. Supp. at 1226 ("[R]ather than injuring separation of powers principles, the [Grand] Jury sustains them by lending its aid to the House in the exercise of that body's constitutional jurisdiction [over impeachment]."). Some courts have, however, concluded that an impeachment inquiry is preliminary to a "judicial proceeding" within the meaning of Rule 6(e)(3)(E)(i) or that impeachment is a sufficiently exceptional circumstance to warrant disclosure pursuant to a court's inherent authority. These bases for disclosure of grand jury matters to Congress in connection with impeachment are discussed *infra* in their respective sections.

[280] 1979-2 Trade Cas. 78,639 (D.D.C. 1979).

[281] *Id.* at 78,640.

no indictments.[282] In seeking court-ordered disclosure of the grand jury materials, the committee asserted, among other things, that it was not required to establish the applicability of a Rule 6(e) exception or make a showing of particularized need because the Speech or Debate Clause entitled it to the materials.[283] The court, however, considered "the suggestion that Rule 6(e) does not apply to disclosures to Congress" to be "[un]acceptable."[284] The court noted that Rule 6(e) "contains no reservations in favor of Congress" and rejected the *Ven-Fuel* court's suggestion that the Speech or Debate Clause may be "used as a sword to enable Congress to penetrate an otherwise secret function of one of the other branches."[285] While, in the court's view, the Clause would protect Congress from collateral interference if it were attempting to "acquire materials which it has a legal right to obtain," the Clause would not sanction expansion of Congress's legal rights "to manufacture a new right to obtain grand jury materials" that could be affirmatively employed.[286]

As the court in *Uranium Industry* recognized, the *Ven-Fuel* decision's reliance on the Speech or Debate Clause as a font of constitutional authority permitting congressional access to grand jury materials finds little support in the broader case law on the Clause. Though the Clause functions to *protect* congressional activity, including lawful use of the subpoena power, from judicial interference when such activity is challenged by a third party,[287] courts have not viewed the Clause to constitute a sword that Congress may use to affirmatively seek judicial authorization for disclosure of information in the possession of a

---

[282] *Id.*
[283] *Id.*
[284] *Id.* at 78,641-42.
[285] *Id.* at 78,642.
[286] *Id. See also In re* Grand Jury Impaneled Oct. 2, 1978 (79-2), 510 F. Supp. 112, 116 (D.D.C. 1981) (denying congressional committee request for grand jury materials "to fulfill its oversight responsibilities" because no Rule 6(e) exception applied); William E. Weinberger, *Congressional Access to Grand Jury Transcripts*, 33 STAN. L. REV. 155, 167-68 (1980) ("[T]he speech or debate clause protects congressional use of compulsory process to obtain only those materials to which it has a legal right.").
[287] *See In re* Grand Jury, 821 F.2d 946, 957 (3d Cir. 1987) (explaining that the Clause "shields Congressmen from suit to block a Congressional subpoena").

coordinate branch.[288] That said, the extent to which the rule of grand jury secrecy applies more generally along the "theoretical fault line[]"[289] that exists between executive branch activity and Congress's Article I investigative authority remains unsettled.[290] It is worth noting in this regard that although Congress's power to obtain information for legitimate legislative purposes is broad, it is not limitless.[291]

Though no federal appellate courts have spoken directly to the issue,[292] decisions addressing the now-lapsed independent counsel statute appear to lend some support to the position that Congress enjoys no special constitutional solicitude in obtaining otherwise-secret grand jury materials. That statute required a duly appointed independent counsel to file a pre-termination "final report" with the court "setting forth fully and completely a description of the work of the independent counsel," and the statute permitted the court to release "to the Congress, the public, or any appropriate person, such portions of [the] report . . . as the division of the court considers appropriate."[293] In several decisions considering whether to authorize such release of independent counsel reports to Congress and the public, the D.C. Circuit has recognized that Rule 6(e) applies to an independent counsel, meaning that "any release of grand jury material" in the final report authorized by statute "falls within the protective provisions" of the Rule

---

[288] *See* United States v. Am. Tel. & Tel. Co., 567 F.2d 121, 129 (D.C. Cir. 1977) ("Congress' investigatory power is not, itself, absolute.").

[289] *Ven-Fuel*, 441 F. Supp. at 1307.

[290] For additional information on the scope of the Speech or Debate Clause, see CRS Report R45043, *Understanding the Speech or Debate Clause*, by Todd Garvey.

[291] *See* Watkins v. United States, 354 U.S. 178, 187 (1957) ("There is no general authority to expose the private affairs of individuals without justification in terms of the functions of the Congress."); Barenblatt v. United States, 360 U.S. 109, 112 (1959) ("Congress, in common with all branches of the Government, must exercise its powers subject to the limitations placed by the Constitution on governmental action, more particularly in the context of this case, the relevant limitations of the Bill of Rights.").

[292] The Eleventh Circuit affirmed the district court's decision in *Grand Jury No. 81-1, Miami* on the ground that the disclosure of materials to a House committee contemplating impeachment fell within the exception for disclosures "preliminarily to or in connection with a judicial proceeding." *See* 833 F.2d 1438, 1446 (11th Cir. 1987). The appellate court did note, however, that "[d]eference to principles of comity" would "not entail simply giving the House any materials it requests," but would be "a factor to be weighed in favor of disclosure when making the Rule 6(e) analysis." *Id.* at 1445.

[293] 28 U.S.C. § 594(h)(1)-(2).

unless an exception applies.[294] Nevertheless, the court has read a provision of the independent counsel statute permitting a court to authorize disclosure of the report as establishing a "judicial proceeding" such that release of the report may fall within that exception to Rule 6(e).[295] Pursuant to the exception, the court has proceeded to consider multiple factors in deciding whether to authorize the report's release.[296] In other words, rather than finding an independent constitutional entitlement to grand jury material when faced with the question of whether to authorize the release to Congress of a report containing such material, the D.C. Circuit has simply applied Rule 6(e).[297] It could be argued, however, that because these cases did not involve a congressional subpoena, the court was not faced with a direct exercise of Congress's constitutional power of inquiry.

The Department of Justice, for its part, agrees that it may release grand jury material to Congress in response to a subpoena only to the extent that disclosure is permitted under Rule 6(e).[298] It takes the opposite position from the *Ven-Fuel* court with respect to separation-of-powers implications when Congress requests grand jury material: in the department's view, recognizing a congressional "independent right of access" to grand jury material would amount to "legislative encroachment into the Executive's exclusive authority to enforce the law."[299]

---

[294] *In re* Cisneros, 426 F.3d 409, 412 (D.C. Cir. 2005).

[295] *In re* Espy, 259 F.3d 725, 729 (D.C. Cir. 2001); *see also In re* North, 16 F.3d 1234, 1244 (D.C. Cir. 1994).

[296] *Cisneros*, 426 F.3d at 415.

[297] *Id.* It is worth noting that the court's consideration of whether to release to Congress a report containing grand jury material in *Cisneros* was cursory, with the court merely acknowledging that the subject of the report was "a matter within the responsibility and concern of the Congress." *Id.* The court also authorized the report at issue to be delivered to Congress inclusive of a section that it found should not be disclosed to the public. *Id.* Thus, the court arguably did view Congress's constitutional role as uniquely deserving of consideration in determining whether disclosure was appropriate; but the court did not conclude, as the *Ven-Fuel* court did, that Rule 6(e) and its exceptions were irrelevant.

[298] U.S. Dep't of Justice, Office of Legal Counsel, *Congressional Subpoenas of Department of Justice Investigative Files*, 8 U.S. Op. Off. Legal Counsel 252, 259-60 (1984).

[299] U.S. Dep't of Justice, Office of Legal Counsel, Legislation Providing for Court-Ordered Disclosure of Grand Jury Materials to Congressional Committees, 9 U.S. Op. Off. Legal Counsel 86, 87 (1985).

Requests for Materials Not Constituting Grand Jury Matters

Assuming that Rule 6(e) does apply to congressional requests, it is clear that Congress may nevertheless obtain materials that do not constitute "matters occurring before the grand jury" within the meaning of the Rule.

Rule 6(e) protects from disclosure only those materials that "tend to reveal some secret aspect of the grand jury's investigation."[300] Thus, where a congressional committee has an interest in the subject matter of an ongoing grand jury investigation, the committee may be able to obtain most, if not all, of the same evidence the grand jury is considering from other sources.[301]

For instance, although the court in *Ven-Fuel* viewed Congress as constitutionally entitled to disclosure of documents that had been presented to a grand jury, the court also determined that the documents were not necessarily cloaked in secrecy under Rule 6(e) in the first instance.[302] And while not all courts may take such a narrow view of grand jury "matters,"[303] the principle that "[t]here is no *per se* rule against disclosure of any and all information which has reached the grand jury chambers" is a well-recognized one.[304]

---

[300] Lopez v. Dep't of Justice, 393 F.3d 1345, 1349 (D.C. Cir. 2005) (quoting Senate of the Commonwealth of P.R. v. Dep't of Justice, 823 F.2d 574, 582 (D.C. Cir. 1987)); *see supra* § Disclosure of Matters Occurring Before the Grand Jury.

[301] Congress could, for example, subpoena grand jury witnesses, who are not obligated to maintain the secrecy of grand jury proceedings. *See supra* § Persons Subject to Rule 6(e).

[302] *In re* Grand Jury Investigation of Ven-Fuel, 441 F. Supp. 1299, 1303-04 (M.D. Fla. 1977); *see also In re* Senate Banking Comm. Hearings, 19 F.R.D. 412 (N.D. Ill. 1956) (authorizing disclosure to Senate Banking Committee of documents shown to grand jury because "when the fact or document is sought for itself, independently, rather than because it was stated before or displayed to the grand jury, there is no bar of secrecy").

[303] *See In re* Grand Jury Subpoenas, 454 F.3d 511, 522 (6th Cir. 2006) (applying rebuttable presumption that nonpublic documents obtained by grand jury by coercive means are secret).

[304] Senate of Commonwealth of P.R. v. Dep't of Justice, 823 F.2d 574, 582 (D.C. Cir. 1987); *see also, e.g.*, United States v. Interstate Dress Carriers, Inc., 280 F.2d 52, 54 (2d Cir. 1960) (acknowledging that Rule 6(e) does not "foreclose from all future revelation to proper authorities the same information or documents which were presented to the grand jury").

Applicability of Rule 6(e) Exceptions to Congress

Although no exception to grand jury secrecy explicitly encompasses disclosures to Congress, a few of the exceptions could apply to Congress in particular situations, which are discussed below in turn.

Disclosures to Congress Without Judicial Authorization

Members of Congress as Government Personnel

As discussed, Rule 6(e) permits disclosure of grand jury matters, excluding grand jury deliberations and votes, to "any government personnel—including those of a state, state subdivision, Indian tribe, or foreign government—that an attorney for the government considers necessary to assist in performing that attorney's duty to enforce federal criminal law."[305]

The term "government personnel" is not defined in the Rule,[306] and the provision's legislative history reflects a concern with information-sharing between federal prosecutors and federal law enforcement officers or agency subject-matter experts who were needed to understand certain issues in complex cases.[307] That said, during the hearings on the proposed amendments that added the exception, there was some testimony indicating that the breadth of the term "government personnel" could mean that "even Members of Congress or the military" would be included.[308]

---

[305] FED. R. CRIM. P. 6(e)(3)(A)(ii).

[306] An Advisory Committee note indicates that the term "includes, but is not limited to, employees of administrative agencies and government departments." FED. R. CRIM. P. 6(e) advisory committee's note to 1977 amendments. Although there is reason to think that employees of government "agencies" and "departments" would be limited to the executive branch, *see* Hubbard v. United States, 514 U.S. 695, 715 (1995) (concluding that agencies and departments do not include the judiciary), the fact that the Advisory Committee viewed government personnel as extending *beyond* agency and department employees suggests that Members of Congress could be included.

[307] *See generally In re* Grand Jury Proceedings, 158 F. Supp. 2d 96, 107-15 (D. Mass. 2001).

[308] Proposed Amendments to the Federal Rules of Criminal Procedure: Hearings Before the Subcomm. on Criminal Justice of the House Comm. on the Judiciary, 95th Cong. 149 (1977) (testimony of Bernard J. Nussbaum, Esq.).

It is thus possible that a Member of Congress, or congressional staff, could be considered "government personnel" to whom disclosure could be made without a court order under this exception.

Any such disclosure, however, would be exceedingly circumscribed in light of the exception's other requirements. First, disclosure would be at the discretion of the attorney for the government, and would be limited to a situation in which the attorney believed that the Member or staff was needed to assist the attorney in enforcing federal criminal law.[309] Second, the Member or staff to whom disclosure was made could use the grand jury information only for the same purpose, that is, to assist the attorney in prosecuting the federal crimes to which the information related.[310]

Third, the Member or staff would be obligated to maintain the secrecy of the information and could further disclose it only in accordance with Rule 6(e).[311]

As such, even assuming Members of Congress or congressional staff fall within the meaning of "government personnel," the exception would not permit Congress to seek grand jury materials for broader independent investigative or legislative purposes.

Congressional Access to Intelligence and National Security Information

Rule 6(e)(3)(D) permits an attorney for the government to disclose, among other things, any grand jury matter involving threats of attack or intelligence gathering by foreign powers or threats of sabotage or terrorism to "any appropriate federal . . . government official" (among others).[312] Similar to the exception for "government personnel," the Rule does not define the term "appropriate . . . government official." Nonetheless, other statutory provisions suggest that the term "government official" could be

[309] See FED. R. CRIM. P. 6(e)(3)(A)(ii).
[310] FED. R. CRIM. P. 6(e)(3)(B).
[311] FED. R. CRIM. P. 6(e)(2)(B)(vii).
[312] FED. R. CRIM. P. 6(e)(3)(D).

construed to include a Member of Congress.[313] As with the "government personnel" exception, however, disclosure under this exception would be limited: only grand jury information pertaining to the specified subject matter would be available, at the discretion of the attorney for the government, and the Member receiving the information could use it "only as necessary in the conduct of [her] official duties subject to any limitations on the unauthorized disclosure of such information."[314]

Disclosures to Congress with Judicial Authorization

Congressional Activities as "Judicial Proceedings"

Rule 6(e)'s "judicial proceeding" exception may also be relevant to Congress. As previously described, the Rule provides that a court may authorize disclosure of a grand jury matter "preliminarily to or in connection with a judicial proceeding,"[315] with the term "judicial proceeding" generally contemplating some necessary resort to the judicial system.[316] Two courts have determined that a congressional committee's request for grand jury materials pursuant to its ordinary investigative and oversight functions does not qualify under this exception, as the possibility that "the actions it is investigating may wind up in the courts if wrongdoing is uncovered" is "too remote to trigger the Rule 6(e) exception."[317] By contrast, where a congressional committee has sought grand jury materials in connection with the contemplated impeachment of a specific public official, several courts have recognized that court-ordered disclosure may be available pursuant to the "judicial proceeding"

---

[313] *See* 18 U.S.C. § 201 (defining "public official" to include Members of Congress for purposes of criminal bribery provision); *but see* 18 U.S.C. § 1116(b)(3) (defining "foreign official" to mean executive-equivalent officers, among others, for purposes of criminal homicide provision).

[314] FED. R. CRIM. P. 6(e)(3)(D)(i).

[315] FED. R. CRIM. P. 6(e)(3)(E)(i).

[316] *E.g.*, *In re* Grand Jury 89-4-72, 932 F.2d 481, 485 (6th Cir. 1991) (concluding the possibility of eventual, discretionary court review did not make nonjudicial disciplinary process "preliminary to" a judicial proceeding).

[317] *In re* Grand Jury Investigation of Uranium Industry, 1979-2 Trade Cas. 78,639, 78,643-45 (D.D.C. 1979); *see also In re* Grand Jury Impanelled Oct. 2, 1978 (79-2), 510 F. Supp. 112, 114 (D.D.C. 1981) (citing *Uranium Industry* for the proposition that a Senate "Subcommittee's general oversight proceedings do not constitute a 'judicial proceeding'").

exception.[318] Under this view, though "impeachment proceedings before Congress . . . are not by a 'court,'"[319] a "contemplated trial" in the Senate is still "very much a judicial proceeding."[320]

A committee seeking court-authorized disclosure on the basis of this exception must establish a "particularized need" for the materials at issue, which requires a showing that the need outweighs the public interest in secrecy.[321] In the context of impeachment, courts have concluded that a congressional committee's need is sufficient to warrant disclosure, at least where the grand jury's work has concluded.[322] Nevertheless, given that mere "relevance" or "efficiency" is generally insufficient[323] to establish a particularized need for grand jury materials, the context of the request and

---

[318] *See In re* Request for Access to Grand Jury Materials Grand Jury No. 81-1, Miami, 833 F.2d 1438, 1440 (11th Cir. 1987) (noting in case where House Judiciary Committee sought materials for impeachment inquiry that lower court held and parties agreed that "a Senate impeachment trial qualifies as a 'judicial proceeding'" and "a House impeachment inquiry is 'preliminary to' the Senate trial"); *In re* Report and Recommendation of June 5, 1972 Grand Jury Concerning Transmission of Evidence to House of Representatives, 370 F. Supp. 1219, 1230 (D.D.C. 1974), *mandamus denied sub nom.* Haldeman v. Sirica, 501 F.2d 714 (D.C. Cir. 1974) (considering whether to transmit grand jury report to House Judiciary Committee and concluding that it would be "incredible" to view a police disciplinary investigation, but not "a proceeding of so great import as an impeachment investigation," as a judicial proceeding); *see also Uranium Industry*, 1979-2 Trade Cas. at 78,644 (distinguishing a case involving impeachment).

[319] *Grand Jury Materials*, 735 F.2d at 1271.

[320] *Uranium Industry*, 1979-2 Trade Cas. at 78,644; *see also In re* Grand Jury Proceedings of Grand Jury No. 81-1 (Miami), 669 F. Supp. 1072, 1075-76 (S.D. Fla. 1987) ("There can be little doubt that an impeachment trial by the Senate is a 'judicial proceeding' in every significant sense and that a House investigation preliminary to impeachment is within the scope of the Rule."). There is, however, dictum suggesting a contrary view. *See In re* Petition to Inspect & Copy Grand Jury Materials, 735 F.2d 1261, 1271 (11th Cir. 1984) (suggesting that a congressional committee's impeachment inquiry may "not [be] ancillary to a 'judicial proceeding,' in the strict sense").

[321] Douglas Oil Co. v. Petrol Stops Nw., 441 U.S. 211, 223 (1979).

[322] *See Grand Jury No. 81-1, Miami*, 833 F.2d 1438, 1442 (11th Cir. 1987) (concluding that the "interest in conducting a full and fair impeachment inquiry" was sufficient, especially given that the events took place years ago); *June 5, 1972 Grand Jury*, 370 F. Supp. at 1229-30 (considering that grand jury had concluded its work and President did not object as factors in determination of whether disclosure was appropriate); *see also* Application of U.S. for Order Pursuant to Provisions of Rule 6(e), Federal Rules of Criminal Procedure, 505 F. Supp. 25, 27 (W.D. Pa. 1980) (recognizing entitlement to disclosure "where petitioner demonstrated that state investigations of official improprieties would be stymied").

[323] Pizzuti v. United States, 809 F. Supp. 2d 164, 194 (S.D.N.Y. 2011).

the materials at issue could influence whether a committee can show such a need.[324]

"Inherent Authority" to Release Grand Jury Materials to Congress

As discussed, some federal courts have recognized that courts have "inherent authority" to order the release of grand jury information in "special" or "exceptional" circumstances, regardless of whether an explicit Rule 6(e) exception would otherwise apply.[325]

One lower court has relied on this inherent authority over grand jury matters, among other things, to authorize the release to the House Judiciary Committee of a report prepared by the grand jury investigating the alleged—and potentially impeachable—improprieties of President Nixon.[326] The D.C. Circuit essentially affirmed that decision, expressing "general agreement" with the lower court decision.[327]

Another court has also relied on its inherent authority to order the release of the records of a grand jury that had indicted a federal judge to an investigating committee of the judiciary, relying on the "exceptional circumstance[]" that the "question under investigation"—whether a federal judge should be recommended for impeachment or otherwise disciplined—was "of great societal importance."[328] Recognizing that the investigating committee still was required to show a sufficient need for the grand jury materials, the court concluded such a showing had been made (and was not outweighed by the interest in secrecy) because (1) the investigating

---

[324] *See* Senate Select Committee on Presidential Campaign Activities v. Nixon, 498 F.2d 725, 732 (D.C. Cir. 1974) ("The sufficiency of the Committee's showing of need has come to depend . . . entirely on whether the subpoenaed materials are critical to the performance of its legislative functions."); *but cf. In re* Petition to Inspect and Copy Grand Jury Materials, 735 F.2d 1261, 1273 (11th Cir. 1984) (viewing requirement that petitioner "must exhaust other means of securing the relevant information before being granted access" to grand jury materials "inappropriate" in context of petition by investigating committee of the judiciary because of committee's "unique investigatory mission and the necessity that, when the investigation is over, the public [will] be assured that it was complete").

[325] *See supra* § Courts' Inherent Authority to Order Disclosure.

[326] *June 5, 1972 Grand Jury*, 370 F. Supp. at 1228 ("The Court can see no justification for a suggestion that th[e] codification [in Rule 6(e)] of a 'traditional practice' should act, or have been intended to act, to render meaningless a historically proper function of the grand jury by enjoining courts from any disclosure of reports in any circumstance.").

[327] Haldeman v. Sirica, 501 F.2d 714, 715 (D.C. Cir. 1974).

[328] *Grand Jury Materials*, 735 F.2d at 1269-70.

committee was composed of federal judges who were acting pursuant to express statutory authority; (2) the grand jury investigation and trial of the judge had already concluded; and (3) only by "examining all of the record" could the committee "determine the true state of the evidence for or against the charge."[329]

Assuming a court adopts the inherent authority view of Rule 6(e) based on the above decisions, it is possible that a court would be willing to authorize the disclosure of grand jury materials to a congressional committee pursuant to the court's inherent authority.[330] Precedential support for disclosure is strongest in the context of an impeachment inquiry (assuming the court did not view such an inquiry as being "preliminar[y] to . . . a judicial proceeding").[331] It is less certain that an "inherent authority" disclosure order would be available to a congressional petitioner when not tied to a contemplated impeachment proceeding. In an appropriately "exceptional" situation, a court could be amenable to exercising its inherent authority to order the release of grand jury information in the face of a pressing congressional request. The outcome would depend in large part on whether Congress could establish a sufficiently weighty need for the materials, which would implicate a variety of circumstantial factors.[332]

Limitations on Further Disclosure by Congress

Once grand jury materials find their way into the possession of a Member or committee of Congress, the question arises as to what limits exist on further dissemination of those materials. As previously discussed, Federal Rule of Criminal Procedure 6(e) imposes an obligation of secrecy

---

[329] *Id.* at 1272-75.

[330] This option would not be available in a jurisdiction where binding precedent forecloses authorizing disclosures outside of the exceptions contained in Rule 6(e). As noted previously, the D.C. Circuit is currently considering a case that could settle the issue with respect to federal courts in the District of Columbia, unless or until the Supreme Court decides to weigh in. *See* McKeever v. Sessions, No. 17-5149 (D.C. Cir. June 26, 2017).

[331] *See supra* notes 326-29.

[332] *See supra* § Courts' Inherent Authority to Order Disclosure.

only on specified persons, of which Congress (or, more generally, a recipient of grand jury information pursuant to the "judicial proceeding" or "inherent authority" exceptions) is not one.[333]

That said, Rule 6(e) does explicitly make court-authorized disclosures "subject to any . . . conditions that [the court] directs."[334] It is thus conceivable that in ordering the release of grand jury information, a court could impose a requirement that the information not be further distributed. However, such a requirement would be in tension with the Constitution's Speech or Debate Clause in the case of Congress, at least where further dissemination occurs in the course of legitimate legislative activity, as the Clause prevents a court from blocking disclosure of information in Congress's possession in such a circumstance.[335] In any event, courts will "presume that the committees of Congress will exercise their powers responsibly and with due regard for the rights of affected parties,"[336] though a court may consider the extent to which Congress has taken specific precautions to protect against further dissemination of grand jury materials in deciding whether disclosure is appropriate.[337]

---

[333] *See supra* § Persons Subject to Rule 6(e).

[334] FED. R. CRIM. P. 6(e)(3)(E)(i).

[335] *See* FTC v. Owens-Corning Fiberglas Corp., 626 F.2d 966, 970 (D.C. Cir. 1980) ("A court may not block disclosure of information in Congress's possession, at least when the disclosure would serve a valid legislative purpose."); *In re* Request for Access to Grand Jury Materials Grand Jury No. 81-1, Miami, 833 F.2d 1438, 1446 (11th Cir. 1987) (acknowledging that "what the Committee does *after* disclosure is outside of [the court's] jurisdiction" because the "Speech and Debate Clause prevents [the court] from questioning Congress about actions taken in the impeachment process"); *see also* Doe v. McMillan, 412 U.S. 306, 312 (1973) (holding that Members of Congress were immune from suit over inclusion of confidential information in report and distribution of report to other Members "for legislative purposes"). This is not to say, however, that *public* dissemination of grand jury materials would necessarily be protected, *see* Gravel v. United States, 408 U.S. 606, (1972) (holding that arrangement for private publication of the Pentagon Papers was not protected "speech or debate"), or that Congress or a committee itself could not impose sanctions for leaks of grand jury information in accordance with its own rules.

[336] Exxon Corp. v. FTC, 589 F.2d 582, 589 (D.C. Cir. 1978).

[337] *In re* Report and Recommendation of June 5, 1972 Grand Jury Concerning Transmission of Evidence to House of Representatives, 370 F. Supp. 1219, 1230 (D.D.C. 1974), *mandamus denied sub nom.* Haldeman v. Sirica, 501 F.2d 714 (D.C. Cir. 1974) (noting that the committee had "taken elaborate precautions to insure against unnecessary and inappropriate disclosure of [the] materials" and finding "no basis on which to assume that the Committee's use of [them] will be injudicious").

Legal Considerations for Congress

Past Congresses, faced with potential limitations on the ability to obtain grand jury materials, have considered legislation that would amend Federal Rule of Criminal Procedure 6(e) to, among other things, permit a court to authorize disclosure of grand jury matters "upon a showing of substantial need"[338] to "any committee of Congress . . . for use in relation to any matter within the jurisdiction of such . . . congressional committee."[339]

A bill to this effect was introduced during the 99th Congress, prompting the Department of Justice's Office of Legal Counsel to issue a memorandum opinion "strongly oppos[ing] any provision that would permit Congress independently to petition the courts for Rule 6(e) material."[340] In the Office's view, such a provision would "codify legislative encroachment into the Executive's exclusive authority to enforce the law."[341] In other words, the Office took the position that creating a mechanism for Congress to obtain grand jury materials from the court, without any opportunity for interposition by the executive branch, would be inconsistent with the Constitution's separation of powers and would invite "legislative pressures" that would interfere with prosecutorial discretion and due process of law.[342]

The Senate Judiciary Committee held a hearing on the legislation and a similar bill as to their impacts on Rule 6(e) and grand jury disclosure practices, during which the bill's sponsor, Senator Charles Grassley, expressed concern that Rule 6(e) had been "utilized by the Justice

---

[338] "Substantial need" is a less demanding standard than "particularized need" in that it does not require a showing that the grand jury materials at issue cannot be obtained through other avenues. *See* BRENNER & SHAW, *supra* note 141, § 18:9 (citing 135 CONG. REC. S2396 (daily ed. Mar. 8, 1989); S. REP. NO. 101-337 (1990)).

[339] S. 1562, 99th Cong. § 5 (as introduced, Aug. 1, 1985).

[340] U.S. Dep't of Justice, Office of Legal Counsel, *Legislation Providing for Court-Ordered Disclosure of Grand Jury Materials to Congressional Committees*, 9 U.S. Op. Off. Legal Counsel 86, 87 (1985).

[341] Id.

[342] Id. at 87-88. The Office also pointed out that the proposed legislation had the potential to impact executive privilege claims by effectively "handing over" privilege disputes to the courts "for their frequent adjudication." Id. at 92.

Department as a shield against legitimate congressional inquiry."[343] The Senator pointed out that the bill did not provide "automatic congressional access to grand jury information," but rather allowed "congressional committees[,] in performance of their constitutional duty to oversee the executive agencies, an opportunity to demonstrate to the court a 'substantial need' for access[.]"[344]

An Associate Deputy Attorney General reiterated in testimony the Department of Justice's position that the provision for congressional access "would raise substantial constitutional concerns in terms of separation of powers as to where the enforcement authority lies; due process issues in terms of fairness and the application of decisionmaking with respect to criminal prosecutions; as well as the issue of opening the door for raising concerns about potential political influence or persuasion upon criminal prosecutions."[345] He did point out, however, that the department had "accommodate[d] requests from particular congressional committees for investigative materials on an ad hoc basis by appropriate application to the courts, and subject to necessary protective conditions," which it would continue to do.[346]

In separate testimony, representatives of the American Bar Association and the National Association of Criminal Defense Lawyers argued that the provision under consideration could violate the separation-of-powers doctrine and undermine the "fundamental tradition of grand jury secrecy" by "subvert[ing] the purpose of the grand jury" to legislative ends.[347]

An attorney with expertise on the subject of congressional access to information also testified at the hearing and expressed the view that a bill permitting a court to provide grand jury materials to a congressional committee "with legitimate oversight functions would not violate

---

343 Grand Jury Disclosure: Hearing on S. 1562 and S. 1676 Before the S. Comm. on the Judiciary, 99th Cong. 2 (1985) (statement of Sen. Charles E. Grassley).

344 Id. at 3.

345 Id. at 12 (statement of Jay B. Stephens, Assoc. Deputy Attorney Gen., Dep't of Justice).

346 Id. at 26.

347 See id. at 57 (statement of Peter F. Vaira, Vice-Chairperson, ABA Section of Crim. Justice, Grand Jury Comm.); id. at 66 (statement of David W. Russell, President, Nat. Assoc. of Crim. Defense Lawyers).

separation-ofpowers principles."[348] However, he believed that Congress should have access to grand jury materials only "in very limited circumstances" and suggested that an amendment to Rule 6(e) "should instruct a Federal court to weigh congressional needs against grand jury secrecy requirements in determining whether to grant access."[349] In the attorney's view, this weighing would include consideration of whether the committee could acquire sufficient information from non-grand-jury sources, whether the grand jury proceedings for which information was sought had terminated or were ongoing, and whether the committee had "in place special provisions to protect the confidentiality of grand jury material."[350] The attorney did not view the provision under consideration, as written, to be adequate in light of the considerations he identified.[351]

Ultimately, the bill was reported out of committee with the changes to Rule 6(e), including the congressional-access provision, excised, and it does not appear that the legislation was further pursued.[352] Consequently, ambiguity remains regarding the relationship between grand jury secrecy and congressional access to grand jury materials. As the debate in the 99th Congress reflects, any change to the Rule could raise potentially difficult constitutional, interpretive, and policy questions. In any event, should Congress desire to create further exceptions to the secrecy framework beyond Rule 6(e), the Supreme Court has instructed that it must "affirmatively express its intent to do so."[353]

---

[348] *Id.* at 46 (statement of James Hamilton, Attorney, Ginsburg, Feldman & Bress).
[349] *Id.* at 39.
[350] *Id.* at 39-40.
[351] *Id.* at 40.
[352] S. 1562, 99th Cong. (as reported by S. Comm. on the Judiciary, July 28, 1986).
[353] Illinois v. Abbott & Assoc., Inc., 460 U.S. 557, 572-73 (1983).

In: Insights into Secrecy and Information Policy ISBN: 978-1-53615-408-5
Editor: Clarence Armstrong

Chapter 2

EXECUTIVE BRANCH ETHICS AND FINANCIAL CONFLICTS OF INTEREST: DISCLOSURE*

Cynthia Brown

ABSTRACT

Recent media reports indicate that the 116th Congress may address government ethics reform, including conflicts of interest among executive branch officials. Federal officials have a basic duty not to allow private gain to influence their government service, which includes "not hold[ing] financial interests that conflict with the conscientious performance of duty." Federal statutes, as well as a code of conduct for executive branch employees, make this principle part of a federal regulatory scheme intended to prevent officials from benefitting personally from their offices. The current federal statutory scheme regulating conflicts between an official's personal financial interests and his or her official duties has three prongs: disclosure, disqualification, and divestiture (i.e., a "3-D

* This is an edited, reformatted and augmented version of Congressional Research Service, Publication No. Congressional Research Service, dated January 2, 2019.

system"). This sidebar is the first in a three-part series examining conflicts of interest in the executive branch.

CURRENT SCOPE OF DISCLOSURE REQUIREMENTS

To make conflicts of interest between officials' public duties and private financial interests transparent, Congress enacted mandatory disclosure requirements to "promote the integrity of public officials and institutions." The Ethics in Government Act requires high-level elected and appointed officials to disclose a range of personal interests at various times, including upon entering public service, annually during such service, and upon departing their position. In 2012, Congress enacted the STOCK Act, which amended the Ethics in Government Act to increase transparency, in part, through more frequent reporting requirements and broader availability of disclosure reports.

Under these statutes, financial disclosure reports must be filed at various stages of a covered official's government service. An initial report, which must be filed upon entering government service, discloses information about that individual's (1) income; (2) financial assets, (3) liabilities; (4) outside positions; and (5) agreements and continuing relationships with other employers. Following an individual's appointment or election, he must file an annual report that includes three additional categories of information: gifts, financial transactions, and the cash value of any interest in a blind trust. In addition to annual reports, covered officials must file periodic transaction reports when they engage in certain financial transactions. Finally, officials must provide final reports covering all eight information categories when they leave a covered position.

Prior to passage of the STOCK Act and its subsequent amendments, mandatory financial disclosures were available for public inspection only by request to the official's employing agency. Although the STOCK Act originally required all disclosures to be posted to the internet for public inspection, the current provisions require internet disclosure for only the most senior officials in the executive branch—the President, Vice

President, and appointees and nominees to positions classified at Level 1 and Level 2 of the Executive Service. Disclosures by officials in those positions are available on the Office of Government Ethics' website for immediate public access. Financial disclosure forms filed by other high-ranking employees who are subject to these rules are available by request.

CONSTITUTIONALITY OF FINANCIAL DISCLOSURE REQUIREMENTS GENERALLY

In addition to upholding the constitutionality of disclosure requirements in other contexts (e.g., campaign finance), the Supreme Court has let stand a lower court decision recognizing the constitutionality of financial disclosures by officials under ethics laws. In that case, the U.S. Court of Appeals for the Fifth Circuit considered a challenge brought by federal judges who alleged that their disclosure requirements violated several constitutional principles, including separation of powers and privacy. The court upheld the law, rejecting each claim challenging Congress's authority to require them to disclose their financial interests. Although that challenge concerned members of the judicial branch, the court's opinion appears to address the constitutional issues broadly.

Noting that Congress intended the disclosure requirements "to increase public confidence in all three branches of the federal government," the court's opinion indicates that public officials, regardless of whether they are elected or appointed, can be subject to transparency standards. The court rejected the judges' assertion that Congress lacked authority to impose disclosure requirements because they were unelected officials in the judicial branch. Instead, it upheld the statute as "justified by the promotion of important objectives within the constitutional authority of Congress." To that end, the court explained that even unelected officials like judges "are important governmental officers in whom the public at large has a substantial interest."

Likewise, the court rejected the argument that mandatory disclosure would interfere with officials' personal right to privacy, citing its previous agreement with "the majority of courts considering the matter" when it held that disclosure requirements for elected officials was constitutional. It cited precedent acknowledging that disclosure of personal information, like any government action, may have some influence on the official's personal life but concluded that "any influence does not rise to the level of a constitutional problem." The Fifth Circuit relied upon a balancing test, "weigh[ing] the injuries imposed by a legislative act against the governmental interests furthered by the act," to conclude that the government's interest in deterring public officials from misusing their influence outweighed the burdens of disclosure on individual officials. The court expressly stated again in the context of the privacy claim that the governmental interests prevailed regardless of whether the officials subject to the disclosure requirements were elected or appointed to their posts.

More recently, a federal district court in Maryland recognized some limits to federal disclosure requirements based on employee rights to privacy. In a challenge to public posting requirements initially enacted under the STOCK Act, the court recognized that the governmental interest in disclosure, though compelling, "is not insurmountable." The STOCK Act, in part, requires public posting of financial disclosures on the internet, as well as creation of an online database to allow the public to search, sort, and download the posted information. Considering a challenge brought by senior executive employees (excluding the President, Vice President, cabinet secretaries, and other presidentially appointed positions requiring Senate confirmation), the district court held that the government's compelling interests in deterring corruption and conflicts of interests "fail to outweigh [the claimant officials'] privacy and security interests." The court contrasted making the disclosure forms publicly available via the internet with the traditional method by which the public could request disclosures from the employing agency. The court described a "unique confluence of circumstances" in the case, including the degree of disclosure because of "unfettered Internet access" to the disclosed information and the security concerns associated with posting "complete personal financial information of all senior officials on the internet." Consistent with the court's decision, Congress amended the STOCK Act to require posting for public access of only the most senior government officials' disclosures on the internet (i.e., the President, Vice President, and positions classified at Level 1 and Level 2 of the Executive Service).

APPLICABILITY OF DISCLOSURE REQUIREMENTS TO SENIOR EXECUTIVE OFFICIALS

Disclosure is the only prong of the 3-D system governing conflicts of interest that applies to the President and Vice President. Congress expressly exempted both positions from disqualification requirements and neither position is subject to agency specific divestiture rules, which may apply to other executive branch officials. Thus, disclosure is the principal mechanism regulating potential conflicts between a President or Vice President's financial interests and public office. Accordingly, the current regulatory scheme appears to rely on the electorate addressing any potential conflicts through the ballot box.

To that end, candidates for President and Vice President must file initial financial disclosure forms after declaring their candidacy and annually thereafter for "each successive year an individual continues to be a candidate," as well as reports that are required if the candidate is elected. Additionally, federal campaign finance law requires disclosure of campaign contributions received and spent. Under the Federal Election Campaign Act (FECA), candidate campaign committees must register with the Federal Election Commission (FEC) and comply with periodic disclosure requirements. Thus, candidates must file reports that show the total amount of all contributions received, including those from individuals, political action committees (PACs), and parties, and the identity of any person who contributes more than $200 during a calendar year. There are no additional requirements for disclosure of other financial information, e.g., tax returns, by candidates, although candidates may release their returns or related data voluntarily.

Similarly, the Ethics in Government Act also requires nominees for appointment to positions that require Senate confirmation to file an initial financial disclosure report within five days of the President's transmittal of the nomination to the Senate. The nominee must provide updated information no later than the date of the first hearing to consider the nomination, and the statute expressly allows the committee considering the nomination to request "as a condition of confirmation, any additional financial information from any Presidential nominee." Because these officials are not elected, authority to request additional information to identify potential conflicts of interest before exercising the constitutional power to consent to the nomination provides an additional safeguard against conflicts of interest in the highest executive branch positions.

While disclosure requirements' applicability to the most senior executive branch officials has not been subject to a direct legal challenge, the judicial opinions discussed suggest that such a challenge likely would not be successful. The Fifth Circuit emphasized the significance of the government's interest in accountability of government officials across all branches of government and particularly those whose official actions "have dramatic impact upon the lives of every citizen in this country." The federal district court in Maryland expressly noted that it was not ruling the internet publication requirements as facially unconstitutional, specifically citing their continued applicability to these most senior government officials. Furthermore, disclosure requirements do not appear to interfere with the President's or Vice President's constitutional duties because they do not bar the President or Vice President from carrying out any executive actions, but instead only require the individual to report financial interests.

CONCLUSION

Should Congress consider legislation addressing financial conflicts of interests for executive branch officials, it may revisit disclosure requirements. Disclosure requirements provide transparency so that the electorate, the Senate, and employing agencies are aware of potential conflicts of interest that presidential candidates, executive branch nominees, and other high-ranking executive officials may have. Existing precedent has consistently upheld disclosure requirements, although public access to such information over the internet may be limited in some instances.

In: Insights into Secrecy and Information Policy ISBN: 978-1-53615-408-5
Editor: Clarence Armstrong

Chapter 3

DO COURTS HAVE INHERENT AUTHORITY TO RELEASE SECRET GRAND JURY MATERIALS?*

Michael A. Foster

The U.S. Constitution requires that any prosecution of a serious federal crime be initiated by "a presentment or indictment of a Grand Jury." The "[g]rand [j]ury" contemplated by the Constitution is a temporary, citizen-comprised body that obtains evidence and considers whether it is sufficient to justify criminal charges in a particular case. Though a grand jury works with federal prosecutors and functions under judicial auspices, it is considered an independent "constitutional fixture in its own right" that "belongs to no branch of the institutional Government, serving as a kind of buffer . . . between the Government and the people." One long-established principle that has been deemed essential to the grand jury's functioning and independence is that matters occurring before it are to be kept secret. Secrecy prevents those under scrutiny from fleeing or importuning the

* This is an edited, reformatted and augmented version of Congressional Research Service Publication No. LSB10201, dated October 5, 2018.

grand jurors, encourages full disclosure by witnesses, and protects the innocent from unwarranted prosecution. For these and other reasons, prosecutors, the jurors themselves, and most others involved in grand jury proceedings are generally prohibited from revealing "such matters as the identities or addresses of witnesses or jurors, the substance of testimony, the strategy or direction of the investigation, the deliberations or questions of jurors, and the like." The prohibition endures even after a grand jury's work is completed.

That said, Federal Rule of Criminal Procedure 6(e), which enshrines the traditional rule of grand jury secrecy, establishes exceptions that allow grand jury materials (such as transcripts of witness testimony) to be disclosed to certain outside parties in limited circumstances. Some of these exceptions allow for automatic disclosure—to necessary government personnel, for example—but many of the exceptions require that disclosure be authorized by the federal district court in the jurisdiction where the jury is convened, as the court ultimately has some degree of "supervisory authority" over the grand jury. Rule 6(e)(3)(E) provides in relevant part that the court "may authorize disclosure . . . of a grand-jury matter" (1) preliminarily to or in connection with a judicial proceeding; (2) to a defendant who shows grounds may exist to dismiss the indictment because of something that occurred before the grand jury; or (3) at the request of the government, to a foreign court or prosecutor or to an "appropriate" state, state-subdivision, Indian tribal, military, or foreign government official for the purpose of enforcing or investigating a violation of the respective jurisdiction's criminal law. Persons seeking court authorization under one of these exceptions must make a "strong showing of particularized need" that "outweighs the public interest in secrecy."

Relying on a robust conception of a court's "supervisory authority over the grand juries that they have empaneled," three Circuit Courts of Appeals—the Second, Seventh, and Eleventh—and a number of district courts have determined that the list of court-authorized exceptions in Rule 6(e) is not exclusive, and that courts in fact have the inherent authority to permit disclosure of grand jury information and materials in circumstances not expressly contemplated by the text of the Rule. The courts that have found such authority have emphasized the proposition, supported by early Supreme Court precedent, that Rule 6 is merely "'declaratory' of the long-standing 'principle' that 'disclosure' of grand jury materials is 'committed to the discretion of the trial court.'" As such, according to these courts, Rule 6(e)'s enumeration of circumstances in which courts may authorize disclosure of matters occurring before a grand jury "does not, by itself, eliminate the court's power to address situations that the Rule does not describe." Courts that have found they possess inherent authority to permit disclosure of grand jury materials beyond the text of Rule 6(e) have nonetheless generally cabined the exercise of such authority to "special circumstances," most frequently where there is significant public interest in proceedings that have already concluded.

It is by no means settled whether the authority of courts to permit disclosure of grand jury materials extends beyond the exceptions found in Rule 6(e), however, as a case currently under consideration by the U.S. Court of Appeals for the District of Columbia Circuit illustrates. In *McKeever v. Sessions*, Stuart McKeever, a researcher and author, filed a motion in the D.C. district court seeking grand jury records from the investigation of a man who was suspected of, but never charged with, murdering a university professor. McKeever sought the records in connection with a book he was researching on the subject of the professor's disappearance. Though McKeever's request clearly did not fall within any of the textual Rule 6(e) exceptions permitting court-authorized disclosure, he maintained that the court could exercise its inherent authority to release the records based on historical interest in the case. In a 2017 order, the court agreed that it had such authority but determined that the scope of McKeever's request made disclosure inappropriate on the facts of the particular case. McKeever has now appealed the order to the D.C. Circuit, and the government has argued in opposition that the records cannot be released because Rule 6(e)'s exceptions constitute an exclusive enumeration of the circumstances in which court-authorized disclosure is appropriate.

A three-judge panel of the D.C. Circuit heard oral argument in *McKeever* on September 21, 2018 and, according to at least one commentator, appeared skeptical that courts have authority to release grand jury materials in situations not governed by Rule 6(e). Weighing against a finding of such authority is language from an otherwise-inapposite Supreme Court case that suggests "any power federal courts may have to fashion, on their own initiative, rules of grand jury procedure is a very limited one, not remotely comparable to the power they maintain over their own proceedings." And on other occasions, the Court has expressed "reluctan[ce] to conclude that a breach of [grand jury] secrecy has been authorized" absent "a clear indication in a statute or Rule."

At the same time, the D.C. Circuit panel in *McKeever* may need to reconcile its own arguably inconsistent precedent: in a 1974 ruling affirming the disclosure to the House Judiciary Committee of grand jury materials related to the Watergate investigation, the appellate court appeared to accept a lower court's determination that it had inherent power to permit the disclosure because of the significance of the circumstances, regardless of any textual authority contained in Rule 6(e). Yet a more recent D.C. Circuit opinion, in an unrelated context, expressed disagreement with the proposition that courts have general supervisory authority over grand juries, which could give the court in *McKeever* a basis to disavow the existence of extratextual authority over disclosure of matters occurring before a grand jury.

In any event, the *McKeever* decision could have both significant legal implications and practical implications for Congress in its oversight role. Should the D.C. Circuit in *McKeever* decide that federal district courts do *not* have the power to authorize disclosure of grand jury information beyond the exceptions found in Rule 6(e), it will create a circuit split that ultimately may require Supreme Court resolution or an amendment to the Rule. In the meantime, such a ruling could limit Congress's ability to obtain materials that reveal matters occurring before federal grand juries in the District of Columbia. Assuming Rule 6(e) operates to preclude Congress from obtaining grand jury materials without judicial authorization—which federal courts in the District of Columbia have recognized that it does—any such authorization would have to fall within one of the enumerated exceptions contained in the Rule. Thus, while some case law suggests that an impeachment or other official proceeding could warrant disclosure in accordance with the specific exception concerning "judicial proceeding[s]," for example, a request in the course of an ordinary legislative inquiry potentially would not. Congress is, of course, free to amend Rule 6(e) to permit disclosure in circumstances not currently covered by the Rule, as it has done in the past.

In: Insights into Secrecy and Information Policy ISBN: 978-1-53615-408-5
Editor: Clarence Armstrong

Chapter 4

RECORDS, PAPERS, DECISIONS: KAVANAUGH RECORDS AND THE PRESIDENTIAL RECORDS ACT*

Meghan M. Stuessy

Since Judge Brett Kavanaugh's nomination to be an Associate Justice of the Supreme Court was received on July 10, papers detailing his activities in the George W. Bush Administration and the Office of Independent Counsel Kenneth W. Starr have been the subject of ongoing congressional interest. Specifically, many Members of Congress have discussed the public release of Judge Kavanaugh's records and whether the scope and volume of records released is similar to the records of previous Supreme Court nominees.

The release and maintenance of records pertaining to Judge Kavanaugh's tenure in these offices is governed by the interaction of the Federal Records Act, the Presidential Records Act (PRA), and the Freedom of Information Act (FOIA). While the Federal Records Act applies to all

* This is an edited, reformatted and augmented version of Congressional Research Service Publication No. IN10959, dated August 27, 2018.

federal records, such as Judge Kavanaugh's attorney work files from his tenure with the Office of Independent Counsel, the PRA applies only to records created on behalf of a president, such as records created during the George W. Bush Administration.

After a President leaves office, the legal custody of presidential records transfers from the President to the Archivist of the National Archives and Records Administration (NARA), who oversees the custody, control, preservation, and access to presidential records.

PRA Restrictions

Presidential records are defined as "documentary materials, or any reasonably segregable portion thereof, created or received by the President, the President's immediate staff, or a unit or individual of the Executive Office of the President whose function is to advise or assist the President." Presidential records meeting certain criteria may be subject to a withholding period of up to 12 years after the conclusion of the President's Administration.

The PRA allows the outgoing President to restrict access to six categories of presidential records for specified durations of time, not to exceed 12 years. The records categories for which a President can restrict access include the following:

- Records described in an executive order as in the interest of national defense or foreign policy or that are otherwise classified documents,
- Records relating to appointments to federal office,
- Records specifically exempted from disclosure by statute,
- Records that contain trade secrets and commercial or financial information,
- Records of confidential communications requesting or submitting advice between the President and the

- President's advisers or between such advisers, and
- Records of personnel and medical files whose disclosure would constitute an invasion of personal privacy.

As the length of time between the conclusion of a presidency and the present day increases, records restrictions under the PRA weaken. For example, generally less than five years out from the conclusion of a presidency, presidential records cannot be accessed through FOIA unless the Archivist has completed the processing of the records. Between five and 12 years out from the end of a presidency, the Archivist determines PRA restrictions in consultation with the former President. After 12 years, these PRA restrictions no longer apply, though FOIA exemptions (for example the trade secrets exemption) may still be applicable to presidential records.

EXCEPTIONS TO RESTRICTED ACCESS OF PRESIDENTIAL RECORDS

Although a number of laws safeguard presidential records for particular durations of time, certain federal officials may access presidential records within the 12-year time frame, known as gaining "special access" to presidential records. Per 44 U.S.C. §2205:

[S]ubject to any rights, defenses, or privileges which the United States or any agency or person may invoke, Presidential records shall be made available—

(A) pursuant to subpoena or other judicial process issued by a court of competent jurisdiction for the purposes of any civil or criminal investigation or proceeding;
(B) to an incumbent President if such records contain information that is needed for the conduct of current business of the incumbent President's office and that is not otherwise available; and

(C) to either House of Congress, or, to the extent of matter within its jurisdiction, to any committee or subcommittee thereof if such records contain information that is needed for the conduct of its business and that is not otherwise available.

Observers have questioned what constitutes a House or Senate request for presidential records and who needs to make the request for the records for it to qualify under 44 U.S.C. §2205(C). In a news release dated August 15, 2018, NARA writes that "the National Archives longstanding and consistent practice has been to respond only to requests from the Chair of Congressional Committees, regardless of which political party is in power."

National Archives and Records Administration Efforts to Release

In its August 15 news release, NARA described its efforts to release records related to Judge Kavanaugh's service in the George W. Bush Administration. NARA noted that the Archives processed approximately 70,000 pages of Chief Justice John Roberts's records and 170,000 pages of Justice Elena Kagan's records, whereas it anticipates processing "the equivalent of several million pages of paper and email records" related to Judge Kavanaugh. In response to a congressional "special access" request dated July 27, 2018, NARA is prioritizing the processing of 900,000 pages. NARA anticipates completing its review of the White House Counsel Office emails from Judge Kavanaugh and the textual records related to his tenure as Associate Counsel and Senior Associate Counsel to the President—totaling approximately 300,000 pages—by August and the remaining 600,000 pages by October.

In the same news release, NARA recognized that the George W. Bush Presidential Library is conducting a separate review of such records, which is permissible under 44 U.S.C. Section 2205(3). NARA, however, did note that "the PRA representative of President George W. Bush requested and received from the National Archives a copy of the White House Counsel's Office records and nomination records and has begun to provide copies of those records directly to the Senate Judiciary Committee, which is something that has never happened before." Records related to Judge Kavanaugh that have been released can be found on NARA's webpage.

In: Insights into Secrecy and Information Policy ISBN: 978-1-53615-408-5
Editor: Clarence Armstrong

Chapter 5

Military Service Records, Awards, and Unit Histories: A Guide to Locating Sources*

Nese F. DeBruyne and Barbara Salazar Torreon

Summary

This guide provides information on locating military unit histories and individual service records of discharged, retired, and deceased military personnel. It also provides information on locating and replacing military awards and medals. Included is contact information for military history centers, websites for additional sources of research, and a bibliography of other publications, including related CRS reports.

* This is an edited, reformatted and augmented version of Congressional Research Service Publication No. RS21282, dated August 7, 2018.

Personnel Files: Military Service and Pension Records at the National Archives

The Military Personnel Records division of the National Personnel Records Center (NPRC), a component of the National Archives and Records Administration (NARA) located in St. Louis, Missouri, holds most existing U.S. military personnel, health, and medical records of discharged and deceased veterans of all services from World War I to the present. Official Military Personnel File (OMPF) records may be requested online at https://www.archives.gov/veterans/militaryservice-records, by mail (the appropriate address listed on the back of the form), or fax (314-801- 9195) using the Standard Form 180.

Veterans and their next-of-kin (NOK) may request these records. According to the NPRC, for the Air Force, Navy, Marine Corps, and Coast Guard, the NOK is defined as the unremarried widow or widower, son, daughter, father, mother, brother or sister; for the Army, the NOK is defined as the surviving spouse, eldest child, father or mother, eldest sibling or eldest grandchild.

If an individual does not meet the definition of a NOK, he or she is considered a member of the general public and may request military personnel records via the Freedom of Information Act (FOIA). See "Access to OMPFs by the General Public" at https://www.archives.gov/st-louis/military-personnel/public/general-public.html.

In 1973, a fire at NPRC destroyed approximately 16 million to 18 million Army and Air Force official military personnel files. In such cases where files were lost, NPRC uses alternate sources of information to respond to requests.

More information about obtaining military personnel files can be found on the NPRC website, http://www.archives.gov/st-louis/military-personnel/, or by contacting the center at

National Personnel Records Center
Military Personnel Records

1 Archives Drive

St. Louis, MO 63138

Status Update Request Form: https://www.archives.gov/st-louis/forms

Older military personnel records (generally prior to 1917) are located at National Archives and Records Administration (NARA)

Textual Archives Division Washington, DC 20408

http://www.archives.gov/veterans/military-service-records/pre-ww-1-records.html

Correcting Military Service Records

For guidance on the review of discharges and military corrections boards, see NARA's "Veterans' Service Records: Correcting Military Service Records" at https://www.archives.gov/veterans/military-service-records/correct-service-records.html.

For links to the service review boards (Air Force, Army, Coast Guard, and Navy and Marine Corps) see "Boards for Correction of Military Records (BCMR)/ Discharge Upgrades" at https://www.archives.gov/personnel-records-center/vso/boards-for-correction-of-military-records. NARA's site also provides the following BCMR guidance:

> "Prior to submitting a request to a Board for Correction of Military Records, ALL administrative avenues must be used. Generally, that means a request to NPRC for a correction (minor corrections can be made by NPRC), then a request to the military service department (service departments can make more corrections than NPRC), and finally if both these fail, then submit DD Form 149, with supporting evidence as instructed on the form."[1]

[1] NARA, Boards for Correction of Military Records / Discharge Upgrades" at https://www.archives.gov/personnelrecords-center/vso/boards-for-correction-of-military-records.

MILITARY AWARDS AND DECORATIONS

The NPRC also provides information and guidance on how to request military awards and decorations online and by mail for veterans and their NOK; replacing certain military medals; and obtaining a Cold War Recognition Certificate.[2] Note: This is available for the records of a servicemember who separated before or during 1956. For records for individuals who separated after 1956, these records can be requested through FOIA. The general public may also purchase a copy of the veteran's OMPF to determine the awards due and obtain the medals from a commercial source.

Individuals can request information on military service medals, decorations and awards online through https://www.archives.gov/veterans/military-service-records.

By military service (Army, Navy, Marine Corps, and Air Force including Army Air Corps & Army Air Forces) via mail:

National Personnel Records Center 1 Archives Drive
St. Louis, MO 63138

For Coast Guard:
Coast Guard Personnel Service Center
4200 Wilson Blvd, Suite 900 (PSC-PSD-MA)
Stop 7200
Arlington, VA 20598-7200.

Cold War Recognition Certificate

The National Defense Authorization Act (NDAA) for Fiscal Year 1998 (P.L. 105-85) in Section 1084 required the Secretary of Defense to prepare

---

[2] NARA, Military Awards and Decorations at https://www.archives.gov/st-louis/military-personnel/public/awards-anddecorations.html.

a certificate recognizing the Cold War service of qualifying members of the Armed Forces and civilian personnel of DOD and other government agencies contributing to national security. This certificate, known as the "Cold War Recognition Certificate," may be awarded upon individual request to all members of the armed forces and qualified federal government civilian personnel who served the United States during the Cold War era from September 2, 1945, to December 26, 1991.[3]

Additional information regarding requesting a Cold War Recognition Certificate is available at https://www.archives.gov/st-louis/military-personnel/public/awards-and-decorations.html#cwc.

FINDING UNIT HISTORIES

The Modern Military Records office of NARA has custody of records relating to World War I, World War II, Korea, and Vietnam. The records vary by conflict and branch of service; for example, the records for Army units active during the interwar periods (1920-1939 and 1945- 1950) are incomplete. For more information, contact the Textual Records office at

Textual Records Office
National Archives and Records Administration at College Park
8601 Adelphi Road
College Park, MD 20740-6001

If a military unit record is not publicly available, a FOIA request may be submitted to the agency where the record is held. For example, for special access records held at the National Archives at College Park, contact the Archives FOIA office at the following:

---

[3] NARA, Cold War Recognition Certificate an https://www.archives.gov/personnel-records-center/awards-anddecorations#cwc.

Special Access and FOIA Division National Archives at College Park
8601 Adelphi Road
College Park, MD 20740-6001

For more information on how to submit a FOIA request, visit https://www.foia.gov/how-to.html.

Other types of auxiliary and organizational records, including Army morning reports, Army unit rosters, Army officer pay cards, Navy muster rolls, U.S. Army Surgeon General's office records and Veterans Administration index cards are maintained at the National Archives at St. Louis, Missouri. Further information regarding these records, as well as the timespan of available records for each category, are available at http://www.archives.gov/st-louis/archivalprograms/other-records/index.html.

In: Insights into Secrecy and Information Policy ISBN: 978-1-53615-408-5
Editor: Clarence Armstrong

Chapter 6

DOES EXECUTIVE PRIVILEGE APPLY TO THE COMMUNICATIONS OF A PRESIDENT-ELECT?*

Todd Garvey

Former White House Chief Strategist Stephen Bannon and outgoing White House Communications Director Hope Hicks both appeared recently before closed-door meetings of the House Permanent Select Committee on Intelligence as part of the Committee's ongoing investigation into Russian involvement in the 2016 election. According to reports, Mr. Bannon did not answer questions relating to the transition period between the election and inauguration. Ms. Hicks answered "most," but not all, of the Committee's questions relating to that time period. One threshold question that appears central to these reports is whether executive privilege attaches to communications involving a President-elect prior to his inauguration.

---

* This is an edited, reformatted and augmented version of Congressional Research Service Publication No. LSB10094, dated March 8, 2018.

Executive privilege (or what is sometimes referred to by lower courts as the presidential communications privilege) is a relatively nebulous, constitutional privilege that protects the confidentiality of presidential communications on the grounds that "[a] President and those who assist him must be free to explore alternatives in the process of shaping policies and making decisions and to do so in a way many would be unwilling to express except privately." The Supreme Court's only significant analysis of executive privilege (privilege) comes from a pair of cases involving President Nixon's unsuccessful attempts to maintain control over his communications and records. In *United States v. Nixon (Nixon I)*, the Court rejected then-President Nixon's attempts to quash a judicial subpoena issued at the request of a special prosecutor for recordings of conversations the President had in the oval office with close advisors regarding the Watergate break-in. In that case, the Court determined that "absent a [] need to protect military, diplomatic, or sensitive national security secrets," the President's "generalized interest in confidentiality" was outweighed by the "demonstrated, specific need for evidence in a pending criminal trial."

Three years later, after President Nixon had resigned, the Court again disagreed with the former President's broad conception of the privilege—this time in relation to the disposition of his records after he left office. In *Nixon v. GSA (Nixon II)*, the Court rejected Nixon's challenge to the Presidential Recordings and Materials Preservation Act, a statute that nullified an arrangement that gave the former President control over his own presidential records and instead established a process to secure and preserve Nixon's records with the General Services Administration. Although the Court concluded that a former President may assert the privilege over communications that occurred while in office, any ongoing expectation of confidentiality was "subject to erosion over time...."

Both opinions acknowledged the "legitimate governmental interest in the confidentiality of communications between high government officials," and specifically recognized the privilege as an implied constitutional principle, derived from "the supremacy of the Executive Branch within its assigned area of constitutional responsibilities" and "inextricably rooted in the separation of powers." In addition, however, the cases established two key limiting principles. First, the privilege is not "absolute" and must be assessed in a manner that "preserves the essential functions of each branch." Most claims of privilege, therefore, require a balancing of the President's need for confidentiality with either the judicial or legislative branches' need for the information sought. In *Nixon I*, the Court expressly abstained from addressing the appropriate balancing if Congress (in the context of a congressional investigation) was seeking the information rather than a prosecutor (in the context of a criminal case). The D.C. Circuit, however, has held that in order to overcome the privilege, Congress would need to show that "the subpoenaed evidence is demonstrably critical to the responsible fulfillment of the [investigating] Committee's functions." Second, "the privilege is limited to communications 'in performance of the President's responsibilities,' 'of his office,' and made 'in the process of shaping policies and making decisions....'" Thus, not all presidential communications are protected.

Neither of the *Nixon* opinions had any reason to reference whether the privilege applies to communications made prior to taking office. However, the opinions do suggest that the privilege attaches to the "office" of the President, originating from the President's Article II powers and protecting those communications made in connection to the exercise of the powers of the Presidency. For example, in *Nixon I*, the Court suggested that the privilege applies to communications made in the "discharge of a President's powers" or in the "performance" of the "responsibilities" of "his office." In *Nixon II*, the Court noted that although the protections of the privilege survive the end of a President's term, it is "only the incumbent [that] is charged with performance of the executive duty under the Constitution." Other lower courts have similarly viewed the privilege as "the President's alone." Similar reasoning has been applied to other Presidential privileges. For example, in *Clinton v. Jones*, the Supreme Court did not extend the protections of presidential immunity to acts taken before assuming office on the grounds that such "unofficial acts" do not relate to the "performance of particular functions of [the President's] office."

The President-elect is not the President and does not exercise statutory or constitutional powers or responsibilities of that office. This conclusion flows from the text of the Constitution itself, which vests "[t]he executive Power" only in a single "President of the United States." Moreover, the Constitution prevents the President-elect from "enter[ing] on the Execution of his Office" until he has taken the constitutionally required oath, which cannot occur until the expiration of his predecessor's term on January 20th, at which point the new President's term "shall begin." The only federal court to directly address the privilege's application to a President-elect (a Kansas district court) adopted this line of reasoning, concluding that neither *Nixon I* nor *Nixon II* can be read to "extend the privilege to presidents-elect."

It is conceivable, however, that a court could apply a more functional analysis to extend aspects of the privilege to a President-elect. This line of argument would likely stem from the fact that the Court has viewed the privilege as protecting the "effectiveness of the executive decision-making process." In *Nixon I*, the Court explained that the privilege exists to ensure that the President and his advisors are "free to explore alternatives in the process of shaping policies and making decisions" without fear of disclosure. Similarly, in *Nixon II*, the Court suggested that the privilege encourages the "the full and frank submissions of facts and opinions upon which effective discharge of his duties depends." Numerous important decisions occur during a transition, and indeed, advice provided to a President-elect may then later serve as the basis for a decision made after assuming office. For example, a President-elect and his transition staff typically engage in discussions and deliberations regarding appointments to be made once the President-elect becomes the President. To the extent that protecting such communications is essential to defend the "the public interest in candid, objective, and even blunt or harsh opinions in Presidential decisionmaking," it could potentially be covered by the privilege. It should be noted, however, that no court to date has ever adopted such a view.

Even if, for purposes of argument, the privilege is viewed as extending to certain communications between a President-elect and his transition staff, it nevertheless would seem arguable that the privilege may apply with less weight given that such an extension would appear to lack the same direct grounding in the Constitution that characterizes the privilege for incumbent Presidents. Courts have previously identified a variety of situations in which covered communications receive diminished protections; for example, after significant time has passed, when the incumbent president does not support the assertion of a former president, or where the President has made public disclosures about the communications. If this reasoning were adopted, it would likely influence the weight a reviewing court would accord to the President-elect's "confidentiality interests" when balancing those interests against Congress's need for the communications as part of a congressional investigation.

In: Insights into Secrecy and Information Policy ISBN: 978-1-53615-408-5
Editor: Clarence Armstrong

Chapter 7

RESOLUTIONS OF INQUIRY: AN ANALYSIS OF THEIR USE IN THE HOUSE, 1947-2017*

Christopher M. Davis

SUMMARY

A resolution of inquiry is a simple resolution making a direct request or demand of the President or the head of an executive department to furnish the House with specific factual information in the Administration's possession. Under the rules and precedents of the House of Representatives, such resolutions, if properly drafted, are given a privileged parliamentary status. This means that, under certain circumstances, a resolution of inquiry can be brought to the House floor for consideration even if the committee to which it was referred has not reported it and the majority party leadership has not scheduled it for action.

Between 1947 and October 20, 2017, 313 resolutions of inquiry were submitted in the House of Representatives. Two periods in particular, 1971-1975 and 2003-2006, saw the highest levels of activity on resolutions of inquiry during the 70 years studied. Early evidence

---

* This is an edited, reformatted and augmented version of Congressional Research Service Publication No. R40879, dated November 9, 2017.

suggests that the House may be entering another period of heightened activity on resolutions of inquiry: The number of such resolutions submitted thus far in the 115th Congress (2017-2018) already exceeds the number introduced in the previous three Congresses combined.

Although nearly every standing House committee has been referred at least one resolution of inquiry during the post-World War II period, the Committees on Armed Services, Foreign Affairs, and the Judiciary have received the largest share of references because the most commonly sought information has related to matters of defense, foreign relations, and intelligence. Most resolutions of inquiry are directed to the President himself, but other executive branch officials have been the subject of such information requests as well.

Just over half of the resolutions of inquiry introduced between 1947 and October 20, 2017, were reported by the House committee to which they were referred—in most cases adversely, indicating that the committee opposed the resolution. This opposition might be because the resolution had been made moot by the executive branch complying in whole or in part with the request, or because such a request would, in the view of the committee, compromise an ongoing investigation, endanger sensitive information, or seek already-available information. Approximately one-fifth of the resolutions of inquiry introduced during the period studied received House floor action, the last one in 1995.

Although Representatives of both political parties have utilized resolutions of inquiry, in recent Congresses, such resolutions have overwhelmingly become a tool of the minority party in the House. This development has led some to question whether resolutions of inquiry are being used primarily for partisan gain or are unduly increasing the workload of certain House committees. Others have attributed the increase to a frustration among minority party Members over their inability to readily obtain information from the executive branch.

Available data suggest that 28% of the time, a resolution of inquiry has resulted in the production of information to the House. In half of the cases examined here, however, it is simply unknown, unclear, or in dispute whether the resolution of inquiry produced any of the requested information, a fact which might suggest the need for additional investigation of the efficacy of this parliamentary oversight tool by policymakers.

RESOLUTIONS OF INQUIRY GENERALLY

A resolution of inquiry is a resolution that formally calls on the executive branch to provide specified factual information to Congress. The use of resolutions of this type as a tool of oversight dates to the earliest days of Congress.[1] Although there are historical examples of resolutions of inquiry being used in the Senate,[2] they are far more common in the House of Representatives, and this chapter examines their use only in that chamber between 1947 and October 20, 2017.[3]

House resolutions of inquiry are simple resolutions (designated "H.Res."), which are submitted in the same manner as other legislation.[4] Under House rules and precedents, however, resolutions of inquiry, if properly drafted and under specific circumstances, are afforded a privileged parliamentary status.[5] Clause 7 of House Rule XIII makes a resolution of inquiry privileged for consideration at any time after it is reported or discharged from committee, consistent with the normal three-day layover period required of most committee reports.[6]

If a resolution of inquiry is not reported to the House within 14 legislative days after its introduction (not counting the days of introduction and discharge), a motion to discharge a committee from its further consideration is in order on the House floor.[7] Should the committee or

---

[1] For more information on resolutions of inquiry, see CRS Report RL31909, *House Resolutions of Inquiry*, by Christopher M. Davis. Also: U.S. Congress, House, *Constitution, Jefferson's Manual, and Rules of the House of Representatives*, H.Doc. 114-192, 114th Cong., 2nd sess. (Washington: GPO, 2017), §864, pp. 670-672.

[2] *Riddick's Senate Procedure*, the official compilation of Senate precedents, lists several examples of resolutions of inquiry from the 19th century and one from 1926. See pp. 799 and 1205.

[3] 1947 was chosen as year to begin this examination because it is the first year in which most provisions of the Legislative Reorganization Act of 1946 (P.L. 79-753, 60 Stat. 812) became effective, a milestone which is widely viewed as the beginning of the "modern" U.S. Congress.

[4] Members have occasionally called on the Executive Branch to provide information to the House and Senate in an inquiry framed as a concurrent, rather than simple, resolution. In modern practice, however, resolutions of inquiry are simple resolutions introduced, and acted upon, in one chamber. See Asher C. Hinds, *Hinds' Precedents of the House of Representatives of the United States* (Washington: GPO, 1907), vol. 3, §1875.

[5] House rules and precedents place certain types of legislation in a special "privileged" category which gives measures of this kind the ability to be called up for consideration when the House is not considering another matter.

[6] House Rule XIII, clause 4. For more information on House layover requirements, see CRS Report RS22015, *Availability of Legislative Measures in the House of Representatives (The "Three-Day Rule")*, by Elizabeth Rybicki.

[7] The current time period of 14 legislative days for a committee to report was established in the 98th Congress (1983- 1984). Prior to 1983, House rules required resolutions of inquiry to be reported within one week.

committees of referral report (or be discharged under a time limit imposed by the Speaker) within the 14-day period, however, only a Member acting at the formal direction of the committee may move to proceed to its consideration on the floor.[8] Thus, even when a House committee opposes a resolution of inquiry, the committee will virtually always mark it up and report it, often adversely, in order to retain control over the measure and prevent a supporter from making the privileged motions on the House floor to discharge the committee and call up the resolution.

To retain the privileged parliamentary status described above, resolutions of inquiry may not contain a preamble and must call only for facts within the executive branch's control. Such resolutions may not seek opinions or require an investigation and are traditionally framed as "requesting" the President or "directing" the head of a Cabinet-level agency to respond. As is the case with other types of privileged business, committee reports accompanying resolutions of inquiry are presented from the floor, rather than submitted through the hopper.

If the House chooses to consider a resolution of inquiry, it is considered under the One-Hour Rule.[9] When raised, such resolutions may be agreed to, rejected, or tabled by majority vote. In prior eras it was common for the majority party Member managing a resolution of inquiry on the House floor to quickly move to table it, either because he or she opposes its provisions, or because the request has been rendered moot by the executive branch having provided some or all of the requested information.

Finally, but importantly, as simple resolutions, resolutions of inquiry have no legal force. Thus, compliance by the executive branch with the

---

[8] In cases of multiple referral, all committees must report or be discharged before a resolution of inquiry may be considered on the floor. For a discussion of who may call up a multiply referred resolution of inquiry, see Charles W. Johnson, John V. Sullivan, and Thomas J. Wickham Jr., *House Practice: A Guide to the Rules, Precedents and Procedures of the House* (Washington: GPO, 2017), ch. 49, §7, p. 849.

[9] Clause 2 of Rule XVII, which limits to one hour the amount of time that a Member may occupy in debate on a pending question, is the default setting for consideration and debate in the House. In most cases, the Member in control of the hour of debate will move the previous question at the conclusion of the hour, cutting off further debate and bringing the pending measure to a final vote. For more information, see CRS Report 98-427, *Considering Measures in the House Under the One-Hour Rule*, by James V. Saturno.

House's request for factual information in such a resolution is entirely voluntary, resting largely on a sense of comity between co-equal branches of government and recognition of the necessity for Congress to be well-informed as it legislates. While there is no direct way for the House to enforce its request for information, executive branch compliance with resolutions of inquiry might be indirectly influenced by a general respect for congressional legislative and oversight power, including Congress's power to appropriate or withhold money for agency functions.

USE OF RESOLUTIONS OF INQUIRY: 1947-2017

Some Congresses Show High Levels of Activity

The Congressional Research Service has identified 313 resolutions of inquiry submitted in the House between 1947 and October 20, 2017—an average of just under nine per Congress. These statistics are represented in *Table 1* and the resolutions are described in detail in *Table 7*.

The number of resolutions of inquiry introduced in individual Congresses over this 70-year period varies widely. Two distinct periods, however (as shown in *Figure 1*), saw a number of resolutions of inquiry introduced in the House that far exceeded the overall average: the 92nd-94th Congresses (1971-1976), during which a total of 87 resolutions of inquiry were introduced, and the 108th and 109th Congresses (2003-2006), during which 53 resolutions were put forward. The number of resolutions of inquiry introduced in these five Congresses alone account for a full 45 percent of all such resolutions submitted during the 70-year period examined.

The number of House resolutions of inquiry introduced in the 108th (2003-2004) and 109th (2005- 2006) Congresses reflected a sharp increase in the number introduced over the preceding decade. In each Congress between the 102nd (1991-1992) and 107th (2001-2002) Congresses, an average of one resolution of inquiry was introduced. In the 108th Congress, 14 such resolutions were introduced, and 39 resolutions of inquiry were submitted in the 109th Congress. The 53 resolutions of inquiry introduced in these two Congresses exceeded the total number of such resolutions introduced in the previous two decades combined.

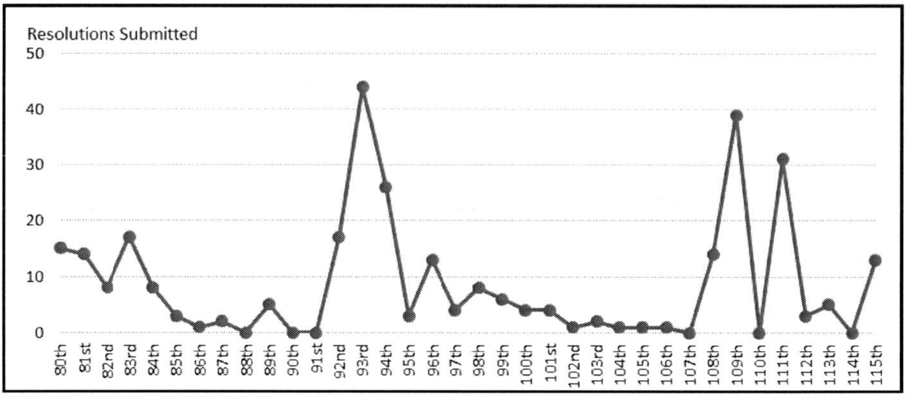

Source: CRS analysis of data from the Legislative Information System of the U.S. Congress (LIS) and relevant issues of the Journal of the House of Representatives of the United States.

Figure 1. Resolutions of Inquiry Submitted in the House of Representatives. (1947-October 20, 2017)

During the period under examination (1947-October 20, 2017), the 39 resolutions of inquiry introduced in the 109th Congress are exceeded only by the 44 resolutions introduced in the 93rd Congress (1973-1974). But this latter total may be misleadingly high due to parliamentary rules in effect at that time. In the 93rd Congress, House rules limited the co-sponsorship of measures to a maximum of 25 Representatives.[10] Several of the 44 resolutions of inquiry introduced in the 93rd Congress appear to be identically worded resolutions introduced separately, apparently to enable more than 25 Members to cosponsor them. When these "doubles" are taken into account, more resolutions of inquiry were introduced in the 109th Congress than in any single Congress since World War II. In the 111th Congress (2009-2010), 29 resolutions of inquiry were introduced.

Subsequent Congresses have seen activity on House resolutions of inquiry below historic averages. Three resolutions of inquiry were

[10] U.S. Congress, *House, Constitution, Jefferson's Manual, and Rules of the House of Representatives*, §825, p. 635.

submitted in the 112th Congress (2011-2012), five were submitted in the 113th Congress (2013-2014), and no resolutions of inquiry were put forward in the 114th Congress (2015-2016). Early indications suggest, however, that the House may be entering a another period of high resolution of inquiry activity: The 13 resolutions submitted thus far in the 115th Congress (2017-2018) exceed the average for a Congress and are more than the number of resolutions of inquiry put forward in the previous three Congresses combined.

The reason for the sharp increase in the number of such resolutions introduced during some recent Congresses is open to interpretation. Some have charged that instead of using resolutions of inquiry as an oversight tool to obtain information from the executive branch, in at least some instances, minority party Members have purposely used the privileged status such resolutions enjoy as a way to "force" committees to act on a given subject or get Members to record votes on politically controversial policy questions, in essence, enabling the minority party to "schedule" a committee markup meeting on a subject of its choosing. Those holding this view point to the high number of resolutions introduced during periods when the House and the President are of the same political party as evidence of the "political" use of resolutions of inquiry. The sharp uptick in such resolutions submitted in the GOP-controlled 115th Congress, where a Republican President has taken over for a Democratic chief executive, arguably supports this viewpoint.

One 2005 committee report took a skeptical view of several resolutions of inquiry referred to the committee that sought information on pre-Iraq war intelligence, saying, "[these] resolutions are politically-calculated attacks on the ... administration."[11] Still another report argued that "the Minority [party] is attempting to use this parliamentary tool for political means. Perhaps most importantly, as a matter of procedure, [the resolution of inquiry] challenges the Majority's prerogatives and its right to set the

[11] U.S. Congress, House Committee on International Relations, *Report to Accompany H.Res. 549*, 109th Cong., 1st sess., H.Rept. 109-351 (Washington: GPO, 2005), p. 2.

legislative agenda, and for that reason alone should be rejected."[12] Members holding this viewpoint argue that recent activity on resolutions of inquiry is more about "message politics" than obtaining information from the executive branch.

Other Members have taken a different view, arguing that resolutions of inquiry have increased in number recently because the executive branch has frequently responded "grudgingly" to information requests from Congress, particularly those made by minority party Members relating to politically sensitive issues. Such Members argue that the White House has treated letters from lawmakers requesting information "as if they are junk mail, routinely tossing them aside without responding."[13] This executive branch behavior, these Members contend, coupled with what they characterize as an ambivalence by majority parties to the rights of the minority in the House, has led to the increased use of such resolutions. Members holding this view argue that resolutions of inquiry, precisely because they are privileged, are one of the few parliamentary tools available to individual Representatives—including those in the minority—to hold the executive branch to account.

Most Resolutions Relate to Defense or Foreign Affairs

The most commonly identified subjects of House resolutions of inquiry over the past seven decades have been defense, foreign affairs, and intelligence. This may help to explain in part the significant increases noted above during the 92nd-94th (1971-1976) and 108th-109th (2003-2006) Congresses, periods where Members were focused on military conflicts in Vietnam, Iraq, and Afghanistan and on foreign affairs and intelligence issues stemming from the so-called Global War on Terrorism.

---

[12] U.S. Congress, House Committee on Education and the Workforce, *Adverse Report to Accompany H.Res. 467*, 109th Cong., 1st sess., H.Rept. 109-258 (Washington: GPO, 2005), p. 6.

[13] U.S. Congress, House Committee on the Judiciary, *Adverse Report to Accompany H.Res. 643*, 109th Cong., 2nd sess., H.Rept. 109-382 (Washington: GPO, 2006), p. 185.

When resolutions of inquiry are submitted, the Speaker, acting through the Parliamentarian, refers them to committee based on the subject matter of the measure and the jurisdiction of House committees as codified in clause 1 of Rule X.

With the exception of the Committees on Budget, Rules, and Ethics, every standing committee of the House has, at some point over the 70 years examined, had at least one resolution of inquiry referred to it. However, as is reflected in *Figure 2*, and as may be inferred from the most common subjects of such resolutions mentioned above, three House committees have received the greatest share of such referrals: Armed Services, which was referred 74 resolutions of inquiry over this period; Foreign Affairs, with 71; and Judiciary, which received 42. These three panels were the committees of primary referral for 60% of all resolutions of inquiry introduced between 1947 and October 20, 2017.

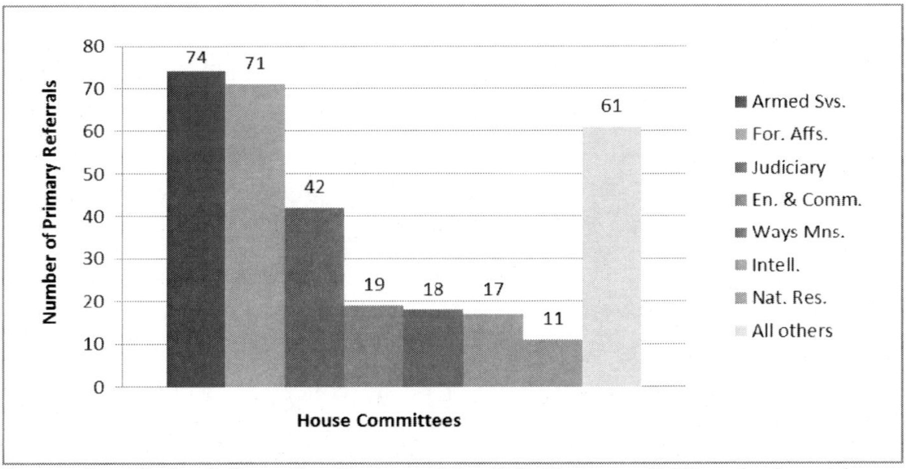

Source: Legislative Information System of the U.S. Congress (LIS) and relevant issues of the Journal of the United States House of Representatives.

Notes: For purposes of consistency and clarity, committees are identified by their designation in clause 1 of House Rule X as adopted by the 115th Congress.

Figure 2. Committees of Primary Referral for Resolutions of Inquiry. (1947-October 20, 2017)

The referral of legislation to more than one House committee has been permitted in the House since 1975, and over the period examined, several resolutions of inquiry were multiply referred. The House Parliamentarian has recently written, however, that "the modern practice is to refer [resolutions of inquiry] to a single committee only."[14] Since 2004, three resolutions of inquiry have been multiply referred. It is not clear if this is the case because the subject of recent resolutions fell exclusively into the jurisdiction of one committee, because resolution sponsors have introduced separate resolutions directed to different officials (as opposed to one multiply-referred resolution directed to all of them), or because House Speakers, acting through the Parliamentarian, have consciously chosen to avoid the multiple referral of resolutions of inquiry wherever possible.

Most Resolutions of Inquiry Are Directed to the President

As has been noted, privileged resolutions of inquiry are directed to the President of the United States, or, under House Rule XIII, to the "head of an executive department." Under chamber precedents, the "head of an executive department" has been interpreted to mean the Secretary of a Cabinet-level executive agency—that is, those listed in 5 U.S.C. 101, not subordinate government officials such the Administrator of the Environmental Protection Agency or the Director of National Intelligence.[15] As such, although a resolution of inquiry directed to an officer below the Cabinet level could be introduced, it would not enjoy privileged status. The inclusion of lesser officials is viewed as destroying the privilege of an entire resolution, even in cases where the resolution is also directed to the President or a Cabinet Secretary.

Since 1947, 114 of the 313 resolutions of inquiry introduced in the House (36%) have been directed to the President of the United States; 59 (19%) have been directed to the Secretary of Defense or his predecessor;

---

[14] *House Practice*, ch. 49, §6, p. 848.

[15] Asher C. Hinds, *Hinds' Precedents of the House of Representatives of the United States* (Washington: GPO, 1907), vol. 3, §1861, p. 169.

38 resolutions (12%) sought information from the Secretary of State; and 27 (9%) from the Attorney General. Various other executive branch officials, including the Secretaries of Commerce, Energy, Health and Human Services, Homeland Security, Labor, and the Treasury have been the target of House resolutions of inquiry. These statistics are represented in *Figure 3*.

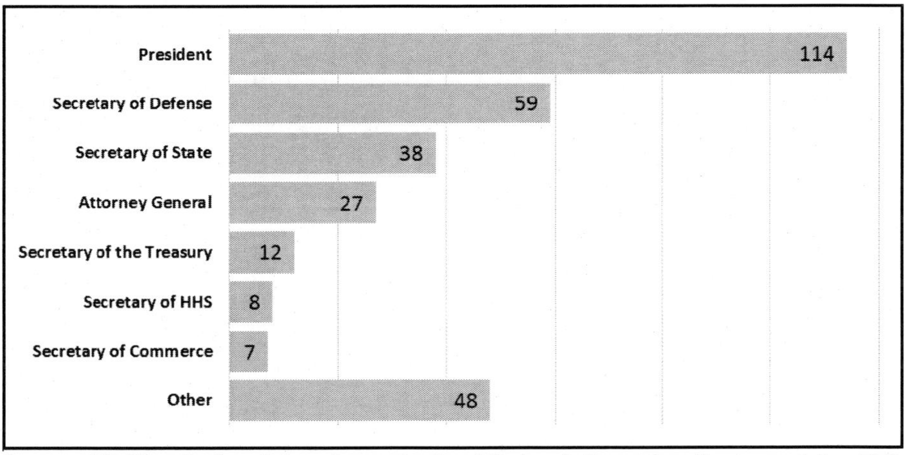

Source: CRS analysis of data from the Legislative Information System of the U.S. Congress (LIS) and relevant issues of the Journal of the United States House of Representatives.

Notes: As of October 20, 2017. In cases in which a resolution was addressed to more than one executive branch official, the first listed official was counted.

Figure 3. Primary Official to Whom House Resolutions of Inquiry Were Directed. (1947-October 20, 2017)

A small number of resolutions of inquiry introduced during the period examined were directed solely or in part to sub-Cabinet officials, including the Directors of Central Intelligence and National Intelligence, the Chairman of the Nuclear Regulatory Commission, and the Internal Revenue Service Commissioner. As noted, such resolutions were arguably not privileged for consideration in the House, and, in at least once instance, the Speaker sustained a point of order to that effect when an effort was made to raise the measure on the floor.[16]

HOUSE ACTION ON RESOLUTIONS OF INQUIRY

Committees Are Acting on More Resolutions of Inquiry

A committee has a number of choices after a resolution of inquiry is referred to it. It may mark up and report the resolution without amendment, or it may recommend amendments to it. It may report the resolution to the House favorably, adversely, or without recommendation. It may also take no action; however, as has been noted, in failing to act, it risks a Member, after the expiration of the 14-legislative-day period, making a privileged motion on the House floor to discharge the committee of further consideration of the resolution.

Just over half of the resolutions of inquiry introduced between 1947 and October 20, 2017, were acted on by the primary House committee of referral. Approximately 52% (162 of 313) of the resolutions of inquiry submitted were actively considered at the committee level. As is discussed in more detail below, however, in recent Congresses, House committees have chosen to mark up virtually every privileged resolution of inquiry referred to them, presumably in order to retain control of the resolution and prevent another Member from triggering floor votes on the motion to discharge the committee.

As is reflected in *Table 2*, during the period examined, committees which chose to mark up a resolution of inquiry and report it to the House chose frequently (73%) to report the resolution "adversely," a parliamentary designation which means that the committee did not recommend that the House agree to the resolution. In a smaller percentage of cases during the time period examined, House committees have chosen

---

[16] Deschler's *Precedents of the United States House of Representatives*, H. Doc. 94-661, 94th Cong., 2nd sess., vol. 4, ch. 15, §2.1.

to report resolutions of inquiry favorably (13%) or without recommendation (14%). On occasion, the committees have reported amendments to the resolution, oftentimes recommending the adoption of a full substitute.

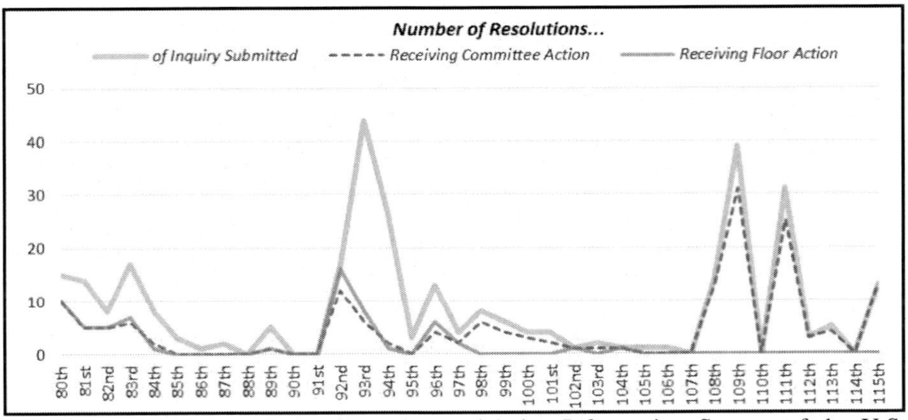

Source: CRS analysis of data from the Legislative Information System of the U.S. Congress (LIS) and relevant issues of the Journal of the House of Representatives of the United States.

Figure 4. House Activity on Resolutions of Inquiry (1947-October 20, 2017)

No generalizations can be made about adverse reports on resolutions of inquiry. A House committee may choose to report a resolution adversely because they oppose it or to ensure that no Member except a designee of the committee may try to call up the resolution on the floor. In several instances over the period examined, however, an adverse report was clearly made because the executive branch had produced some or all of the requested information, and the committee did not want the House to expend its time on a moot question. It has also been common for committees to report adversely with the rationale that production of the information would compromise an ongoing investigation. An adverse report might also occur because, in the view of the committee, the requested information was too sensitive to be provided or, conversely, was already widely available, and thus, not the proper subject of a privileged resolution.

As mentioned, data show that since the 108th Congress (2003-2004), committees have almost universally marked up every properly-drafted resolution of inquiry referred to them regardless of its subject, sponsor, or how the committee viewed the resolution. This was not the case in earlier Congresses during the 70-year period studied. This suggests that, today, committees are acting on resolutions of inquiry at least in part to retain control of the resolution.

The fact that more resolutions of inquiry have been introduced in some recent Congresses, and House committees are marking up virtually every such resolution referred to them, has led some to question whether resolutions of inquiry are improperly increasing the workload of House committees. Those holding such a view argue that if committees feel they "have to" mark up a resolution of inquiry because it is privileged, the potential exists for minority party Members to flood a committee with such resolutions and wrest partial control over a committee's markup agenda from the majority.

Those holding this view note that certain House committees are disproportionately affected by such resolutions, and they argue that using resolutions of inquiry in this way is not the purpose such measures were created for or given privileged status under chamber rules. They note, for example, that in the 109th Congress (2005-2006), 45% (10 out of 22) of the reports made to the House by the Committee on International Relations (now named Foreign Affairs) were on minority-party sponsored resolutions of inquiry.[17] During the same period, 21% (3 out of 14) of the reports made to the House by the Committee on Armed Services were on minority-party sponsored resolutions of inquiry.[18]

Members holding the opposite view argue that although resolutions of inquiry may have increased in number in recent years, they still represent a small fraction of the overall legislative workload and are easily managed by the chamber's committee system. They further argue that such resolutions actually aid the House, by compelling its committees to seek information

---

[17] See U.S. Congress, House Committee on International Relations, *Legislative Review Activities*, 109th Cong., 2nd sess., H.Rept. 109-747 (Washington: GPO, 2007), pp. 27-28.

[18] Legislative Information System of the U.S. Congress (LIS).

from the executive branch that Members need to legislate effectively. Those holding this view might argue that resolutions of inquiry motivate committees to focus not just on legislating but also on the oversight responsibilities they have been charged with by the House.

Few Resolutions of Inquiry Reach the House Floor

As is reflected in *Table 3*, House floor consideration of resolutions of inquiry during the 70-year period examined was generally rare. In recent Congresses it has been virtually non-existent. In the last 26 years, two resolutions of inquiry have received action on the House floor.

Between 1947 and October 20, 2017, 64 resolutions of inquiry have been considered on the House floor, about 20% of those introduced, and approximately 40% of those reported by the chamber's committees. Of the resolutions receiving floor action, 52 (81%) were laid on the table by majority vote, effectively killing them. Eleven resolutions of inquiry have been agreed to by the House since 1947, the most recent occurring in the 104th Congress (1995-1996). It is worth reiterating that the tabling of a resolution on the House floor may have been undertaken because the question had been made moot by the executive branch being in substantial compliance with the request. For example, in a handful of instances during the period examined, it was the sponsor of the resolution of inquiry who moved to lay the resolution on the table, apparently satisfied it had produced the desired result.

During the 91st-95th Congresses, several resolutions of inquiry that were submitted received no action either in committee or on the floor. This might be due to the fact that, as has been noted, several of the resolutions of inquiry introduced during this period appear to be identically worded resolutions introduced separately, apparently to enable more Members to cosponsor them. One might speculate that no action was taken on other resolutions during this period because the executive branch provided the requested information. In current practice, House committees will virtually always mark up and report a resolution of inquiry in order to retain control of the measure and avoid floor votes.

Resolutions of Inquiry Are Increasingly a Minority Party Tool

Resolutions of inquiry are sometimes assumed to be an oversight tool that is used disproportionately, or even exclusively, by congressional minorities. This view is, in a sense, understandable. The majority party in the House arguably has far more effective oversight tools at its disposal than non-binding resolutions of inquiry: committee hearings, subpoenas, and the ability to pass legislation.

An examination of resolutions of inquiry introduced between 1947 and October 20, 2017, however, reveals a far more bipartisan overall picture than this view might suggest. Over the 70 years examined, the party affiliation of resolution of inquiry sponsors is fairly evenly divided. Of the 313 resolutions of inquiry introduced between 1947 and October 20, 2017, 132 were introduced by Members of the congressional majority party and 181 by minority party Members.[19] The political affiliation of resolution of inquiry sponsors versus that of the President is more divided. Of the 313 resolutions of inquiry submitted in the House between 1947 and October 20, 2017, 239 (76%) were introduced by Members of Congress belonging to the opposite political party of the President.

If one examines only recent Congresses, the statistical picture is much starker and supports the view that resolutions of inquiry have become overwhelmingly a minority party tool. In recent years, the sponsorship of resolutions of inquiry has become far more partisan, and more lopsided in party division than at any time during the seven decades studied. Since 2005, two of the 91 resolutions of inquiry submitted were authored by a Member of Congress having the same political party as the President. The

---

[19] Two resolutions of inquiry introduced over the period were sponsored by Members with a political affiliation other than Democratic or Republican. For purposes of this analysis, both sponsors were grouped with the Democratic Party, which is the party they voluntarily affiliated with for purposes of House committee assignment.

others were submitted by Members directed at Presidents of the opposite party.

Effectiveness of Resolutions of Inquiry Is Unclear

Because resolutions of inquiry are primarily intended to be an information-gathering tool, one question is whether available evidence suggests such resolutions have been successful in producing information from the executive branch.

The data in *Table 6* and in *Figure 3* are gleaned from an examination of legislative history documents, such as committee reports and floor debate, accompanying resolutions of inquiry introduced between 1947 and October 20, 2017. Based on these documents and the measures themselves, resolutions of inquiry were divided into three categories: (1) Yes, evidence suggests the resolution did produce full or partial information from the executive branch; (2) No, the evidence suggests that no information was received from the executive branch in response to the resolution; or (3) Whether information was produced is unknown, unclear, or in dispute.

In half of the resolutions submitted between 1947 and October 20, 2017, whether the resolution resulted in the production of information was unknown, unclear, or in dispute based on an examination of the legislative history. Twenty-eight percent of the resolutions of inquiry introduced over the period studied appear to have resulted in the production of some or all of the information requested of the executive branch. Twenty-two percent of the resolutions authored during this period appear to have failed to produce any requested information. When a similar examination is limited to the most recent period of high resolution of inquiry activity noted above, 2003-2006, the effectiveness of such resolutions in producing information from the executive branch is far less. During these years, such resolutions failed to produce information 64% of the time and succeeded in 19% of cases.

As these statistics suggest, making determinations about the "success" of resolutions of inquiry can be difficult. As has been noted, slightly under half of the resolutions of inquiry introduced between 1947 and October 20, 2017 were never marked up by House committee or considered on the chamber floor. In such cases there are no legislative history documents to examine to find clues as to whether the Member's information request was answered or ignored. It is easy to imagine that, in at least some of these instances, information was in fact obtained. This supposition seems particularly likely in cases of resolutions introduced in the early years studied, where requests were commonly made for routine, non-controversial data, such as labor statistics or documents about the government's use of railroad cars. It seems reasonable to suppose that such resolutions' sponsors never tried to call the measures up on the floor precisely because their request had been satisfied; in such a scenario, inaction on a resolution would be an indication of its success. But that is only a supposition. Likewise, the very introduction of a resolution of inquiry might encourage an executive department to hand over information, but it may not be immediately apparent that the resolution was the motivating factor.

Although the established purpose of a resolution of inquiry is to acquire factual information, that may not be the only goal a Member has when authoring such legislation. Calling attention to an issue, seizing a committee's agenda from the majority party, forcing other legislative action (such as a hearing), getting Members on the record with difficult policy votes, or demonstrating interest in a particular subject area may all be possible goals for introducing a resolution of inquiry. As has been noted above, in recent Congresses, some have argued that the increase in resolutions of inquiry introduced is precisely because the resolutions are being used for goals such as these, rather than as a purely information-gathering mechanism.

CONCLUSION AND QUESTIONS FOR CONSIDERATION

An examination of resolutions of inquiry introduced in the House between 1947 and October 20, 2017, raises several questions for the potential consideration of policymakers. Overall, the data suggest that resolutions of inquiry have become more common in some recent Congresses, have resulted in more work at the committee level, and have increasingly been used by minority party Members in the House.

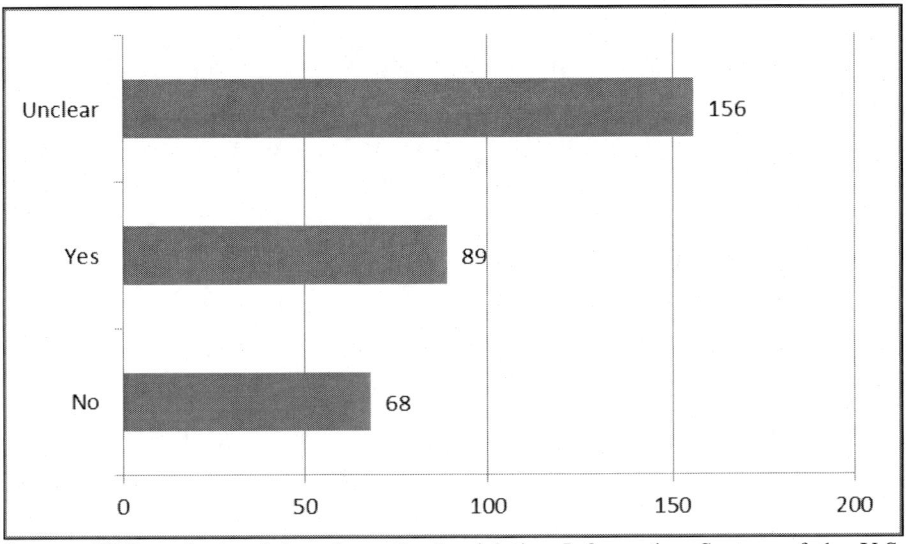

Source: CRS analysis of data from the Legislative Information System of the U.S. Congress (LIS) and relevant issues of the Journal of the House of Representatives of the United States.

Notes: Categories based solely on examination of resolutions and related legislative history documents.

Figure 5. Have House Resolutions of Inquiry Produced Information? (1947-October 20, 2017)

As noted, the data examined raise the question of whether increases in the number of House resolutions of inquiry submitted in some recent Congresses are affecting the workload of certain chamber committees. If policymakers were to determine that this is the case, and that it merits action, they might consider whether changes in the treatment of such resolutions under House rules are warranted. The House might respond, for example, by making such resolutions privileged only if a House committee chose to report them favorably. Or, the House might choose instead to extend the time period that committees have to report a privileged resolution of inquiry from the present 14 legislative days to a longer period of time. A change of this latter type might preserve the traditional use of resolutions of inquiry for all Members and give committees more freedom to choose when they will act on them. It might also discourage resolutions of inquiry from being introduced in an attempt to gain political advantage by highlighting important, but transient, hot-button political issues.

Perhaps the clearest picture emerging from a systematic examination of resolution of inquiry activity in the post-WWII period, however, relates to the efficacy of such resolutions. Although the data show that in some cases—particularly in earlier eras—such resolutions have produced information, half the time it is unclear if resolutions of inquiry result in the production of any information to the House, and if so, to what degree.

The possibility that the standing committees of the House are spending an increased amount of time acting on resolutions whose efficacy is largely unknown may lead policymakers to try to institute a more rigorous accounting of future resolutions of this type. Lawmakers might do so in a number of ways. Committees, for example, might direct the agencies they oversee to formally catalogue and submit to them what response, if any, they have made to recently introduced resolutions of inquiry. Committees might be encouraged to report this information to the House in the activities report they are already required to submit to the House each Congress under clause 1(d)(1) of Rule XI, or by some other mechanism. Executive branch communications to the House in response to a resolution of inquiry might be designated as such in the *Congressional Record*, or noted in a special category when received by the Clerk of the House, so that the cause and effect (or lack thereof) of such resolutions might become clearer. Policymakers might also consider standardizing the procedures House committees use to handle resolutions of inquiry, for example, by requiring them to transmit the resolution to the executive branch within a stated timeframe with a letter from the chairman formally requesting executive comment on the resolution.[20]

---

[20] In the early years of the period studied, it appeared to be universal practice for a House committee receiving referral of a resolution of inquiry to immediately request formal executive comment on the resolution. The executive's response to this request was

Other options also exist. The House Committee on Rules, as the panel with jurisdiction over chamber rules, might examine whether resolutions of inquiry, as a mechanism rooted in the earliest days of Congress, should continue to enjoy privileged parliamentary status considering advances in information technology, including the development of oversight tools available to Members in recent decades. The House Oversight and Government Reform Committee, which has special duties under House Rule X to report committee oversight plans to the House along with any recommendations to promote "more effective and coordinated oversight," might also consider examining the use of such resolutions as oversight tools.

Whether policymakers ultimately determine that changes in the use of resolutions of inquiry are warranted or not, such an examination might arguably give all Members of the House a better understanding of the resolution's use in the ongoing oversight relationship between the legislative and executive branches of government.

Table 1. House Resolutions of Inquiry and Associated Action, 1947-October 20, 2017

Congress and Years	Resolutions of Inquiry Introduced	Resolutions Receiving Committee Action	Resolutions Receiving Floor Action
80th (1947-1948)	15	10	10
81st (1949-1950)	14	5	5
82nd (1951-1952)	8	5	5
83rd (1953-1954)	17	6	7
84th (1955-1956)	8	2	1
85th (1957-1958)	3	0	0
86th (1959-1960)	1	0	0
87th (1961-1962)	2	0	0
88th (1963-1964)	0	0	0

commonly printed in the committee's report to the House on the resolution. In recent Congresses, however, it is not clear from the legislative history documents examined if House committees are still routinely making such requests for formal executive comment on resolutions of inquiry, and if so, to what extent.

Table 1. (Continued)

Congress and Years	Resolutions of Inquiry Introduced	Resolutions Receiving Committee Action	Resolutions Receiving Floor Action
89th (1965-1966)	5	1	1
90th (1967-1968)	0	0	0
91st (1969-1970)	0	0	0
92nd (1971-1972)	17	12	16
93rd (1973-1974)	44	6	8
94th (1975-1976)	26	2	1
95th (1977-1978)	3	0	0
96th (1979-1980)	13	4	6
97th (1981-1982)	4	2	2
98th (1983-1984)	8	6	0
99th (1985-1986)	6	4	0
100th (1987-1988)	4	3	0
101st (1989-1990)	4	2	0
102nd (1991-1992)	1	1	1
103rd (1993-1994)	2	1	0
104th (1995-1996)	1	1	1
105th (1997-1998)	1	0	0
106th (1999-2000)	1	0	0
107th (2001-2002)	0	0	0
108th (2003-2004)	14	13	0
109th (2005-2006)	39	31	0
110th (2007-2008)	0	0	0
111th (2009-2010)	31	25	0
112th (2011-2012)	3	3	0
113th (2013-2014)	5	4	0
114th (2015-2016)	0	0	0
115th (2017-2018)	13	13	0
TOTAL	313	162	64

Source: Legislative Information System of the U.S. Congress (LIS) and relevant issues of the Journal of the United States House of Representatives.

Notes: Table reflects resolutions of inquiry introduced through October 20, 2017.

Table 2. Form of Report on Resolutions of Inquiry, 1947-October 20, 2017

Congress and Years	Adverse	Favorable	Without Recommendation
80th (1947-1948)	6	3	1
81st (1949-1950)	4	1	0
82nd (1951-1952)	1	1	3
83rd (1953-1954)	6	0	0
84th (1955-1956)	1	0	1
85th (1957-1958)	0	0	0
86th (1959-1960)	0	0	0
87th (1961-1962)	0	0	0
88th (1963-1964)	0	0	0
89th (1965-1966)	1	0	0
90th (1967-1968)	0	0	0
91st (1969-1970)	0	0	0
92nd (1971-1972)	12	0	0
93rd (1973-1974)	6	0	0
94th (1975-1976)	2	0	0
95th (1977-1978)	0	0	0
96th (1979-1980)	3	1	0
97th (1981-1982)	1	0	1
98th (1983-1984)	5	0	1
99th (1985-1986)	4	0	0
100th (1987-1988)	2	1	0
101st (1989-1990)	2	0	0
102nd (1991-1992)	0	0	1
103rd (1993-1994)	1	0	0
104th (1995-1996)	0	1	0
105th (1997-1998)	0	0	0
106th (1999-2000)	0	0	0
107th (2001-2002)	0	0	0
108th (2003-2004)	13	0	0
109th (2005-2006)	26	0	5
110th (2007-2008)	0	0	0
111th (2009-2010)	7	10	8
112th (2011-2012)	1	2	0
113th (2013-2014)	2	0	2

Table 2. (Continued)

Congress and Years	Adverse	Favorable	Without Recommendation
114th (2015-2016)	0	0	0
115th (2017-2018)	12	1	0
TOTAL	118	21	23

Source: CRS analysis of data from the Legislative Information System of the U.S. Congress (LIS) and relevant issues of the Journal of the United States House of Representatives.

Notes: Reflects activity as of October 20, 2017.

Table 3. House Floor Action on Resolutions of Inquiry, 1947-October 20, 2017

Congress and Years	Tabled	Agreed to
80th (1947-1948)	6	4
81st (1949-1950)	4	1
82nd (1951-1952)	3	2
83rd (1953-1954)	7	0
84th (1955-1956)	1	0
85th (1957-1958)	0	0
86th (1959-1960)	0	0
87th (1961-1962)	0	0
88th (1963-1964)	0	0
89th (1965-1966)	1	0
90th (1967-1968)	0	0
91st (1969-1970)	0	0
92nd (1971-1972)	14	1
93rd (1973-1974)	8	0
94th (1975-1976)	0	1
95th (1977-1978)	0	0
96th (1979-1980)	4	2
97th (1981-1982)	2	0
98th (1983-1984)	0	0
99th (1985-1986)	1	0
100th (1987-1988)	0	0
101st (1989-1990)	0	0
102nd (1991-1992)	1	0
103rd (1993-1994)	0	0

Congress and Years	Tabled	Agreed to
104th (1995-1996)	0	1
105th (1997-1998)	0	0
106th (1999-2000)	0	0
107th (2001-2002)	0	0
108th (2003-2004)	0	0
109th (2005-2006)	0	0
110th (2007-2008)	0	0
111th (2009-2010)	0	0
112th (2011-2012)	0	0
113th (2013-2014)	0	0
114th (2015-2016)	0	0
115th (2017-2018)	0	0
TOTAL	52	12

Source: CRS analysis of data from the Legislative Information System of the U.S. Congress (LIS) and relevant issues of the Journal of the United States House of Representatives.

Notes: Reflects activity as of October 20, 2017.

Table 4. Party of Resolution of Inquiry Sponsors vs. Congress, 1947-October 20, 2017

Congress and Years	Congressional Majority Party	Sponsor Member of Majority Party	Sponsor Member of Minority Party
80th (1947-1948)	R	15	0
81st (1949-1950)	D	5	9
82nd (1951-1952)	D	0	8
83rd (1953-1954)	R	13	4
84th (1955-1956)	D	2	6
85th (1957-1958)	D	1	2
86th (1959-1960)	D	0	1
87th (1961-1962)	D	2	0
88th (1963-1964)	D	0	0
89th (1965-1966)	D	0	5
90th (1967-1968)	D	0	0
91st (1969-1970)	D	0	0
92nd (1971-1972)	D	9	8

Table 4. (Continued)

Congress and Years	Congressional Majority Party	Sponsor Member of Majority Party	Sponsor Member of Minority Party
93rd (1973-1974)	D	27	17
94th (1975-1976)	D	23	3
95th (1977-1978)	D	1	2
96th (1979-1980)	D	5	8
97th (1981-1982)	D	4	0
98th (1983-1984)	D	7	1
99th (1985-1986)	D	5	1
100th (1987-1988)	D	3	1
101st (1989-1990)	D	1	3
102nd (1991-1992)	D	1	0
103rd (1993-1994)	D	0	2
104th (1995-1996)	R	0	1
105th (1997-1998)	R	0	1
106th (1999-2000)	R	0	1
107th (2001-2002)	R	0	0
108th (2003-2004)	R	0	14
109th (2005-2006)	R	1	38
110th (2007-2008)	D	0	0
111th (2009-2010)	D	0	31
112th (2011-2012)	R	2	1
113th (2013-2014)	R	5	0
114th (2015-2016)	R	0	0
115th (2017-2018)	R	0	13
TOTAL	-	132	181

Source: CRS analysis of data from the Legislative Information System of the U.S. Congress (LIS) and relevant issues of the Journal of the United States House of Representatives.

Notes: Reflects activity as of October 20, 2017. "D" signifies Democratic Party. "R" signifies Republican Party.

Table 5. Party of Resolution of Inquiry Sponsors vs. President, 1947-October 20, 2017

Congress and Years	President's Party	Sponsor Party Same As President	Sponsor Party Different Than President
80th (1947-1948)	D	0	15
81st (1949-1950)	D	5	9
82nd (1951-1952)	D	0	8
83rd (1953-1954)	R	13	4
84th (1955-1956)	R	6	2
85th (1957-1958)	R	2	1
86th (1959-1960)	R	1	0
87th (1961-1962)	D	2	0
88th (1963-1964)	D	0	0
89th (1965-1966)	D	0	5
90th (1967-1968)	D	0	0
91st (1969-1970)	R	0	0
92nd (1971-1972)	R	8	9
93rd (1973-1974)	R	17	27
94th (1975-1976)	R	3	23
95th (1977-1978)	D	1	2
96th (1979-1980)	D	5	8
97th (1981-1982)	R	0	4
98th (1983-1984)	R	1	7
99th (1985-1986)	R	1	5
100th (1987-1988)	R	1	3
101st (1989-1990)	R	3	1
102nd (1991-1992)	R	0	1
103rd (1993-1994)	D	0	2
104th (1995-1996)	D	1	0
105th (1997-1998)	D	1	0
106th (1999-2000)	D	1	0
107th (2001-2002)	R	0	0

Table 5. (Continued)

Congress and Years	President's Party	Sponsor Party Same As President	Sponsor Party Different Than President
108th (2003-2004)	R	0	14
109th (2005-2006)	R	1	38
110th (2007-2008)	R	0	0
111th (2009-2010)	D	0	31
112th (2011-2012)	D	1	2
113th (2013-2014)	D	0	5
114th (2015-2016)	D	0	0
115th (2017-2018)	R	0	13
TOTAL	-	74	239

Source: CRS analysis of data from the Legislative Information System of the U.S. Congress (LIS) and relevant issues of the Journal of the United States House of Representatives.

Notes: Reflects activity as of October 20, 2017. "D" signifies Democratic Party. "R" signifies Republican Party.

Table 6. Have House Resolutions of Inquiry Produced Requested Information? 1947-October 20, 2017

Congress and Years	Yes (or Partial)	No	Unknown, Unclear, or Disputed
80th (1947-1948)	10	1	4
81st (1949-1950)	4	1	9
82nd (1951-1952)	5	0	3
83rd (1953-1954)	8	0	9
84th (1955-1956)	2	0	6
85th (1957-1958)	0	0	3
86th (1959-1960)	0	0	1
87th (1961-1962)	0	0	2
88th (1963-1964)	0	0	0

Congress and Years	Yes (or Partial)	No	Unknown, Unclear, or Disputed
89th (1965-1966)	2	0	3
90th (1967-1968)	0	0	0
91st (1969-1970)	0	0	0
92nd (1971-1972)	10	4	3
93rd (1973-1974)	8	0	36
94th (1975-1976)	1	1	24
95th (1977-1978)	0	0	3
96th (1979-1980)	3	2	8
97th (1981-1982)	3	0	1
98th (1983-1984)	5	1	2
99th (1985-1986)	3	1	2
100th (1987-1988)	2	0	2
101st (1989-1990)	2	0	2
102nd (1991-1992)	1	0	0
103rd (1993-1994)	0	1	1
104th (1995-1996)	1	0	0
105th (1997-1998)	0	0	1
106th (1999-2000)	0	0	1
107th (2001-2002)	0	0	0
108th (2003-2004)	6	8	0
109th (2005-2006)	4	26	9
110th (2007-2008)	0	0	0
111th (2009-2010)	8	4	19
112th (2011-2012)	1	0	2
113th (2013-2014)	0	5	0
114th (2015-2016)	0	0	0
115th (2017-2018)	0	13	0
TOTAL	89	68	156

Source: CRS Analysis of data from the Legislative Information System of the U.S. Congress (LIS) and relevant issues of the Journal of the United States House of Representatives.

Notes: Reflects activity as of October 20, 2017. Categories based on CRS examination of resolutions and related legislative history documents.

Table 7. Identified Resolution of Inquiry Submitted in the U.S. House of Representatives, 1947- October 20, 2017

Resolution, Introduction, and Sponsorship	Official(s) to Whom Inquiry Is Directed	Subject of Inquiry	Committee(s) of Referral and Consideration	House Floor Action
H.Res. 38 01/06/1947 Rep. Lawrence H. Smith (R-WI)	Secretary of War Secretary of the Navy	Materials in the possession of the War and Navy Departments suitable for use in relieving the housing shortage	Armed Services -	-
H.Res. 80 01/30/1947 Rep. Edith N. Rogers (R-MA)	Secretary of State	Withdrawal of U.S. troops from China	Foreign Affairs Reported adversely 02/05/1947 H.Rept. 80-16	Laid on the table 02/05/1947
H.Res. 254 06/24/1947 Rep. Ellsworth Buck (R-NY)	Secretary of State	Documents, records, and memorandum related to Serge Rubenstein	Judiciary Reported adversely 07/11/1947 H.Rept. 80-886	Laid on the table 07/11/1947
H.Res. 255 06/24/1947 Rep. Ellsworth Buck (R-NY)	Attorney General	Documents, records, and memorandum related to Serge Rubenstein	Judiciary Reported adversely 07/11/1947 H.Rept. 80-887	Laid on the table 07/11/1947
H.Res. 257 06/26/1947 Rep. Edith N. Rogers (R-MA)	Secretary of the Treasury	Food and meat being shipped from Greece and the Mediterranean to the United States	Ways and Means -	-

Resolution, Introduction, and Sponsorship	Official(s) to Whom Inquiry Is Directed	Subject of Inquiry	Committee(s) of Referral and Consideration	House Floor Action
H.Res. 258 06/25/1947 Rep. Edith N.Rogers (R-MA)	Secretary of State	Food and meat being shipped from Greece and the Mediterranean to the United States	Foreign Affairs Reported adversely 07/09/1947 H.Rept. 80-814	Laid on the table 07/09/1947
H.Res. 365 11/24/1947 Rep. Karl E. Mundt (R-SD)	Secretary of Defense	Decommissioning of certain factories in post-war Germany	Foreign Affairs Reported favorably (amended) 12/18/1947 H.Rept. 80-1225	Agreed to 12/18/1947
H.Res. 366 11/24/1947 Rep. Karl E. Mundt (R-SD)	Secretary of Commerce	Sale of supplies to the Soviet Union by firms and individuals located in the United States	Interstate and Foreign Commerce Reported favorably (amended) 12/05/1947 H.Rept. 80-1155	Agreed to 12/05/1947
H.Res. 380 11/28/1947 Rep. Edith N. Rogers (R-MA)	Secretary of Commerce	Amount of coal and oil being sent to Canada and other countries by the United States	Interstate and Foreign Commerce -	-
H.Res. 381 11/28/1947 Rep. Edith N. Rogers (R-MA)	United States Maritime Commission	Information relative to oil: Idle tankers and why said tankers have not been put into operation	Merchant Marine and Fisheries -	-

Table 7. (Continued)

Resolution, Introduction, and Sponsorship	Official(s) to Whom Inquiry Is Directed	Subject of Inquiry	Committee(s) of Referral and Consideration	House Floor Action
H.Res. 382 11/28/1947 Rep. Edith N. Rogers (R-MA)	Director of the Office of Defense Transportation	Shortage of coal cars used in transportation of coal to New England and whether coal cars from Great Lakes terminals may be transferred to New England	Interstate and Foreign Commerce -	-
H.Res. 383 11/28/1947 Rep. Edith N. Rogers (R-MA)	Secretary of the Navy	Whether full use is being made of oil tankers under the control of the Navy	Armed Services Reported adversely 12/04/1947 H.Rept. 80-1154	Laid on the table 12/04/1947
H.Res. 385 12/02/1947 Rep. Edith N. Rogers (R-MA)	Secretary of the Interior	The amount of fuel, gasoline, petroleum products, and coal available in the United States	Public Lands Reported without recommendation 12/19/1947 H.Rept. 80-1231	Agreed to 02/16/1948
H.Res. 511 03/24/1948 Rep. John Z. Anderson (R-CA)	Secretary of Agriculture	Research on price spreads between the producer and consumer of agricultural products	Agriculture Reported adversely 04/07/1948 H.Rept. 80-1662	Laid on the table 04/07/1948

Resolution, Introduction, and Sponsorship	Official(s) to Whom Inquiry Is Directed	Subject of Inquiry	Committee(s) of Referral and Consideration	House Floor Action
H.Res. 522 04/07/1948 Rep. John P. Thomas (R-NJ)	Secretary of Commerce	A letter authored by FBI Director, J. Edgar Hoover, relating to Dr. Edward U. Condon, Director of the National Bureau of Standards	Interstate and Foreign Commerce Reported favorably 04/19/1948 H.Rept. 80-1753	Agreed to 04/22/1948
H.Res. 50 01/13/1949 Rep. Jacob K. Javits (R-NY)	Secretary of State	Situation in Palestine	Foreign Affairs Reported adversely 01/31/1949 H.Rept. 81-10	Laid on the table 01/31/1949
H.Res. 80 02/03/1949 Rep. Edwin Arthur Hall (R-NY)	Secretary of Defense	Administrative action on the program of national defense preparedness	Armed Services Reported adversely 02/09/1949 H.Rept. 81-36	Laid on the table 02/09/1949
H.Res. 147 03/11/1949 Rep. Clark W. Thompson (D- TX)	Secretary of State	Effect of imports on the domestic fishing industry	Merchant Marine and Fisheries Reported favorably (amended) 03/30/1949 H.Rept. 81-355	Agreed to 04/22/1948
H.Res. 196 04/27/1949 Rep. Vito Marcantonio (American Laborite-NY)	Secretary of State	Denial of visas to certain foreign officials (Pierre Cot of the Republic of France and Konni Zilliacus of Great Britain)	Foreign Affairs Reported adversely 05/04/1949 H.Rept. 81-504	Laid on the table 05/04/1949

Table 7. (Continued)

Resolution, Introduction, and Sponsorship	Official(s) to Whom Inquiry Is Directed	Subject of Inquiry	Committee(s) of Referral and Consideration	House Floor Action
H.Res. 198 04/29/1949 Rep. Thomas J. Lane (D-MA)	United States Tariff Commission	Statistics relating to the woolen and worsted manufacturing industry	Ways and Means	-
H.Res. 199 04/29/1949 Rep. Thomas J. Lane (D-MA)	Secretary of Labor	Employment statistics relating to the woolen and worsted manufacturing industry	Education and Labor -	-
H.Res. 200 04/29/1949 Rep. Thomas J. Lane (D-MA)	Secretary of the Treasury	Corporate income tax statistics relating to the woolen and worsted manufacturing industry	Ways and Means -	-
H.Res. 424 01/12/1950 Rep. Edith N. Rogers (R-MA)	Administrator of Veterans' Affairs	Personal finances of mental patients hospitalized by the Veterans' Administration	Veterans' Affairs-	-
H.Res. 449 01/26/1950 Rep. Edgar A.Jonas (R-IL)	Secretary of the Treasury	Receipts from taxes paid on tips and gratuities received by taxpayers	Ways and Means -	-
H.Res. 452 01/27/1950 Rep. John D. Lodge (R-CT)	President	Foreign policy of the United States in the far east	Foreign Affairs Reported adversely 02/09/1950 H.Rept. 81-1618	Laid on the table 02/09/1950

Resolution, Introduction, and Sponsorship	Official(s) to Whom Inquiry Is Directed	Subject of Inquiry	Committee(s) of Referral and Consideration	House Floor Action
H.Res. 477 02/16/1950 Rep. Edith N. Rogers (R-MA)	Secretary of the Treasury	The number of watches, clocks, and parts of watches and clocks imported into the U.S. over the previous five years	Ways and Means -	-
H.Res. 478 02/16/1950 Rep. Edith N. Rogers (R-MA)	Secretary of Commerce	The number of watches, clocks, and parts of watches and clocks manufactured in the U.S. over the previous five years	Interstate and Foreign Commerce-	-
H.Res. 829 08/28/1950 Rep. Donald L. Jackson (R-CA)	Attorney General	Arrest and detention, and deportation of Rafael Garcia Travesi-Carral	Judiciary -	-
H.Res. 870 11/30/1950 Rep. Edith N. Rogers (R-MA)	Secretary of the Army Chairman of the Interstate Commerce Commission	Railroad accidents involving troop transport trains	Armed Services -	-
H.Res. 125 02/07/1951 Rep. Edith N. Rogers (R-MA)	Secretary of Commerce	Railroad accident which occurred near Woodbridge, New Jersey, on February 6, 1951	Interstate and Foreign Commerce -	-

Table 7. (Continued)

Resolution, Introduction, and Sponsorship	Official(s) to Whom Inquiry Is Directed	Subject of Inquiry	Committee(s) of Referral and Consideration	House Floor Action
H.Res. 514 01/31/1952 Rep. Ellis Y. Berry (R-SD)	Secretary of State	Any agreements made between the President of the United States and the Prime Minister of Great Britain during their recent conversations	Foreign Affairs Reported adversely 02/20/1952 H.Rept. 82-1381	Agreed to 02/20/1952
H.Res. 609 04/24/1952 Rep. Matthew H. Ellsworth (R- OR)	President	Information related to the President's actions during the 1952 steel strike	Education and Labor -	-
H.Res. 661 05/28/1952 Rep. Edith N. Rogers (R-MA)	Secretary of the Army	Insurgency in prisoner-of-war camps in Korea and communist- inspired disturbances of the peace in Japan since the departure of General MacArthur	Armed Services Reported without recommendation 06/10/1952 H.Rept. 82-2128	Laid on the table 06/10/1952
H.Res. 662 05/28/1952 Rep. Edith N. Rogers (R-MA)	Secretary of Defense	Insurgency in prisoner-of-war camps in Korea and communist- inspired disturbances of the peace in Japan since the departure of General MacArthur	Armed Services Reported without recommendation 06/10/1952 H.Rept. 82-2129	Laid on the table 06/10/1952

Resolution, Introduction, and Sponsorship	Official(s) to Whom Inquiry Is Directed	Subject of Inquiry	Committee(s) of Referral and Consideration	House Floor Action
H.Res. 663 05/28/1952 Rep. Edith N. Rogers (R-MA)	Secretary of the Army	Reduction in grade of Colonel Charles F. Colson relating to his conduct during the riot at Koje Island, Korea	Armed Services Reported without recommendation 06/10/1952 H.Rept. 82-2130	Laid on the table 06/10/1952
H.Res. 664 05/28/1952 Rep. Edith N. Rogers (R-MA)	Secretary of State	Insurgency in prisoner-of-war camps in Korea and communist- inspired disturbances of the peace in Japan since the departure of General MacArthur	Foreign Affairs Reported favorably 06/10/1952 H.Rept. 82-2131	Agreed to 06/10/1952
H.Res. 716 06/28/1952 Rep. Edmund P. Radwan (R-NY)	Secretary of State	Any agreement made by the Secretary of State and the government of Great Britain during their recent meetings and conversations which may affect the conduct of the war in Korea	Foreign Affairs -	-
H.Res. 121 01/29/1953 Rep. Clare Hoffman (R-MI)	Secretary of Defense	The military operation in Korea codenamed "Operation Smack"	Armed Services-	-

Table 7. (Continued)

Resolution, Introduction, and Sponsorship	Official(s) to Whom Inquiry Is Directed	Subject of Inquiry	Committee(s) of Referral and Consideration	House Floor Action
H.Res. 134 02/06/1953 Rep. John D. Dingell (D-MI)	Civil Service Commission	Federal employees not falling under civil service rules and regulations	Post Office and Civil Services -	-
H.Res. 171 03/09/1953 Rep. Clare Hoffman (R-MI)	Secretary of Defense	The military operation in Korea codenamed "Operation Smack"	Armed Services Reported adversely 03/17/1953 H.Rept. 83-164	Laid on the table 03/17/1953
H.Res. 278 06/11/1953 Rep. Edith N. Rogers (R-MA)	Atomic Energy Commission	Effect on the weather of certain atomic bomb explosions	Joint Committee on Atomic Energy -	-
H.Res. 279 06/11/1953 Rep. Edith N. Rogers (R-MA)	Secretary of the Army	Effect on the weather of certain atomic bomb explosions	Armed Services Reported adversely 06/23/1953 H.Rept. 83-646	Laid on the table 06/23/1953
H.Res. 280 06/11/1953 Rep. Edith N. Rogers (R-MA)	Federal Civil Defense Administrator	Effect on the weather of certain atomic bomb explosions	Armed Services Reported adversely 06/23/1953 H.Rept. 83-641	Laid on the table by rule 06/26/1953
H.Res. 281 06/11/1953 Rep. Edith N. Rogers (R-MA)	Secretary of the Navy	Effect on the weather of certain atomic bomb explosions	Armed Services Reported adversely 06/23/1953 H.Rept. 83-647	Laid on the table 06/23/1953

Resolution, Introduction, and Sponsorship	Official(s) to Whom Inquiry Is Directed	Subject of Inquiry	Committee(s) of Referral and Consideration	House Floor Action
H.Res. 282 06/11/1953 Rep. Edith N. Rogers (R-MA)	Secretary of the Air Force	Effect on the weather of certain atomic bomb explosions	Armed Services Reported adversely 06/23/1953 H.Rept. 83-648	Laid on the table 06/23/1953
H.Res. 283 06/11/1953 Rep. Edith N. Rogers (R-MA)	Secretary of Commerce	Effect on the weather of certain atomic bomb explosions	Interstate and Foreign Commerce Reported adversely 06/27/1953 H.Rept. 83-682	Laid on the table 06/27/1953
H.Res. 387 08/01/1953 Rep. Edith N. Rogers (R-MA)	Secretary of the Treasury	Unexpended balances of appropriations	Appropriations -	-
H.Res. 388 08/01/1953 Rep. Edith N. Rogers (R-MA)	Comptroller General	Unexpended balances of appropriations	Appropriations -	-
H.Res. 434 02/08/1954 Rep. George M. Rhodes (D-PA)	President	Discharge of federal officers and employees for security reasons during the past year	Post Office and Civil Service -	-
H.Res. 435 02/08/1954 Rep. George M. Rhodes (D-PA)	Chairman of the United States Civil Service Commission	Discharge of federal officers and employees for security reasons during the past year	Post Office and Civil Service -	-

Table 7. (Continued)

Resolution, Introduction, and Sponsorship	Official(s) to Whom Inquiry Is Directed	Subject of Inquiry	Committee(s) of Referral and Consideration	House Floor Action
H.Res. 436 02/08/1954 Rep. George M. Rhodes (D-PA)	Attorney General	Discharge of federal officers and employees for security reasons during the past year	Judiciary -	-
H.Res. 560 05/26/1954 Rep. Edith N. Rogers (R-MA)	Secretary of the Navy	Facts concerning the explosion on the aircraft carrier Bennington	Armed Services -	Discharged by unanimous consent and laid on the table 06/07/1954
H.Res. 602 06/28/1954 Rep. Jacob K. Javits (R-NY)	Postmaster General	Transmission of hate propaganda through the mails	Post Office and Civil Service -	-
H.Res. 632 07/14/1954 Rep. Jacob K. Javits (R-NY)	Postmaster General	Transmission of hate propaganda through the mails	Post Office and Civil Service -	-
H.Res. 134 02/07/1955 Rep. Clare Hoffman (R-MI)	President Administrator of Veterans' Affairs	Veterans' Administration expenditures	Veterans' Affairs-	-
H.Res. 136 02/07/1955 Rep. Clare Hoffman (R-MI)	Secretary of Defense	Extent and cost of certain military installations	Armed Services Reported adversely 02/16/1955 H.Rept. 84-56	Laid on the table 02/16/1955

Resolution, Introduction, and Sponsorship	Official(s) to Whom Inquiry Is Directed	Subject of Inquiry	Committee(s) of Referral and Consideration	House Floor Action
H.Res. 207 04/14/1955 Rep. John P. Pillion (R-NY)	Secretary of the Interior	Information related to Antarctica	Interior and Insular Affairs -	-
H.Res. 209 04/18/1955 Rep. Craig Hosmer (R-CA)	Secretary of the Interior	Information related to Antarctica	Interior and Insular Affairs -	-
H.Res. 238 05/09/1955 Rep. Clare Hoffman (R-MI)	Secretary of Health, Education, and Welfare	Statistical information relating to the staffing and workload of Social Security field offices in Michigan and Indiana	Ways and Means -	-
H.Res. 245 05/16/1955 Rep. James A. Haley (D-FL)	Secretary of the Interior	Information related to Antarctica	Interior and Insular Affairs -	-
H.Res. 475 04/16/1956 Rep. Herman P. Eberharter (D- PA)	Secretary of the Treasury	Settlement of the American Distilling Company income tax case by the Internal Revenue Service	Ways and Means Reported without recommendation 07/21/1956 H.Rept. 84-2867	-
H.Res. 525 06/06/1956 Rep. Clare Hoffman (R-MI)	Secretary of Labor	Statistical information related to salaries and employment in the manufacturing industry	Education and Labor -	-
H.Res. 454 01/27/1958 Rep. Clare Hoffman (R-MI)	Secretary of Labor	Violence related to labor strikes	Education and Labor -	-

Table 7. (Continued)

Resolution, Introduction, and Sponsorship	Official(s) to Whom Inquiry Is Directed	Subject of Inquiry	Committee(s) of Referral and Consideration	House Floor Action
H.Res. 593 06/16/1958 Rep. Joseph M. Montoya (D-NM)	Secretary of the Interior	Information related to the school-age Indian population of the United States	Interior and Insular Affairs -	
H.Res. 612 06/30/1958 Rep. Clare Hoffman (R-MI)	Secretary of Labor	Activity by Labor Department employees in relation to the Aiken Brothers Company of Greenville, South Carolina	Education and Labor -	
H.Res. 290 06/08/1959 Rep. Clare Hoffman (R-MI)	Secretary of Labor	Statistical information about the amount of money paid to various labor unions	Education and Labor -	
H.Res. 593 04/10/1962 Rep. Leonard Farbstein (D-NY)	Secretary of State	Reasons underlying U.S. sponsorship and active support of the censure of Israel by the United Nations Security Council	Foreign Affairs -	
H.Res. 610 04/18/1962 Rep. Barratt O'Hara (D-IL)	Secretary of State	Reasons underlying U.S. sponsorship and active support of the censure of Israel by the United Nations Security Council	Foreign Affairs -	

Resolution, Introduction, and Sponsorship	Official(s) to Whom Inquiry Is Directed	Subject of Inquiry	Committee(s) of Referral and Consideration	House Floor Action
H.Res. 529 08/18/1965 Rep. Albert Quie (R-MN)	Postmaster General	Temporary summer employment at the U.S. Postal Service	Post Office and Civil Service -	
H.Res. 574 09/08/1965 Rep. Albert Quie (R-MN)	Postmaster General	Temporary summer employment at the U.S. Postal Service	Post Office and Civil Service Reported adversely 09/16/1965 H.Rept. 89-10 1 0	Laid on the table 09/16/1965
H.Res. 575 09/12/1965 Rep. Robert H. Michel (R-IL)	President	Reports of the White House Education Task Force chaired by John W. Gardner	Education and Labor -	
H.Res. 576 09/12/1965 Rep. Robert H. Michel (R-IL)	Secretary of Health, Education, and Welfare	Specified proposals and position papers relating to education in the states and in big city schools	Education and Labor -	
H.Res. 1018 09/14/1966 Rep. Melvin R. Laird (R-WI)	President	Certain information regarding the 1967 budget	Appropriations -	-
H.Res. 489 06/21/1971 Rep. Bella S. Abzug (D-NY) Cosponsors: (10)	President	The report "U.S.-Vietnam Relationships, 1945-1967" (Also known as "The Pentagon Papers")	Armed Services Reported adversely 06/30/1971 H.Rept. 92-318	Laid on the table 06/30/1971

Table 7. (Continued)

Resolution, Introduction, and Sponsorship	Official(s) to Whom Inquiry Is Directed	Subject of Inquiry	Committee(s) of Referral and Consideration	House Floor Action
H.Res. 490 06/21/1971 Rep. Bella S. Abzug (D-NY) Cosponsors: (14)	President	The report "U.S.-Vietnam Relationships, 1945-1967" (Also known as "The Pentagon Papers")	Armed Services Reported adversely 06/30/1971 H.Rept. 92-319	Laid on the table 06/30/1971
H.Res. 491 06/21/1971 Rep. Bella S. Abzug (D-NY) Cosponsors: (17)	President Secretary of State Director of the Central Intelligence Agency	The report "U.S.-Vietnam Relationships, 1945-1967" (Also known as "The Pentagon Papers")	Armed Services -	Motion to discharge fell on a point of order 07/07/1971
H.Res. 492 06/21/1971 Rep. Paul N. "Pete" McCloskey, Jr. (R-CA) Cosponsors: (none)	Secretary of State	U.S. operations in Laos	Foreign Affairs Reported adversely 07/01/1971 H.Rept. 92-327	Laid on the table 07/07/1971
H.Res. 493 06/21/1971 Rep. Paul N. "Pete" McCloskey, Jr. (R-CA) Cosponsors: (none)	Secretary of State	The Phoenix Program	Foreign Affairs Reported adversely 07/01/1971 H.Rept. 92-328	Laid on the table 07/07/1971
H.Res. 494 06/21/1971 Rep. Paul N. "Pete" McCloskey, Jr. (R-CA) Cosponsors: (none)	Secretary of State	The report "U.S. Vietnam Relationships, 1945-1967" (Also known as "The Pentagon Papers")	Foreign Affairs Reported adversely 07/01/1971 H.Rept. 92-329	Laid on the table 07/07/1971

Resolution, Introduction, and Sponsorship	Official(s) to Whom Inquiry Is Directed	Subject of Inquiry	Committee(s) of Referral and Consideration	House Floor Action
H.Res. 495 06/21/1971 Rep. Paul N. "Pete" McCloskey, Jr. (R-CA) Cosponsors: (none)	Secretary of State	Bombing operations in northern Laos	Foreign Affairs Reported adversely 07/01/1971 H.Rept. 92-330	Laid on the table 07/07/1971
H.Res. 530 07/08/1971 Rep. James M. Collins (R-TX) Cosponsors: (1)	Secretary of Health, Education, and Welfare	Busing to achieve racial balance in the public schools	Education and Labor -	-
H.Res. 539 07/14/1971 Rep. James M. Collins (R-TX) Cosponsors: (1)	Secretary of Health, Education, and Welfare	Busing to achieve racial balance in the public schools	Education and Labor -	Discharged and agreed to 08/02/1971
H.Res. 557 07/21/1971 Rep. Bertram L. Podell (D-NY) Cosponsors: (none)	Secretary of Defense	Extent of military assistance to certain foreign countries	Armed Services -	Discharged and laid on the table 08/03/1971
H.Res. 595 09/14/1971 Rep. Bella S. Abzug (D-NY) Cosponsors: (none)	Secretary of State	Communications pertaining to the upcoming Vietnamese presidential election	Foreign Affairs Reported adversely 09/27/1971 H.Rept. 92-512	Laid on the table 09/30/1971
H.Res. 619 09/27/1971 Rep. Bella S. Abzug (D-NY) Cosponsors: (1)	Secretary of State	Communications pertaining to the upcoming Vietnamese presidential election	Foreign Affairs -	Discharged and laid on the table 09/30/1971

Table 7. (Continued)

Resolution, Introduction, and Sponsorship	Official(s) to Whom Inquiry Is Directed	Subject of Inquiry	Committee(s) of Referral and Consideration	House Floor Action
H.Res. 632 09/27/1971 Rep. Lester Wolff (D-NY) Cosponsors: (24)	Secretary of State	Role of the U.S. government in events leading to an uncontested presidential election in South Vietnam on October 3, 1971	Foreign Affairs Reported adversely 10/14/1971 H.Rept. 92-567	Laid on the table 10/20/1971
H.Res. 638 10/06/1971 Rep. Lester Wolff (D-NY) Cosponsors: (14)	Secretary of State	Role of the U.S. government in events leading to an uncontested presidential election in South Vietnam on October 3, 1971	Foreign Affairs Reported adversely 10/14/1971 H.Rept. 92-568	Laid on the table 10/20/1971
H.Res. 918 04/11/1972 Rep. Bella S. Abzug (D-NY) Cosponsors: (none)	President Secretary of Defense	Statistics relating to U.S. military involvement in Indochina	Armed Services Reported adversely 04/19/1972 H.Rept. 92-1003	Laid on the table 04/26/1972
H.Res. 1078 08/02/1972 Rep. Paul N. "Pete" McCloskey, Jr. (R-CA) Cosponsors: (none)	Secretary of Defense	Statistics relating to U.S. military involvement in North Vietnam	Armed Services Reported adversely 08/10/1972 H.Rept. 92-1330	Laid on the table 08/16/1972

Resolution, Introduction, and Sponsorship	Official(s) to Whom Inquiry Is Directed	Subject of Inquiry	Committee(s) of Referral and Consideration	House Floor Action
H.Res. 1079 08/02/1972 Rep. Paul N. "Pete" McCloskey, Jr. (R-CA) Cosponsors: (none)	Secretary of Defense	Statistics relating to U.S. military involvement in North Vietnam	Armed Services Reported adversely 08/10/1972 H.Rept. 92-1331	Laid on the table 08/16/1972
H.Res. 26 01/03/1973 Rep. Michael J. Harrington (D- MA) Cosponsors: (21)	President Secretary of Defense	Statistics relating to U.S. military involvement in Vietnam	Armed Services Reported adversely 03/01/1973 H.Rept. 93-40	Laid on the table 03/01/1973
H.Res. 114 01/11/1973 Rep. Michael J. Harrington (D- MA) Cosponsors: (13)	Secretary of Defense	Data relating to the extent of the bombing of North Vietnam from December 17, 1972, through January 10, 1973	Armed Services Reported adversely 03/01/1973 H.Rept. 93-38	Laid on the table 03/06/1973
H.Res. 115 01/11/1973 Rep. Michael J. Harrington (D- MA) Cosponsors: (13)	Secretary of Defense	Data relating to the extent of the bombing of North Vietnam from December 17, 1972, through January 10, 1973	Armed Services Reported adversely 03/01/1973 H.Rept. 93-39	Laid on the table 03/06/1973
H.Res. 143 01/18/1973 Rep. Michael J. Harrington (D- MA) Cosponsors: (1)	Secretary of Defense	Data relating to the extent of the bombing of North Vietnam from December 17, 1972, through January 10, 1973	Armed Services Reported adversely 03/01/1973 H.Rept. 93-41	Laid on the table 03/06/1973

Table 7. (Continued)

Resolution, Introduction, and Sponsorship	Official(s) to Whom Inquiry Is Directed	Subject of Inquiry	Committee(s) of Referral and Consideration	House Floor Action
H.Res. 220 02/19/1973 Rep. Bella S. Abzug (D-NY) Cosponsors: (3)	Attorney General	Basis of the venue in the northern district of Texas of the grand jury investigation before which Kenneth Tierney, Thomas Laffey, Matthias Reilly, Paschal Morahan, and Daniel Crawford were summoned	Judiciary -	-
H.Res. 223 02/20/1973 Rep. Bella S. Abzug (D-NY) Cosponsors: (1)	Attorney General	Basis of the venue in the northern district of Texas of the grand jury investigation before which Kenneth Tierney, Thomas Laffey, Matthias Reilly, Paschal Morahan, and Daniel Crawford were summoned	Judiciary -	-

Resolution, Introduction, and Sponsorship	Official(s) to Whom Inquiry Is Directed	Subject of Inquiry	Committee(s) of Referral and Consideration	House Floor Action
H.Res. 258 02/28/1973 Rep. Hugh L. Carey (D-NY) Cosponsors: (2)	Attorney General	Record of the Department of Justice which led to the determination of the venue in the Northern District of Texas of the grand jury investigation before which Kenneth Tierney, Thomas Laffey, Matthias Reilly, Paschal Morahan, and Daniel Crawford were summoned	Judiciary -	-
H.Res. 262 03/01/1973 Rep. James V. Stanton (D-OH) Cosponsors: (none)	Attorney General	Basis of the venue in the northern district of Texas of the grand jury investigation before which Kenneth Tierney, Thomas Laffey, Matthias Reilly, Paschal Morahan, and Daniel Crawford were summoned	Judiciary -	-

Table 7. (Continued)

Resolution, Introduction, and Sponsorship	Official(s) to Whom Inquiry Is Directed	Subject of Inquiry	Committee(s) of Referral and Consideration	House Floor Action
H.Res. 281 03/08/1973 Rep. Bella S. Abzug (D-NY) Cosponsors: (none)	Attorney General	Basis of the venue in the northern district of Texas of the grand jury investigation before which Kenneth Tierney, Thomas Laffey, Matthias Reilly, Paschal Morahan, and Daniel Crawford were summoned	Judiciary -	-
H.Res. 346 04/09/1973 Rep. Ogden R. Reid (D-NY) Cosponsors: (none)	Secretary of Health, Education, and Welfare	Regulations governing social services proposed in the Federal Register of February 16, 1973 (38 F.R. 4608-4613)	Ways and Means -	-
H.Res. 350 04/10/1973 Rep. Bella S. Abzug (D-NY) Cosponsors: (none)	Secretary of Health, Education, and Welfare	Regulations governing social services proposed in the Federal Register of February 16, 1973 (38 F.R. 4608-4613)	Ways and Means -	-
H.Res. 379 05/03/1973 Rep. Robert L. Leggett (D-CA) Cosponsors: (15)	Secretary of Defense	Bombing and other activities in Cambodia and Laos during the period January 27, 1973, to April 30, 1973	Armed Services Reported adversely 05/09/1973 H.Rept. 93-170	Laid on the table 05/09/1973

Resolution, Introduction, and Sponsorship	Official(s) to Whom Inquiry Is Directed	Subject of Inquiry	Committee(s) of Referral and Consideration	House Floor Action
H.Res. 508 07/25/1973 Rep. Michael J. Harrington (D-MA) Cosponsors: (none)	Secretary of Defense	Data concerning the extent of the bombing of Cambodia and Laos from January 20, 1969, through April 30, 1970	Armed Services -	-
H.Res. 519 07/31/1973 Rep. Michael J. Harrington (D- MA) Cosponsors: (24)	Secretary of Defense	Data concerning the extent of the bombing of Cambodia and Laos from January 20, 1969, through April 30, 1970	Armed Services -	-
H.Res. 520 08/01/1973 Rep. Michael J. Harrington (D- MA) Cosponsors: (5)	Secretary of Defense	Data concerning the extent of the bombing of Cambodia and Laos from January 20, 1969, through April 30, 1970	Armed Services -	-
H.Res. 522 08/02/1973 Rep. Michael J. Harrington (D- MA) Cosponsors: (3)	Secretary of Defense	Data concerning the extent of the bombing of Cambodia and Laos from January 20, 1969, through April 30, 1970	Armed Services -	-

Table 7. (Continued)

Resolution, Introduction, and Sponsorship	Official(s) to Whom Inquiry Is Directed	Subject of Inquiry	Committee(s) of Referral and Consideration	House Floor Action
H.Res. 525 08/03/1973 Rep. Michael J. Harrington (D- MA) Cosponsors: (none)	Secretary of Defense	Data concerning the extent of the bombing of Cambodia and Laos from January 20, 1969, through April 30, 1970	Armed Services -	-
H.Res. 537 09/10/1973 Rep. Michael J. Harrington (D- MA) Cosponsors: (1)	Secretary of Defense	Data concerning the extent of the bombing of Cambodia and Laos from January 20, 1969, through April 30, 1970	Armed Services -	-
H.Res. 572 10/01/1973 Rep. Paul Findley (R-IL) Cosponsors: (none)	Attorney General	Allegations that Spiro T. Agnew accepted bribes or received consideration for services rendered	Judiciary -	Discharged and laid on the table 10/10/1973
H.Res. 634 10/23/1973 Rep. Paul N. "Pete" McCloskey, Jr. (R-CA) Cosponsors: (none)	Attorney General	Papers, documents, recordings, memorandums, and items of evidence in the custody of the Special Prosecutor, Archibald Cox, as of noon, Saturday, October 20, 1973	Judiciary -	Discharged and laid on the table 11/01/1973

Resolution, Introduction, and Sponsorship	Official(s) to Whom Inquiry Is Directed	Subject of Inquiry	Committee(s) of Referral and Consideration	House Floor Action
H.Res. 1002 03/25/1974 Rep. Michael J. Harrington (D- MA) Cosponsors: (1)	Secretary of State	The military alert declared by the President on October 24, 1974	Foreign Affairs Reported adversely 04/04/1974 H.Rept. 93-970	Laid on the table 04/09/1974
H.Res. 1040 04/22/1974 Rep. Andrew J. Hinshaw (R-CA) Cosponsors: (none)	Secretary of Defense	Expenditure of Federal moneys on private property owned by: (1) Franklin D. Roosevelt; (2) Harry S. Truman; (3) Dwight D. Eisenhower; (4) John F. Kennedy; and (5) Lyndon B. Johnson	Armed Services -	-
H.Res. 1041 04/22/1974 Rep. Andrew J. Hinshaw (R-CA) Cosponsors: (none)	Secretary of Defense	Expenditure of Federal moneys on private property owned by: (1) Franklin D. Roosevelt; (2) Harry S. Truman; (3) Dwight D. Eisenhower; (4) John F. Kennedy; and (5) Lyndon B. Johnson	Armed Services -	-

Table 7. (Continued)

Resolution, Introduction, and Sponsorship	Official(s) to Whom Inquiry Is Directed	Subject of Inquiry	Committee(s) of Referral and Consideration	House Floor Action
H.Res. 1042 04/22/1974 Rep. Andrew J. Hinshaw (R-CA) Cosponsors: (none)	Secretary of the Army	Expenditure of Federal moneys on private property owned by: (1) Franklin D. Roosevelt; (2) Harry S. Truman; (3) Dwight D. Eisenhower; (4) John F. Kennedy; and (5) Lyndon B. Johnson	Armed Services -	-
H.Res. 1043 04/22/1974 Rep. Andrew J. Hinshaw (R-CA) Cosponsors: (none)	Secretary of the Army	Expenditure of Federal moneys on private property owned by: (1) Franklin D. Roosevelt; (2) Harry S. Truman; (3) Dwight D. Eisenhower; (4) John F. Kennedy; and (5) Lyndon B. Johnson	H.Res. 1043 04/22/1974 Rep. Andrew J. Hinshaw (R-CA) Cosponsors: (none)	Secretary of the Army

Resolution, Introduction, and Sponsorship	Official(s) to Whom Inquiry Is Directed	Subject of Inquiry	Committee(s) of Referral and Consideration	House Floor Action
H.Res. 1044 04/22/1974 Rep. Andrew J. Hinshaw (R-CA) Cosponsors: (none)	Secretary of the Navy	Expenditure of Federal moneys on private property owned by: (1) Franklin D. Roosevelt; (2) Harry S. Truman; (3) Dwight D. Eisenhower; (4) John F. Kennedy; and (5) Lyndon B. Johnson	Armed Services -	-
H.Res. 1045 04/22/1974 Rep. Andrew J. Hinshaw (R-CA) Cosponsors: (none)	Secretary of the Navy	Expenditure of Federal moneys on private property owned by: (1) Franklin D. Roosevelt; (2) Harry S. Truman; (3) Dwight D. Eisenhower; (4) John F. Kennedy; and (5) Lyndon B. Johnson	Armed Services -	-
H.Res. 1046 04/22/1974 Rep. Andrew J. Hinshaw (R-CA) Cosponsors: (none)	Secretary of the Air Force	Expenditure of Federal moneys on private property owned by: (1) Franklin D. Roosevelt; (2) Harry S. Truman; (3) Dwight D. Eisenhower; (4) John F. Kennedy; and (5) Lyndon B. Johnson	Armed Services -	-

Table 7. (Continued)

Resolution, Introduction, and Sponsorship	Official(s) to Whom Inquiry Is Directed	Subject of Inquiry	Committee(s) of Referral and Consideration	House Floor Action
H.Res. 1047 04/22/1974 Rep. Andrew J. Hinshaw (R-CA) Cosponsors: (none)	Secretary of the Air Force	Expenditure of Federal moneys on private property owned by: (1) Franklin D. Roosevelt; (2) Harry S. Truman; (3) Dwight D. Eisenhower; (4) John F. Kennedy; and (5) Lyndon B. Johnson	Armed Services -	-
H.Res. 1048 04/22/1974 Rep. Andrew J. Hinshaw (R-CA) Cosponsors: (none)	Administrator of the General Services Administration	Expenditure of Federal moneys on private property owned by: (1) Franklin D. Roosevelt; (2) Harry S. Truman; (3) Dwight D. Eisenhower; (4) John F. Kennedy; and (5) Lyndon B. Johnson	Government Operations -	-

Resolution, Introduction, and Sponsorship	Official(s) to Whom Inquiry Is Directed	Subject of Inquiry	Committee(s) of Referral and Consideration	House Floor Action
H.Res. 1049 04/22/1974 Rep. Andrew J. Hinshaw (R-CA) Cosponsors: (none)	Administrator of the General Services Administration	Expenditure of Federal moneys on private property owned by: (1) Franklin D. Roosevelt; (2) Harry S. Truman; (3) Dwight D. Eisenhower; (4) John F. Kennedy; and (5) Lyndon B. Johnson	Government Operations -	-
H.Res. 1050 04/22/1974 Rep. Andrew J. Hinshaw (R-CA) Cosponsors: (none)	Secretary of Transportation	Expenditure of Federal moneys on private property owned by: (1) Franklin D. Roosevelt; (2) Harry S. Truman; (3) Dwight D. Eisenhower; (4) John F. Kennedy; and (5) Lyndon B. Johnson	Interstate and Foreign Commerce -	-
H.Res. 1051 04/22/1974 Rep. Andrew J. Hinshaw (R-CA) Cosponsors: (none)	Secretary of Transportation	Expenditure of Federal moneys on private property owned by: (1) Franklin D. Roosevelt; (2) Harry S. Truman; (3) Dwight D. Eisenhower; (4) John F. Kennedy; and (5) Lyndon B. Johnson	Interstate and Foreign Commerce-	-

Table 7. (Continued)

Resolution, Introduction, and Sponsorship	Official(s) to Whom Inquiry Is Directed	Subject of Inquiry	Committee(s) of Referral and Consideration	House Floor Action
H.Res. 1052 04/22/1974 Rep. Andrew J. Hinshaw (R-CA) Cosponsors: (none)	Director of the Secret Service	Federal funds for administrative support and personnel at or near the private residences of (1) Franklin D. Roosevelt, (2) Harry S. Truman, (3) Dwight D. Eisenhower, (4) John F. Kennedy, and (5) Lyndon B. Johnson during their terms as President and Vice President	House Ways and Means -	-
H.Res. 1053 04/22/1974 Rep. Andrew J. Hinshaw (R-CA) Cosponsors: (none)	Director of the Secret Service	Federal funds for administrative support and personnel at or near the private residences of (1) Franklin D. Roosevelt, (2) Harry S. Truman, (3) Dwight D. Eisenhower, (4) John F. Kennedy, and (5) Lyndon B. Johnson during their terms as President and Vice President	House Ways and Means -	-

Resolution, Introduction, and Sponsorship	Official(s) to Whom Inquiry Is Directed	Subject of Inquiry	Committee(s) of Referral and Consideration	House Floor Action
H.Res. 1189 06/25/1974 Rep. Bella S. Abzug (D-NY) Co-sponsors: (none)	President	Agreements for nuclear cooperation with Egypt and Israel	Foreign Affairs -	-
H.Res. 1219 07/02/1974 Rep. Bella S. Abzug (D-NY) Cosponsors: (16)	President	Agreements for nuclear cooperation with Egypt and Israel	Foreign Affairs -	-
H.Res. 1363 09/12/1974 Rep. Bella S. Abzug (D-NY) Cosponsors: (10)	President	The specific offenses against the United States for which a pardon was granted to Richard M. Nixon on September 8, 1974	Judiciary -	-
H.Res. 1370 09/17/1974 Rep. John Conyers, Jr. (D-MI) Cosponsors: (none)	President	Decision to grant a pardon to Richard M. Nixon	Judiciary -	-
H.Res. 1398 09/30/1974 Rep. Elizabeth Holtzman (D-NY) Cosponsors: (none)	President	Payments to Richard M. Nixon and his family	Government Operations -	-
H.Res. 1404 10/02/1974 Rep. Elizabeth Holtzman (D-NY) Cosponsors: (4)	President	Payments to Richard M. Nixon and his family	Government Operations -	-
H.Res. 1452 10/16/1974 Rep. Robert L. Leggett (D-CA) Cosponsors: (none)	President	The President's proposal to classify as new oil, all oil extracted from domestic oil wells by secondary methods	Interstate and Foreign Commerce-	-

Table 7. (Continued)

Resolution, Introduction, and Sponsorship	Official(s) to Whom Inquiry Is Directed	Subject of Inquiry	Committee(s) of Referral and Consideration	House Floor Action
H.Res. 1467 11/20/1974 Rep. Lester Wolff (D-NY) Cosponsors: (none)	Secretary of Defense	Comments by the Chairman of the Joint Chief of Staff at Duke University on October 10, 1974	Armed Services -	-
H.Res. 1473 11/21/1974 Rep. Andrew J. Hinshaw (R-CA) Cosponsors: (none)	Administrator of the Small Business Administration	Specified facts pertaining to small business investment companies	Banking and Currency -	-
H.Res. 65 01/14/1975 Rep. Elizabeth Holtzman (D-NY) Cosponsors: (1)	President	Specified activities of the Central Intelligence Agency since January 1, 1960	Judiciary -	-
H.Res. 71 01/16/1975 Rep. Elizabeth Holtzman (D-NY) Cosponsors: (1)	President	Specified activities of the Central Intelligence Agency since January 1, 1960	Judiciary -	-

Resolution, Introduction, and Sponsorship	Official(s) to Whom Inquiry Is Directed	Subject of Inquiry	Committee(s) of Referral and Consideration	House Floor Action
H.Res. 72 01/16/1975 Rep. Elizabeth Holtz-man (D-NY) Cosponsors: (1)	President	Information contained in the report of William E. Colby delivered to the President on or about December 26, 1974, relating to activities of the Central Intelligence Agency	Armed Services Reported adversely 02/27/1975 H.Rept. 94-22	-
H.Res. 106 01/28/1975 Rep. Elizabeth Holtzman (D-NY) Cosponsors: (24)	President	Specified activities of the Central Intelligence Agency since January 1, 1960	Judiciary -	-
H.Res. 129 02/03/1975 Rep. Bella S. Abzug (D-NY) Cosponsors: (24)	Secretary of Defense	Reconnaissance flights since January, 1973, over North and South Vietnam as well as other activities in Indochina	Armed Services Reported adversely 02/27/1975 H.Rept. 94-23	-

Table 7. (Continued)

Resolution, Introduction, and Sponsorship	Official(s) to Whom Inquiry Is Directed	Subject of Inquiry	Committee(s) of Referral and Consideration	House Floor Action
H.Res. 134 02/04/1975 Rep. Bella S. Abzug (D-NY) Cosponsors: (5)	Secretary of Defense	Reconnaissance flights since January, 1973, over North and South Vietnam as well as other activities in Indochina	Armed Services -	-
H.Res. 148 02/05/1975 Rep. Elizabeth Holtzman (D-NY) Cosponsors: (4)	President	Specified activities of the Central Intelligence Agency since January 1, 1960	Judiciary -	-
H.Res. 205 02/19/1975 Rep. Michael J. Harrington (D- MA) Cosponsors: (none)	Secretary of Defense	American involvement and knowledge of the coup in Chile	Armed Services -	-
H.Res. 206 02/19/1975 Rep. Michael J. Harrington (D- MA) Cosponsors: (none)	Secretary of State	American involvement and knowledge of the coup in Chile	Foreign Affairs -	-

Resolution, Introduction, and Sponsorship	Official(s) to Whom Inquiry Is Directed	Subject of Inquiry	Committee(s) of Referral and Consideration	House Floor Action
H.Res. 207 02/19/1975 Rep. Michael J. Harrington (D- MA) Cosponsors: (none)	President	American involvement and knowledge of the coup in Chile	Foreign Affairs -	-
H.Res. 313 03/14/1975 Rep. Fortney Pete Stark (D-CA) Cosponsors: (7)	President	Whether any citizen of the United States, since December 31, 1970, has been subjected to incarceration or denial of rights contrary to the laws or Constitution of the Republic of Mexico	Foreign Affairs -	-
H.Res. 391 04/10/1975 Rep. Fortney Pete Stark (D-CA) Cosponsors: (18)	President	Whether any citizen of the United States, since December 31, 1970, has been subjected to incarceration or denial of rights contrary to the laws or Constitution of the Republic of Mexico	International Relations -	-

Table 7. (Continued)

Resolution, Introduction, and Sponsorship	Official(s) to Whom Inquiry Is Directed	Subject of Inquiry	Committee(s) of Referral and Consideration	House Floor Action
H.Res. 400 04/16/1975 Rep. Elizabeth Holtzman (D-NY) Cosponsors: (18)	President	United States nationals in South Vietnam, their employers, the nature of their work and an explanation of why such persons have not been evacuated	International Relations -	-
H.Res. 529 06/11/1975 Rep. Michael J. Harrington (D-MA) Cosponsors: (25)	President	Facts relating to the seizure of the U.S. merchant ship Mayaguez by the Khmer Rouge	Armed Services -	-
H.Res. 530 06/11/1975 Rep. Michael J. Harrington (D-MA) Cosponsors: (6)	President	Facts relating to the seizure of the U.S. merchant ship Mayaguez by the Khmer Rouge	Armed Services -	-

Resolution, Introduction, and Sponsorship	Official(s) to Whom Inquiry Is Directed	Subject of Inquiry	Committee(s) of Referral and Consideration	House Floor Action
H.Res. 536 06/12/1975 Rep. Michael J. Harrington (D-MA) Cosponsors: (23)	Secretary of State	Facts relating to the seizure of the U.S. merchant ship Mayaguez by the Khmer Rouge	International Relations -	-
H.Res. 537 06/12/1975 Rep. Michael J. Harrington (D- MA) Cosponsors: (11)	Secretary of State	Facts relating to the seizure of the U.S. merchant ship Mayaguez by the Khmer Rouge	International Relations -	-
H.Res. 542 06/16/1975 Rep. Michael J. Harrington (D- MA) Cosponsors: (9)	President	Facts relating to the seizure of the U.S. merchant ship Mayaguez by the Khmer Rouge	International Relations -	-
H.Res. 543 06/16/1975 Rep. Michael J. Harrington (D- MA) Cosponsors: (4)	Secretary of State	Facts relating to the seizure of the U.S. merchant ship Mayaguez by the Khmer Rouge	International Relations -	-

Table 7. (Continued)

Resolution, Introduction, and Sponsorship	Official(s) to Whom Inquiry Is Directed	Subject of Inquiry	Committee(s) of Referral and Consideration	House Floor Action
H.Res. 552 06/18/1975 Rep. Benjamin S. Rosenthal (D- NY) Cosponsors: (none)	President	The sale of Hawk and Redeye missiles to Jordan	International Relations -	-
H.Res. 718 09/17/1975 Rep. James M. Collins (R-TX) Cosponsors: (none)	Secretary of Health, Education, and Welfare	List of public school systems in the United States which will be receiving Federal funds and will be engaging in the busing of schoolchildren to achieve racial balance	Education and Labor -	Discharged and agree to 09/29/1975
H.Res. 795 10/21/1975 Rep. Alan Steelman (R-TX) Cosponsors: (none)	President	Whether any citizen of the United States, since December 31, 1970, has been subjected to incarceration or denial of rights contrary to the laws or Constitution of the Republic of Mexico	International Relations -	-

Resolution, Introduction, and Sponsorship	Official(s) to Whom Inquiry Is Directed	Subject of Inquiry	Committee(s) of Referral and Consideration	House Floor Action
H.Res. 1193 05/17/1976 Rep. Philip M. Crane (R-IL) Cosponsors: (none)	Secretary of Defense	The extent of Cuban or other foreign military or paramilitary presence in the Republic of Panama or in the Panama Canal Zone	International Relations -	-
H.Res. 1295 06/11/1976 Rep. Michael J. Harrington (D-MA) Cosponsors: (none)	President	Payment of funds by the United States Armed Forces or Embassy staff to the Italian Christian Democratic Party or the Italian media	International Relations -	-
H.Res. 1324 06/18/1976 Rep. Michael J. Harrington (D-MA) Cosponsors: (5)	President	Payment of funds by the United States Armed Forces or Embassy staff to the Italian Christian Democratic Party or the Italian media	International Relations -	-
H.Res. 1427 07/27/1976 Rep. Michael J. Harrington (D-MA) Cosponsors: (7)	President	The payment of funds by any person acting under the direction of the United States Government or any agency or other instrumentality of the United States Government to any political party in Italy or the Italian media	International Relations -	-

Table 7. (Continued)

Resolution, Introduction, and Sponsorship	Official(s) to Whom Inquiry Is Directed	Subject of Inquiry	Committee(s) of Referral and Consideration	House Floor Action
H.Res. 285 02/09/1977 Rep. Chalmers P. Wylie (R-OH) Cosponsors: (none)	Attorney General	All communications and documents received by the Department of Justice from Kim Sang Keun of South Korea respecting Members and employees of Congress	Judiciary -	-
H.Res. 709 07/25/1977 Rep. Tim Lee Carter (R-KY) Cosponsors: (none)	Secretary of Defense	The service serial number of each individual who was present at the explosion of the atomic device known as "Smokey" which was detonated at Camp Desert Rock, Nevada, on August 31, 1957	Armed Services -	-
H.Res. 1259 06/29/1978 Rep. Fortney Pete Stark (D-CA) Cosponsors: (6)	Secretary of State	Military equipment shipments to Chile	International Relations -	-

Resolution, Introduction, and Sponsorship	Official(s) to Whom Inquiry Is Directed	Subject of Inquiry	Committee(s) of Referral and Consideration	House Floor Action
H.Res. 197 04/02/1979 Rep. James H. Weaver (D-OR) Cosponsors: (7)	Chairman of the Nuclear Regulatory Commission	The incident at the Three Mile Island nuclear generating plant and on the danger of similar incidents occurring at other nuclear generating plants	Interior and Insular Affairs -	-
H.Res. 201 04/03/1979 Rep. James H. Weaver (D-OR) Cosponsors: (10)	President	The incident at the Three Mile Island nuclear generating plant and on the danger of similar incidents occurring at other nuclear generating plants	Interior and Insular Affairs -	-
H.Res. 291 05/24/1979 Rep. John J. Rhodes (R-AZ) Cosponsors: (101)	President	Oil situation, including data on: 1 shortages, supplies, demand, and allocation of crude oil; and 2 refinery yield reductions and capacity utilization	Interstate and Foreign Commerce Reported adversely 06/11/1979 H.Rept. 96-261	Agreed to 06/15/1979
H.Res. 398 08/02/1979 Rep. Paul Findley (R-Il) Cosponsors: (none)	Secretary of State	Information concerning: (1) Israeli use of military aircraft of U.S. origin outside Israeli borders; and (2) Israeli compliance with the Arms Export Control Act	Foreign Affairs -	Discharged and laid on the table 09/13/1979

Table 7. (Continued)

Resolution, Introduction, and Sponsorship	Official(s) to Whom Inquiry Is Directed	Subject of Inquiry	Committee(s) of Referral and Consideration	House Floor Action
H.Res. 551 01/30/1980 Rep. James M. Collins (R-TX) Cosponsors: (none)	Secretary of State	Human rights objectives and policies with respect to specified countries	Foreign Affairs -	-
H.Res. 571 02/07/1980 Rep. Peter Peyser (R-NY) Cosponsors: (none)	Attorney General	Evidence compiled by the Department of Justice and the Federal Bureau of Investigation against Members of Congress in connection with the Abscam investigation	Judiciary Reported adversely 02/20/1980 H.Rept. 96-778	Laid on the table 02/27/1980
H.Res. 598 02/07/1980 Rep. Elizabeth Holtzman (D-NY) Cosponsors: (2)	President	U.S. decision to vote for the United Nations Security Council resolution on March 1, 1980	Foreign Affairs -	-
H.Res. 626 03/31/1980 Rep. George V. Hansen (R-ID) Cosponsors: (none)	President	Understandings made with the Former Shah of Iran at Lackland Air Force Base and elsewhere	Foreign Affairs -	Discharged and laid on the table 04/23/1980
H.Res. 627 03/31/1980 Rep. George V. Hansen (R-ID) Cosponsors: (1)	President	Commitments, admissions, and/or obligations made to the Government of Iran during March 1980	Foreign Affairs -	Discharged and laid on the table 04/23/1980

Resolution, Introduction, and Sponsorship	Official(s) to Whom Inquiry Is Directed	Subject of Inquiry	Committee(s) of Referral and Consideration	House Floor Action
H.Res. 745 07/22/1980 Rep. Robert E. Bauman (D-MD) Cosponsors: (98)	President	House and Justice Department actions and conversations with regard to Billy Carter's involvement with Libya and State Department cables, communications, or memorandums furnished to Billy Carter	Foreign Affairs Reported favorably (amended) 07/31/1980 H.Rept. 96-1213, pt. I Judiciary Reported favorably (amended) 07/31/1980 H.Rept. 96-1213, pt. II	Agreed to 09/10/1980
H.Res. 777 08/28/1980 Rep. Jim Courter (R-NJ) Cosponsors: (9)	President	Disclosure of classified information relating to the new so-called "Stealth" technology for military aircraft	Armed Services Reported adversely 09/09/1980 H.Rept. 96-1309	-
H.Res. 783 09/08/1980 Rep. Philip M. Crane (R-Il) Cosponsors: (none)	President	Disclosure of classified information relating to the Stealth technology for military aircraft	Armed Services -	
H.Res. 790 09/19/1980 Rep. Fortney Pete Stark (D-CA) Cosponsors: (none)	President	Specified documents containing information about U.S. involvement in Iran	Foreign Affairs -	

Table 7. (Continued)

Resolution, Introduction, and Sponsorship	Official(s) to Whom Inquiry Is Directed	Subject of Inquiry	Committee(s) of Referral and Consideration	House Floor Action
H.Res. 300 12/10/1981 Rep. George W. Crockett, Jr. (D-MI) Cosponsors: (1)	Secretary of State	Pending extradition proceedings against Ziad Abu Eain	Foreign Affairs - Judiciary-	Discharged and laid on the table 01/28/1982
H.Res. 465 05/11/1982 Rep. Fortney Pete Stark (D-CA) Cosponsors: (none)	Secretary of State	Certain information concerning Roberto D'Aubuisson	Foreign Affairs Reported without recommendation (amended) 05/20/1982 H.Rept. 97-579	-
H.Res. 507 06/16/1982 Rep. Toby Moffett (D-CT) Cosponsors: (none)	President Attorney General	Possible Executive interference with the investigation of Secretary of Labor Raymond Donovan	Judiciary -	
H.Res. 512 06/22/1982 Rep. Norman D. Dicks (D-WA) Cosponsors: (10)	Secretary of Defense	Procurement of the C-5B aircraft	Armed Services Reported adversely 07/19/1982 H.Rept. 97-64 1	Laid on the table 08/03/1982
H.Res. 512 06/22/1982 Rep. Norman D. Dicks (D-WA) Cosponsors: (10)	Secretary of Defense	Procurement of the C-5B aircraft	Armed Services Reported adversely 07/19/1982 H.Rept. 97-64 1	Laid on the table 08/03/1982

Resolution, Introduction, and Sponsorship	Official(s) to Whom Inquiry Is Directed	Subject of Inquiry	Committee(s) of Referral and Consideration	House Floor Action
H.Res. 159 04/13/1983 Rep. Tom Harkin (D-IA) Cosponsors: (71)	President	United States activities in Honduras and Nicaragua	Select Intelligence Reported adversely 05/05/1983 H.Rept. 98-88, pt. 1I Armed Services Reported adversely 05/04/1983 H.Rept. 98-88, pt. 1 Foreign Affairs-	-
H.Res. 323 09/29/1983 Rep. Henry B. Gonzalez (D-TX) Cosponsors: (none)	President	Certain financial information on Henry Kissinger and Henry Kissinger and Associates	Government Operations -	-
H.Res. 383 11/18/1983 Rep. Ronald V. Dellums (D-CA) Cosponsors: (22)	President	United States activities regarding Grenada	Armed Services Reported adversely 02/08/1984 H.Rept. 98-597, pt. 1 Foreign Affairs Reported adversely 02/08/1984 H.Rept. 98-597, pt. 1I	-

Table 7. (Continued)

Resolution, Introduction, and Sponsorship	Official(s) to Whom Inquiry Is Directed	Subject of Inquiry	Committee(s) of Referral and Consideration	House Floor Action
H.Res. 437 02/09/1984 Rep. Jim Courter (R-NJ) Cosponsors: (none)	President	A report by the Arms Control and Disarmament Agency entitled "A Quarter Century of Soviet Compliance Practices Under Arms Control Commitments: 1958-1983 (U)," November 1983	Foreign Affairs -	-
H.Res. 463 03/15/1984 Rep. James Michael Shannon (D- MA) Cosponsors: (none)	Secretary of State	Death squads in El Salvador including possible involvement of Roberto D'Aubuisson, a former Army officer	Foreign Affairs Reported without recommendation 04/09/1984 H.Rept. 98-658	-
H.Res. 464 03/15/1984 Rep. James Michael Shannon (D- MA) Cosponsors: (none)	Secretary of State	Possible involvement of Colonel Oscar Edgardo Casanova in the 1980 slayings of four U.S. missionaries in El Salvador, and possible involvement of Minister of Defense Eugenio Vides Casanova in the Salvadoran Government's investigation into the slayings	Foreign Affairs Reported adversely 04/09/1984 H.Rept. 98-657	-

Resolution, Introduction, and Sponsorship	Official(s) to Whom Inquiry Is Directed	Subject of Inquiry	Committee(s) of Referral and Consideration	House Floor Action
H.Res. 467 03/22/1984 Rep. James Michael Shannon (D-MA) Cosponsors: (none)	President	The CIA and death squads in El Salvador	Select Intelligence Reported adversely 04/25/1984 H.Rept. 98-709	-
H.Res. 484 04/10/1984 Rep. Edward J. Markey (D-MA) Cosponsors: (none)	President	Documents relating to: (1) certain military intelligence gathering activities in El Salvador including any possible uses of such intelligence information by El Salvador, Honduras, or Guatemala; (2) military assistance furnished to Honduras and El Salvador; and (3) activities of the United States in El Salvador and Honduras related to hostile action against Nicaragua or against the governments of those nations	Select Intelligence Reported adversely 05/10/1984 H.Rept. 98-742, pt. I Foreign Affairs Ordered reported 05/09/1984	-

Table 7. (Continued)

Resolution, Introduction, and Sponsorship	Official(s) to Whom Inquiry Is Directed	Subject of Inquiry	Committee(s) of Referral and Consideration	House Floor Action
H.Res. 168 05/13/1985 Rep. Don Edwards (D-CA) Cosponsors: (2)	Director of the Central Intelligence Agency	Covert training or other support of counterterrorist units against anti-American terrorists in Lebanon or other parts of the Middle East	Select Intelligence -	-
H.Res. 171 05/14/1985 Rep. Don Edwards (D-CA) Cosponsors: (3)	President	Counterterrorist units which received covert training or other support from the United States	Select Intelligence Reported adversely 06/12/1985 H.Rept. 99-171	-
H.Res. 226 07/17/1985 Rep. William M. Hendon (R-NC) Cosponsors: (19)	Secretary of Defense	All information, including Defense Intelligence Agency analyses, relating to live Americans in Southeast Asia	Select Intelligence Reported adversely 09/10/1985 H.Rept. 99-260, pt. I Armed Services -	-
H.Res. 395 03/11/1986 Rep. Leon Panetta (D-CA) Cosponsors: (48)	President	The use of $27,000,000 appropriated for humanitarian assistance for the Nicaraguan democratic resistance	Foreign Affairs Reported adversely 05/07/1986 H.Rept. 99-585	Laid on the table 05/07/1986

Resolution, Introduction, and Sponsorship	Official(s) to Whom Inquiry Is Directed	Subject of Inquiry	Committee(s) of Referral and Consideration	House Floor Action
H.Res. 485 06/24/1986 Rep. Ronald D. Coleman (D- TX) Cosponsors: (none)	President	Activities of Lieutenant Colonel Oliver North or any other member of the staff of the National Security Council in support of the Nicaraguan resistance	Select Intelligence - Armed Services Reported adversely 07/30/1986 H.Rept. 99-724, pt. I Foreign Affairs-	-
H.Res. 603 10/17/1986 Rep. Don Edwards (D-CA) Cosponsors: (none)	President	Any proposal by the Assistant to the President for National Security Affairs, or anyone outside of the administration, for a plan of real or illusionary events intended to destabilize the Libyan Government	Foreign Affairs -	-
H.Res. 132 03/25/1987 Rep. Richard A. Gephardt (D-MO) Cosponsors: (none)	Secretary of Defense	Documents prepared in accordance with certain report requirements in the 1985, 1986, and 1987 Department of Defense Authorization Acts relating to the Strategic Defense Initiative program and the Anti- Ballistic Missile Treaty	Armed Services Reported favorably (amended) 04/14/1987 H.Rept. 100-53	-

Table 7. (Continued)

Resolution, Introduction, and Sponsorship	Official(s) to Whom Inquiry Is Directed	Subject of Inquiry	Committee(s) of Referral and Consideration	House Floor Action
H.Res. 132 03/25/1987 Rep. Richard A. Gephardt (D-MO) Cosponsors: (none)	Secretary of Defense	Documents prepared in accordance with certain report requirements in the 1985, 1986, and 1987 Department of Defense Authorization Acts relating to the Strategic Defense Initiative program and the Anti- Ballistic Missile Treaty	Armed Services Reported favorably (amended) 04/14/1987 H.Rept. 100-53	-
H.Res. 176 05/27/1987 Rep. Fortney Pete Stark (D-CA) Cosponsors: (1)	Secretary of Energy	Contractor and national laboratory activities performed for the purpose of informing Congress on nuclear testing	Armed Services -	-

Resolution, Introduction, and Sponsorship	Official(s) to Whom Inquiry Is Directed	Subject of Inquiry	Committee(s) of Referral and Consideration	House Floor Action
H.Res. 339 12/18/1987 Rep. Bob Smith (R-NH) Cosponsors: (none)	President	Statements made by Vietnamese Vice Foreign Minister Phan Hein concerning certain civilians and members of the armed forces held as prisoners of war or considered to be missing in action since the beginning of the Vietnam Conflict	Select Intelligence Reported adversely 02/02/1988 H.Rept. 100-500	-
H.Res. 473 06/15/1988 Rep. Leon Panetta (D-CA) Cosponsors: (147)	President	U.S. foreign aid in Central America	Foreign Affairs Reported adversely 07/13/1988 H.Rept. 100-773	-
H.Res. 74 02/09/1989 Rep. Jim Courter (R-NJ) Cosponsors: (3)	Secretary of Defense	Information concerning the actions of the Commission on Base Realignment and Closure with respect to Fort Dix, New Jersey	Armed Services Reported adversely 03/15/1989 H.Rept. 101-9	-
H.Res. 76 02/09/1989 Rep. Larry J. Hopkins (R-KY) Cosponsors: (31)	Secretary of Defense	Actions of the Commission on Base Realignment and Closure with respect to specified military bases	Armed Services Reported adversely 03/15/1989 H.Rept. 101-10	-

Table 7. (Continued)

Resolution, Introduction, and Sponsorship	Official(s) to Whom Inquiry Is Directed	Subject of Inquiry	Committee(s) of Referral and Consideration	House Floor Action
H.Res. 411 06/11/1990 Rep. Henry B. Gonzalez (D-TX) Cosponsors: (1)	President	Payments made by the U.S. Government to Manuel Noriega and Guillermo Endara	Foreign Affairs- Select Intelligence -	-
H.Res. 415 06/14/1990 Rep. Bob Smith (R-NH) Cosponsors: (none)	Secretary of Defense	All unresolved, active live-sighting case files on Americans reported in captivity in Southeast Asia after February 1, 1973	Armed Services - Select Intelligence -	-
H.Res. 19 01/03/1991 Rep. Barbara Boxer (D-CA) Cosponsors: (14)	President	Statistics relating to the conduct and effect of Operation Desert Shield	Armed Services Reported without recommendation 02/20/1991 H.Rept. 102-5, pt. I Foreign Affairs Reported without recommendation 02/21/1991 H.Rept. 102-5, pt. II	Laid on the table 02/21/1991
H.Res. 198 06/16/1993 Rep. Henry J. Hyde (R-IL) Cosponsors: (4)	President	Several specified activities of the White House Travel Office	Judiciary Reported adversely 07/20/1993 H.Rept. 103-183	-

Resolution, Introduction, and Sponsorship	Official(s) to Whom Inquiry Is Directed	Subject of Inquiry	Committee(s) of Referral and Consideration	House Floor Action
H.Res. 360 02/10/1994 Rep. Jan Meyers (R-KS) Cosponsors: (14)	President	Communications between the White House and the Small Business Administration regarding Capital Management Services, Inc., or David Hale; various questions relating to the activities of Vincent Foster	Small Business- Judiciary- Post Office and Civil Service-	-
H.Res. 80 02/10/1995 Rep. Marcy Kaptur (D-OH) Cosponsors: (31)	President	The Mexican economy and certain activities of the International Monetary Fund	Banking and Financial Services Reported favorably (amended) 02/27/1995 H.Rept. 104-53	Agreed to 03/01/1995
H.Res. 334 11/13/1997 Rep. Bernard Sanders (I-VT) Cosponsors: (none)	Secretary of the Treasury	Actions taken by the Secretary of the Treasury and the United States Executive Directors at the inter-national financial institutions to comply with the requirements of 1621 of the Inter-national Financial Institutions Act, relating to encouragement of fair labor practices	Banking and Financial Services -	-

Table 7. (Continued)

Resolution, Introduction, and Sponsorship	Official(s) to Whom Inquiry Is Directed	Subject of Inquiry	Committee(s) of Referral and Consideration	House Floor Action
H.Res. 667 11/14/2000 Rep. David E. Price (D-NC) Cosponsors: (none)	President	Communications between the Archivist of the United States and the primary responsible individual in each State relating to transmission of certificates of ascertainment or of the determination of an electoral controversy involving the presidential election held on November 7, 2000	House Administration -	-
H.Res. 68 02/12/2003 Rep. Dennis J. Kucinich (D-OH) Cosponsors: (1)	President	Documents in the President's possession relating to Iraq's declaration on its weapons of mass destruct-ion that was provided to the United Nations on December 7, 2002	International Relations Reported adversely 03/18/2003 H.Rept. 108-38	-

Resolution, Introduction, and Sponsorship	Official(s) to Whom Inquiry Is Directed	Subject of Inquiry	Committee(s) of Referral and Consideration	House Floor Action
H.Res. 260 06/05/2003 Rep. Dennis J. Kucinich (D-OH) Cosponsors: (41)	President	Documents that provide specific evidence with respect to claims of Iraq's weapons of mass destruction	International Relations Reported adversely 06/23/2003 H.Rept. 108-168	-
H.Res. 286 06/19/2003 Rep. Gene Green (D-TX) Cosponsors: (14)	Secretary of Homeland Security	Any use of Federal agency resources in any task or action involving or relating to Members of the Texas Legislature in the period beginning May 11, 2003, and ending May 16, 2003	Homeland Security Reported adversely 07/21/2003 H.Rept. 108-223	-
H.Res. 287 06/19/2003 Rep. Gene Green (D-TX) Cosponsors: (14)	Attorney General	Any use of Federal agency resources in any task or action involving or relating to Members of the Texas Legislature in the period beginning May 11, 2003, and ending May 16, 2003	Judiciary Reported adversely 07/17/2003 H.Rept. 108-215	-

Table 7. (Continued)

Resolution, Introduction, and Sponsorship	Official(s) to Whom Inquiry Is Directed	Subject of Inquiry	Committee(s) of Referral and Consideration	House Floor Action
H.Res. 288 06/19/2003 Rep. Gene Green (D-TX) Cosponsors: (14)	Secretary of Transportation	Any use of Federal agency resources in any task or action involving or relating to Members of the Texas Legislature in the period beginning May 11, 2003, and ending May 16, 2003	Transportation and Infrastructure Reported adversely 07/21/2003 H.Rept. 108-220	-
H.Res. 358 09/05/2003 Rep. Robert Wexler (D-FL) Cosponsors: (12)	President	The report prepared for the Joint Chiefs of Staff entitled "Operation Iraqi Freedom Strategic Lessons Learned" and other materials relating to the Administration's planning for the reconstruction and security of post-war Iraq	Armed Services-International Relations -	-
H.Res. 364 09/09/2003	President	The report prepared for the Joint Chiefs of Staff entitled "Operation Iraqi Freedom	Armed Services Reported adversely	-

Resolution, Introduction, and Sponsorship	Official(s) to Whom Inquiry Is Directed	Subject of Inquiry	Committee(s) of Referral and Consideration	House Floor Action
Rep. Robert Wexler (D-FL) Cosponsors: (45)		Strategic Lessons Learned" and other materials relating to the Administration's planning for the reconstruction and security of post-war Iraq	10/02/2003 H.Rept. 108-289, pt. II International Relations Reported adversely10/01/2003 H.Rept. 108-289, pt. I	
H.Res. 499 01/21/2004 Rep. Rush D. Holt (D-NJ) Cosponsors: (74)	Secretary of State Secretary of Defense Attorney General	Documents in the possession of the President relating to the disclosure of the identity of Ms. Valerie Plame as an employee of the Central Intelligence Agency during the period beginning on May 6, 2003, and ending on July 31, 2003	Select Intelligence Reported adversely 02/03/2004 H.Rept. 108-413, pt. I Armed Services Reported adversely 02/27/2004 H.Rept. 108-413, pt. IV International Relations Reported adversely 02/27/2004 H.Rept. 108-413, pt. II Judiciary Reported adversely 02/27/2004 H.Rept. 108-413, pt. III	-

Table 7. (Continued)

Resolution, Introduction, and Sponsorship	Official(s) to Whom Inquiry Is Directed	Subject of Inquiry	Committee(s) of Referral and Consideration	House Floor Action
H.Res. 640 05/12/2004 Rep. Chris Bell (D-TX) Cosponsors: (40)	Secretary of Defense	Any picture, photograph, video, communication, or report produced in conjunction with any completed Department of Defense investigation conducted by Major General Antonio M. Taguba relating to allegations of torture or allegations of violations of the Geneva Conventions of 1949 at Abu Ghraib prison in Iraq	Armed Services Reported adversely 06/16/2004 H.Rept. 108-547	-
H.Res. 689 06/23/2004 Rep. John Conyers, Jr. (D-MI) Cosponsors: (47)	President Secretary of State Secretary of Defense Attorney General	Documents relating to the treatment of prisoners or detainees in Iraq, Afghanistan, or Guantanamo Bay and any instructions for handling such documents	Armed Services Reported adversely 07/22/2004 H.Rept. 108-632	-

Resolution, Introduction, and Sponsorship	Official(s) to Whom Inquiry Is Directed	Subject of Inquiry	Committee(s) of Referral and Consideration	House Floor Action
H.Res. 699 06/25/2004 Rep. John Conyers, Jr. (D-MI) Cosponsors: (49)	Secretary of State	Documents relating to the treatment of prisoners or detainees in Iraq, Afghanistan, or Guantanamo Bay and any instructions for handling such documents	International Relations Reported adversely 07/22/2004 H.Rept. 108-631	-
H.Res. 700 06/25/2004 Rep. John Conyers, Jr. (D-MI) Co-sponsors: (49)	Attorney General	Documents relating to the treatment of prisoners or detainees in Iraq, Afghanistan, or Guantanamo Bay and any instructions for handling such documents	Judiciary Reported adversely 09/07/2004 H.Rept. 108-658	-
H.Res. 745 06/25/2004 Rep. John D. Dingell (D-MI) Cosponsors: (4)	President	Specified information respecting the National Energy Policy Development Group	Energy and Commerce Reported adversely 09/23/2004 H.Rept. 108-697	-
H.Res. 776 09/15/2004 Rep. Charles B. Rangel (D-NY) Cosponsors: (4)	President Secretary of Health and Human Services	Estimated cost of the Administration's Medicare prescription drug legislation	Ways and Means Reported adversely 10/07/2004 H.Rept. 108-754, pt. I Energy and Commerce Reported adversely 10/08/2004 H.Rept. 108-754, pt. II	-

Table 7. (Continued)

Resolution, Introduction, and Sponsorship	Official(s) to Whom Inquiry Is Directed	Subject of Inquiry	Committee(s) of Referral and Consideration	House Floor Action
H.Res. 134 03/02/2005 Rep. George Miller (D-CA) Cosponsors: (none)	President	Plan assets and liabilities of single-employer pension plans	Education and the Workforce Reported adversely 04/12/2005 H.Rept. 109-34	-
H.Res. 136 03/03/2005 Rep. John Conyers, Jr. (D-MI) Cosponsors: (33)	Attorney General Secretary of Homeland Security	The security investigations and background checks relating to granting access to the White House of James D. Guckert (also known as Jeff Gannon)	Judiciary Reported adversely 04/05/2005 H.Rept. 109-30	-
H.Res. 170 03/17/2005 Rep. Dennis J. Kucinich (D-OH) Cosponsors: (39)	President	President's remarks on the Social Security trust fund	Ways and Means Reported adversely 04/27/2005 H.Rept. 109-58	-
H.Res. 363 07/14/2005 Rep. Rush Holt (D-NJ) Cosponsors: (80)	President Secretary of State Secretary of Defense Director of the CIA Attorney General	Disclosure of the identity and employment of Ms. Valerie Plame	Select Intelligence- Armed Services- International Relations;- Judiciary-	-

Resolution, Introduction, and Sponsorship	Official(s) to Whom Inquiry Is Directed	Subject of Inquiry	Committee(s) of Referral and Consideration	House Floor Action
H.Res. 375 Rep. Barbara Lee 07/21/2005 (D-CA) Cosponsors: (83)	President Secretary of State	The policy of the United States with respect to Iraq	International Relations Reported adversely 09/16/2005 H.Rept. 109-223	-
H.Res. 408 Rep. Maurice Hinchey (D-NY) 07/28/ 2005 Cosponsors: (none)	President Secretary of Defense	The policy of the United States with respect to Iraq	International Relations Reported adversely 09/16/2005 H.Rept. 109-224	-
H.Res. 417 Rep. Rush Holt (D-NJ) 07/29/2005 Cosponsors: (20)	Secretary of Defense	Disclosure of the identity and employment of Ms. Valerie Plame	Armed Services Reported adversely 09/22/2005 H.Rept. 109-234	-
H.Res. 418 Rep. Rush Holt (D-NJ) 07/29/2005 Cosponsors: (20)	President	Disclosure of the identity and employment of Ms. Valerie Plame	Select Intelligence Reported adversely 09/21/2005 H.Rept. 109-228	-
H.Res. 419 Rep. Rush Holt (D-NJ) 07/29/2005 Cosponsors: (20)	Secretary of State	Disclosure of the identity and employment of Ms. Valerie Plame	International Relations Reported adversely 09/16/2005 H.Rept. 109-225	-
H.Res. 420 Rep. Rush Holt (D-NJ) 07/29/2005 Cosponsors: (20)	Attorney General	Disclosure of the identity and employment of Ms. Valerie Plame	Judiciary Reported adversely 09/22/2005 H.Rept. 109-230	-

Table 7. (Continued)

Resolution, Introduction, and Sponsorship	Official(s) to Whom Inquiry Is Directed	Subject of Inquiry	Committee(s) of Referral and Consideration	House Floor Action
H.Res. 463 Rep. Earl Blumenauer (D-OR) 09/27/2005 Cosponsors: (15)	Secretary of Homeland Security	Reapportionment of airport screeners	Homeland Security Reported adversely 10/28/2005 H.Rept. 109-259	-
H.Res. 467 Rep. George Miller (D-CA) 09/27/2005 Cosponsors: (21)	President	Contracts for services or construction related to Hurricane Katrina recovery	Education and the Workforce Reported adversely 10/28/2005 H.Rept. 109-258	-
H.Res. 488 Rep. Steven C. LaTourette (R-OH) 10/07/2005 Cosponsors: (4)	President	Contracts for services or construction related to Hurricane Katrina recovery	Transportation and Infrastructure Reported without recommendation 11/03/2005 H.Rept. 109-269	-
H.Res. 505 Rep. Dennis J. Kucinich (D-OH) 10/20/2005 Cosponsors: (109)	President Secretary of State	White House Iraq Group	International Relations Reported adversely 11/10/2005 H.Rept. 109-291	-
H.Res. 515 Rep. Dennis J. Kucinich (D-OH) 10/26/2005 Cosponsors: (150)	President	The anticipated effects of climate change on the coastal regions of the United States	Science Reported adversely 11/15/2005 H.Rept. 109-296	-

Resolution, Introduction, and Sponsorship	Official(s) to Whom Inquiry Is Directed	Subject of Inquiry	Committee(s) of Referral and Consideration	House Floor Action
H.Res. 549 Rep. Maurice Hinchey (D-NY) 11/10/2005 Cosponsors: (2)	President	President's October 7, 2002 speech in Cincinnati, Ohio and his January 28, 2003 State of the Union Message	International Relations Reported without recommendation (amended) 12/16/2005 H.Rept. 109-351	-
H.Res. 593 Rep. Edward Markey (D-MA) 12/08/2005 Cosponsors: (3)	President Secretary of State Secretary of Defense Secretary of Homeland Security Attorney General	Extraordinary rendition of certain foreign persons	International Relations Reported adversely 02/10/2006 H.Rept. 109-374	-
H.Res. 624 Rep. Gary Ackerman (D-NY) 12/16/2005 Cosponsors: (14)	President Secretary of State	United States policies under the United Nations Convention Against Torture and Other Cruel, Inhuman or Degrading Treatment or Punishment and the Geneva Conventions	International Relations Reported adversely 02/10/2006 H.Rept. 109-375	-
H.Res. 641 Rep. Barbara Lee (D-CA) 12/18/2005 Cosponsors: 29	President	Electronic surveillance without search warrants on individuals in the United States	Select Intelligence Reported adversely 03/07/2006 H.Rept. 109-385	-

Table 7. (Continued)

Resolution, Introduction, and Sponsorship	Official(s) to Whom Inquiry Is Directed	Subject of Inquiry	Committee(s) of Referral and Consideration	House Floor Action
H.Res. 642 Rep. Barbara Lee (D-CA) 12/18/2005 Cosponsors: (13)	President Secretary of State	The Secretary of State's trip to Europe in December 2005	International Relations Reported adversely 02/10/2006 H.Rept. 109-376	-
H.Res. 643 Rep. John Conyers, Jr. (D-MI) 12/22/2005 Cosponsors: (51)	Attorney General	Warrantless electronic surveillance	Judiciary Reported adversely 03/02/2006 H.Rept. 109-382	-
H.Res. 644 Rep. Louise Slaughter (D-NY) 12/22/2005 Cosponsors: (1)	President Attorney General	Authorization of electronic surveillance of citizens of the United States without court approved warrants	Judiciary Reported adversely 03/02/2006 H.Rept. 109-383	-
H.Res. 645 Rep. Robert Wexler (D-FL) 12/22/2005 Cosponsors: (2)	President Secretary of Defense	Collection of counterterrorism intelligence information pertaining to persons inside the United States without obtaining court-ordered warrants	Armed Services Reported adversely 03/07/2006 H.Rept. 109-384	-

Resolution, Introduction, and Sponsorship	Official(s) to Whom Inquiry Is Directed	Subject of Inquiry	Committee(s) of Referral and Consideration	House Floor Action
H.Res. 685 Rep. Dennis J. Kucinich (D-OH) 02/15/2006 Cosponsors: (15)	President Secretary of State Secretary of Defense	Information relating to any entity (including the Rendon Group and the Lincoln Group) with which the United States has entered into a contract for public relations purposes concerning Iraq	Armed Services Reported adversely 03/16/2006 H.Rept. 109-397	-
H.Res. 717 Rep. Bart Gordon (D-TN) 03/09/2006 Cosponsors: (24)	Secretary of Commerce	The final draft report, produced by the professional staff of the Technology Administration, entitled: "Six-Month Assessment of Workforce Globalization In Certain Knowledge-Based Industries"	Science Reported without recommendation 04/07/2006 H.Rept. 109-415	-
H.Res. 718 Rep. Dennis J. Kucinich (D-OH) 03/09/2006 Cosponsors: (2)	President Secretary of Homeland Security	Dubai Ports World acquisition of six United States commercial ports Leases	Financial Services Reported without recommendation (amended) 04/07/2006 H.Rept109-414.	-

Table 7. (Continued)

Resolution, Introduction, and Sponsorship	Official(s) to Whom Inquiry Is Directed	Subject of Inquiry	Committee(s) of Referral and Consideration	House Floor Action
H.Res. 752 Rep. Henry A. Waxman (D-CA) 03/30/2006 Cosponsors: (11)	President	Receipt and consideration by the Executive Office of the President of any information concerning the variation between the version of S. 1932, the Deficit Reduction Act of 2005, that the House of Representatives passed on February 1, 2006, and the version of the bill that the President signed on February 8, 2006	Government Reform Reported adversely 05/09/2006 H.Rept. 109-457	-
H.Res. 809 Rep. Louise Slaughter (D-NY) 05/09/2006 Cosponsors: (none)	Secretary Homeland Security	Any existing or previous agreement between the Department of Homeland Security and Shirlington Limousine and Transportation, Incorporated of Arlington, VA	Homeland Security Reported adversely 05/25/2006 H.Rept. 109-484	-

Resolution, Introduction, and Sponsorship	Official(s) to Whom Inquiry Is Directed	Subject of Inquiry	Committee(s) of Referral and Consideration	House Floor Action
H.Res. 819 Rep. Robert Wexler (D-FL) 05/17/06 Cosponsors: (none)	President Attorney General	Requests made by the National Security Agency and other Federal agencies to telephone service providers requesting access to telephone communications records of persons in the United States	Judiciary Reported favorably 06/23/2006 H.Rept. 109-527	-
H.Res. 845 Rep. Maurice Hinchey (D-NY) 05/25/2006 Cosponsors: (8)	President, Secretary of Defense Attorney General	Department of Justice's Office of Professional Responsibility's investigation of the National Security Agency's surveillance program	Judiciary Reported adversely 06/26/2006 H.Rept. 109-528	-
H.Res. 846 Rep. Barbara Lee (D-CA) 05/25/2006 Cosponsors: (25)	President Secretary of State	Strategies and plans either designed to cause regime change in or for the use of military force against Iran	International Relations Reported adversely 06/23/2006 H.Rept. 109-526	-
H.Res. 985 Rep. Howard L. Berman (D-CA) 09/07/2006 Cosponsors: (1)	Secretary of State	Documents relating to the report submitted to a House committee on the Iran and Syria Nonproliferation Act	International Relations Reported without recommendation 09/27/2006 H.Rept. 109-689	-

Table 7. (Continued)

Resolution, Introduction, and Sponsorship	Official(s) to Whom Inquiry Is Directed	Subject of Inquiry	Committee(s) of Referral and Consideration	House Floor Action
H.Res. 1020 Rep. Edward J. Markey (D-MA) 09/20/2006 Cosponsors: (none)	Secretary of Defense	Documents relating to Maher Arar	Armed Services -	-
H.Res. 1021 Rep. Edward J. Markey (D-MA) 09/20/2006 Cosponsors: (1)	Secretary of Homeland Security	Documents relating to Maher Arar	Homeland Security-	-
H.Res. 1022 Rep. Edward J. Markey (D-MA) 09/20/2006 Cosponsors: (1)	Secretary of State	Documents relating to Maher Arar	International Relations -	-
H.Res. 1023 Rep. Edward J. Markey (D-MA) 09/20/2006 Cosponsors: (1)	President	Documents relating to Maher Arar	International Relations -	-
H.Res. 1024 Rep. Edward J. Markey (D-MA) 09/20/2006 Cosponsors: (1)	Attorney General	Documents relating to Maher Arar	Judiciary -	-
H.Res. 1043 Rep. John Conyers, Jr. (D-MI) 09/27/2006 Cosponsors: (46)	Director of National Intelligence	National Intelligence Estimate of April 2006 relating to trends in global terrorism	Select Intelligence -	-
H.Res. 1066 Rep. Dennis J. Kucinich (D-OH) 09/29/2006 Cosponsors: (15)	President	U.S. policy towards Iran	Armed Services- International Relations- Select Intelligence-	-

Resolution, Introduction, and Sponsorship	Official(s) to Whom Inquiry Is Directed	Subject of Inquiry	Committee(s) of Referral and Consideration	House Floor Action
H.Res. 251 Rep. Steven C. LaTourette (R- OH) 03/17/2009 Cosponsors: (56)	Secretary of the Treasury	Communications with the American International Group, Inc. (AIG)	Financial Services Reported favorably 04/23/2009 H.Rept. 111-84	-
H.Res. 404 Rep. Peter T. King (R-NY) 05/06/2009 Cosponsors: (14)	Secretary of Homeland Security	Documents relating to the intelligence assessment titled, "Rightwing Extremism: Current Economic and Political Climate Fueling Resurgence in Radicalization and Recruitment"	Homeland Security Reported favorably (amended) 06/04/2009 H.Rept. 111-134	-
H.Res. 446 Rep. F. James Sensenbrenner, Jr. (R-WI) 05/14/2009 Cosponsors: (none)	President Director of Environmental Protection Agency Director of Office of Management and Budget	Information relating to the EPA's finding that greenhouse gas emissions are a danger to public health and public health and welfare	Energy and Commerce -	-
H.Res. 449 Rep. F. James Sensenbrenner, Jr. (R-WI) 05/15/2009 Cosponsors: (none)	President	Information relating to the EPA's finding that greenhouse gas emissions are a danger to public health and welfare	Energy and Commerce Reported without recommendation 06/12/2009 H.Rept. 111-146	-

Table 7. (Continued)

Resolution, Introduction, and Sponsorship	Official(s) to Whom Inquiry Is Directed	Subject of Inquiry	Committee(s) of Referral and Consideration	House Floor Action
H.Res. 462 Rep. Steven C. LaTourette (R- OH) 05/20/2009 Cosponsors: (9)	President	Information relating to communications with Chrysler, L.L.C.	Energy and Commerce Reported without recommendation 06/12/2009 H.Rept. 111-147	-
H.Res. 477 Rep. J. Randy Forbes (R-VA) 05/21/2009 Cosponsors: (8)	Secretary of Defense	Information relating to the FY2010-2030 shipbuilding plan	Armed Services Reported favorably (amended) 06/19/2009 H.Rept. 111-167	-
H.Res. 478 Rep. J. Randy Forbes (R-VA) 05/21/2009 Cosponsors: (8)	Secretary of Defense	Information relating to the FY2010-2030 aviation plan	Armed Services Reported favorably (amended) 06/19/2009 H.Rept. 111-168	-
H.Res. 537 Rep. Mike J. Rogers (R-MI) 06/11/2009 Cosponsors: (3)	President Attorney General	Communications related to detainees and foreign persons suspected of terrorism	Judiciary Reported adversely 06/26/2009 H.Rept. 111-189	-
H.Res. 570 Rep. Mike J. Rogers (R-MI) 06/19/2009 Cosponsors: (3)	Secretary of Homeland Security	The immigration status of any detainees and foreign persons suspected of terrorism	Judiciary -	-

Resolution, Introduction, and Sponsorship	Official(s) to Whom Inquiry Is Directed	Subject of Inquiry	Committee(s) of Referral and Consideration	House Floor Action
H.Res. 591 Rep. John A. Boehner (R-OH) 06/26/2009 Cosponsors: (9)	President	Specific communications with and financial assistance provided to General Motors Corporation and Chrysler LLC	Financial Services Reported favorably (amended) 07/24/2009 H.Rept. 111-231	-
H.Res. 602 Rep. Mike J. Rogers (R-MI) 06/26/2009 Cosponsors: (none)	President Secretary of Defense	Communications regarding detainees and foreign persons suspected of terrorism	Armed Services Reported favorably (amended) 07/23/2009 H.Rept. 111-221	-
H.Res. 636 Rep. Frank R. Wolf (R-VA) 07/13/2009 Cosponsors: (none)	Attorney General	The transfer or release of detainees held at Naval Station, Guantanamo Bay, Cuba, into the United States	Judiciary Reported adversely 07/31/2009 H.Rept. 111-242	-
H.Res. 871 Rep. Lamar Smith (R-TX) 10/27/2009 Cosponsors: (none)	Attorney General	Information received from or referencing the American Association for Justice and any of its members since January 20, 2009, that refers or relates to any recommendation regarding medical malpractice reform	Judiciary Reported without recommendation 11/18/2009 H.Rept. 111-341	-

Table 7. (Continued)

Resolution, Introduction, and Sponsorship	Official(s) to Whom Inquiry Is Directed	Subject of Inquiry	Committee(s) of Referral and Consideration	House Floor Action
H.Res. 920 Rep. Lamar Smith (R-TX) 11/19/2009 Cosponsors: (16)	Attorney General	Detainees held at Naval Station, Guantanamo Bay, Cuba who are transferred into the United States	Judiciary Reported adversely 12/15/2009 H.Rept. 111-378	-
H.Res. 922 Rep. Peter T. King (R-NY) 11/19/2009 Cosponsors: (14)	Secretary of Homeland Security	The Department's planning, information sharing, and coordination with any state or locality receiving detainees held at Naval Station, Guantanamo Bay, Cuba	Homeland Security Reported favorably (amended) 12/15/2009 H.Rept. 111-377	-
H.Res. 923 Rep. Peter Hoekstra (R-MI) 11/19/2009 Cosponsors: (2)	President	Effects on foreign intelligence collection of the transfer of detainees held at Naval Station, Guantanamo Bay, Cuba, into the United States	Select Intelligence Reported favorably (amended) 12/16/2009 H.Rept. 111-384	-
H.Res. 924 Rep. Howard P. "Buck" McKeon (R-CA) 11/19/2009 Cosponsors: (17)	Secretary of Defense	Trial or detention of Khalid Sheikh Mohammed, Walid Muhammad Salih Mubarek Bin 'Attash, Ramzi Binalshibh, Ali Abdul Aziz Ali, or Mustafa Ahmed Adam al Hawsawi	Armed Services Reported favorably (amended) 12/17/2009 H.Rept. 111-383	-

Resolution, Introduction, and Sponsorship	Official(s) to Whom Inquiry Is Directed	Subject of Inquiry	Committee(s) of Referral and Consideration	House Floor Action
H.Res. 978 Rep. Peter Hoekstra (R-MI) 12/16/2009 Cosponsors: (none)	President	Inventory and review of intelligence related to the shooting at Fort Hood, Texas, described by the President in a memorandum dated November 10, 2009	Select Intelligence Reported adversely 01/27/2010 H.Rept. 111-402	-
H.Res. 980 Rep. Charles W. Dent (R-PA) 12/16/2009 Cosponsors: (6)	Secretary of Homeland Security	Transportation Security Administration's Aviation Security Screening Management Standard Operating Procedures manual	Homeland Security Reported adversely 01/27/2010 H.Rept. 111-403	-
H.Res. 983 Rep. Michael C. Burgess (R-TX) 12/16/2009 Cosponsors: (none)	President Secretary of Health and Human Services	Agreements and communications relating to proposed health care reform legislation	Energy and Commerce Reported without recommendation 01/29/2010 H.Rept. 111-408	-
H.Res. 985 Rep. John Boozman (R-AR) 12/16/2009 Cosponsors: (none)	Administrator of the Environmental Protection Agency	Nutrient management of the Illinois River Water-shed, Arkansas and Oklahoma	Transportation and Infrastructure -	-
H.Res. 994 Rep. Frank R. Wolf (R-VA) 012/16/ 2009 Co-sponsors: (none)	Attorney General	Decision to dismiss United States v. New Black Panther Party	Judiciary Reported adversely 01/27/2010 H.Rept. 111-404	-

Table 7. (Continued)

Resolution, Introduction, and Sponsorship	Official(s) to Whom Inquiry Is Directed	Subject of Inquiry	Committee(s) of Referral and Consideration	House Floor Action
H.Res. 995 Rep. John Boozman (R-AR) 12/19/ 2009 Co-sponsors: (none)	President	Nutrient management of the Illinois River Water-shed, Arkansas and Oklahoma	Transportation and Infrastructure Reported without recommendation (amended) 01/20/2010 H.Rept. 111-407	-
H.Res. 1238 Rep. Doc Hastings (R-WA) 04/13/2010 Cosponsors: (1)	Secretary of the Interior	The Secretary's Treasured Landscape Initiative, designation of national monuments, and high priority land-rationalization efforts	Natural Resources -	-
H.Res. 1254 Rep. Doc Hastings (R-WA) 04/15/2010 Cosponsors: (1)	Secretary of the Interior	The Secretary's Treasured Landscape Initiative, designation of national monuments, and high priority land-rationalization efforts	Natural Resources Reported without recommendation 05/11/2010 H.Rept. 111-480	-
H.Res. 1406 Rep. Doc Hastings (R-WA) 05/27/2010 Cosponsors: (1)	Secretary of the Interior	Specified information relating to the potential designation of National Monuments under the Antiquities Act	Natural Resources Reported favorably 06/23/2010 H.Rept. 111-510	-

Resolution, Introduction, and Sponsorship	Official(s) to Whom Inquiry Is Directed	Subject of Inquiry	Committee(s) of Referral and Consideration	House Floor Action
H.Res. 1455 Rep. Lamar Smith (R-TX) 06/17/2010 Cosponsors: (1)	Attorney General	Discussion of administration appointments by White House staff with any candidate for public office in exchange for such candidate's withdrawal from any election	Judiciary Reported adversely 07/15/2010 H.Rept. 111-538	-
H.Res. 1466 Rep. F. James Sensenbrenner, Jr. (R-WI) 06/22/2010 Cosponsors: (none)	President Secretary of Energy	The application to foreclose Yucca Mountain, Nevada from use as a high level nuclear waste repository	Energy and Commerce Reported without recommendation 07/19/2010 H.Rept. 111-550	-
H.Res. 1561 Rep. Michael C. Burgess (R-TX) 07/27/2010 Cosponsors: (none)	Secretary of Health and Human Services	Documents prepared by or for the Centers for Medicare & Medicaid Services regarding the Patient Protection and Affordable Care Act	Energy and Commerce Reported without recommendation 09/29/2010 H.Rept. 111-649	-

Table 7. (Continued)

Resolution, Introduction, and Sponsorship	Official(s) to Whom Inquiry Is Directed	Subject of Inquiry	Committee(s) of Referral and Consideration	House Floor Action
H.Res. 1749 Rep. Peter Hoekstra (R-MI) 12/02/2010 Cosponsors: (8)	President	Documents related to a review by the Office of the Director of National Intelligence described in a document entitled "FACT SHEET: U.S. Government Mitigation Efforts in Light of the Recent Unlawful Disclosure of Classified Information"	Select Intelligence	-
H.Res. 1763 Rep. Ileana Ros-Lehtinen (R-FL) 12/15/2010 Cosponsors: (none)	Secretary of State	Documents unlawfully disclosed and provided to WikiLeaks and select public press outlets, as referenced in a November 27, 2010, letter by a Department of State Legal Adviser	Foreign Affairs	-
H.Res. 208 Rep. Tom Cole (R-OK) 04/07/2011 Cosponsors: (14)	Secretary of Defense	Documents related to consultation with Congress regarding Operation Odyssey Dawn or military actions in or against Libya	Armed Services Reported favorably (amended) 05/12/2011 H.Rept. 112-77	-

Resolution, Introduction, and Sponsorship	Official(s) to Whom Inquiry Is Directed	Subject of Inquiry	Committee(s) of Referral and Consideration	House Floor Action
H.Res. 208 Rep. Tom Cole (R-OK) 04/07/2011 Cosponsors: (14)	Secretary of Defense	Documents related to consultation with Congress regarding Operation Odyssey Dawn or military actions in or against Libya	Armed Services Reported favorably (amended) 05/12/2011 H.Rept. 112-77	-
H.Res. 209 Rep. Tom Cole (R-OK) 04/07/2011 Cosponsors: (17)	Secretary of State	Documents related to consultation with Congress regarding Operation Odyssey Dawn or military actions in or against Libya	Foreign Affairs Reported favorably (amended) 05/12/2011 H.Rept. 112-76	
H.Res. 819 Rep. Dennis J. Kucinich (D-OH) 11/28/2012 Cosponsors: (5)	Attorney General	Documents related to the practice of targeted killing of United States citizens and targets abroad	Judiciary Reported adversely 12/18/2012 H.Rept. 112-704	-
H.Res. 645 Rep. Steve Stockman (R-TX) 06/25/2014 Cosponsors: (none)	President	Emails in the possession of the Executive Office of the President that were transmitted to or from the email account(s) of former Internal Revenue Service Exempt Organizations Division Director Lois Lerner between January 2009 and April 2011	Ways and Means Reported adversely 07/17/2014 H.Rept. 113-524	-

Table 7. (Continued)

Resolution, Introduction, and Sponsorship	Official(s) to Whom Inquiry Is Directed	Subject of Inquiry	Committee(s) of Referral and Consideration	House Floor Action
H.Res. 646 Rep. Steve Stockman (R-TX) 06/25/2014 Cosponsors: (none)	Attorney General	Emails in the possession of the Executive Office of the President that were transmitted to or from the email account(s) of former Internal Revenue Service Exempt Organizations Division Director Lois Lerner between January 2009 and April 2011	Ways and Means Reported without recommendation 07/22/2014 H.Rept. 113-545	-
H.Res. 647 Rep. Steve Stockman (R-TX) 06/25/2014 Cosponsors: (none)	Secretary of the Treasury	Emails in the possession of the Executive Office of the President that were transmitted to or from the email account(s) of former Internal Revenue Service Exempt Organizations Division Director Lois Lerner between January 2009 and April 2011	Ways and Means Reported adversely 07/17/2014 H.Rept. 113-525	-

Resolution, Introduction, and Sponsorship	Official(s) to Whom Inquiry Is Directed	Subject of Inquiry	Committee(s) of Referral and Consideration	House Floor Action
H.Res. 648 Rep. Steve Stockman (R-TX) 06/25/2014 Cosponsors: (none)	Chairman of the Federal Election Commission	Emails in the possession of the Executive Office of the President that were transmitted to or from the email account(s) of former Internal Revenue Service Exempt Organizations Division Director Lois Lerner between January 2009 and April 2011	House Administration	-
H.Res. 649 Rep. Steve Stockman (R-TX) 06/25/2014 Cosponsors: (1)	Secretary of Defense	Emails in the possession of the Executive Office of the President that were transmitted to or from the email account(s) of former Internal Revenue Service Exempt Organizations Division Director Lois Lerner between January 2009 and April 2011	Armed Services Reported without recommendation 07/22/2014 H.Rept. 113-547	-
H.Res. 111 Rep. Jerrold Nadler (D-NY) 02/09/2017 Cosponsors: (143)	Attorney General	Financial practices of the President of the United States	Judiciary Reported adversely (amended) 03/08/2017 H.Rept. 115-28	-

Table 7. (Continued)

Resolution, Introduction, and Sponsorship	Official(s) to Whom Inquiry Is Directed	Subject of Inquiry	Committee(s) of Referral and Consideration	House Floor Action
H.Res. 111 Rep. Jerrold Nadler (D-NY) 02/09/2017 Cosponsors: (143)	Attorney General	Financial practices of the President of the United States	Judiciary Reported adversely (amended) 03/08/2017 H.Rept. 115-28	-
H.Res. 154 Rep. Joseph P. Kennedy III (D-MA) 02/27/2017 Cosponsors: (20)	President Secretary of Health and Human Services	Plans to repeal or replace the Patient Protection and Affordable Care Act and the health-related measures of the Health Care and Education Reconciliation Act of 2010	Energy and Commerce Reported adversely 03/21/2017 H.Rept. 115-54	-
H.Res. 184 Rep. Hakeem S. Jeffries (D-NY) 03/09/2017 Cosponsors: (150)	President Attorney General	Communications with the government of Russia	Judiciary Reported adversely (amended) 03/31/2017 H.Rept. 115-74	-
H.Res. 186 Rep. Bill Pascrell Jr. (D-NJ) 03/09/2017 Cosponsors: (92)	Secretary of the Treasury	Tax returns and other specified financial information of President Donald J. Trump	Ways and Means Reported adversely 03/30/2017 H.Rept. 115-73	-

Resolution, Introduction, and Sponsorship	Official(s) to Whom Inquiry Is Directed	Subject of Inquiry	Committee(s) of Referral and Consideration	House Floor Action
H.Res. 203 Rep. Mike Quigley (D-IL) 03/16/2017 Cosponsors: (9)	President Attorney General	Certain communications by the President of the United States on Twitter	Judiciary Reported adversely (amended) 04/06/2017 H.Rept. 115-83	-
H.Res. 235 Rep. Bennie G. Thompson (D- MS) 03/30/2017 Cosponsors: (11)	Secretary of Homeland Security	Department of Homeland Security's research, integration, and analysis activities relating to Russian government interference in the elections for federal office held in 2016	Homeland Security Reported adversely 04/07/2017 H.Rept. 115-89	-
H.Res. 437 Rep. Peter A. DeFazio (D-OR) 07/12/2017 Cosponsors: (1)	President	General Services Administration documents relating to the lease of the Old Post Office Pavilion to the Trump Organization	Transportation and Infrastructure Reported adversely 07/27/2017 H.Rept. 115-269	-
H.Res. 442 Rep. Maxine Waters (D-CA) 07/13/2017 Cosponsors: (4)	Secretary of the Treasury	President Trump's financial connections to Russia and related information	Financial Services Reported adversely 04/28/2017 H.Rept. 115-265	-
H.Res. 446 Rep. Pramila Jayapal (D-WA) 07/14/2017 Cosponsors: (1)	President Attorney General	The removal of former Federal Bureau of Investigation Director James Comey	Judiciary Reported favorably (amended) 07/26/2017 H.Rept. 115-300	-

Table 7. (Continued)

Resolution, Introduction, and Sponsorship	Official(s) to Whom Inquiry Is Directed	Subject of Inquiry	Committee(s) of Referral and Consideration	House Floor Action
H.Res. 447 Rep. Bonnie Watson Coleman (D-NJ) 07/14/2017 Cosponsors: (5)	Secretary of Homeland Security	Department of Homeland Security policies and activities relating to businesses owned or controlled by President Donald J. Trump	Homeland Security Reported adversely 07/28/2017 H.Rept. 115-270	-
H.Res. 479 Rep. Bill Pascrell Jr. (D-NJ) 07/27/2017 Cosponsors: (8)	Secretary of the Treasury	Tax returns of each business entity disclosed by Donald J. Trump on his Office of Government Ethics Form 278e	Ways and Means Reported adversely 09/14/2017 H.Rept. 115-309	-
H.Res. 488 Rep. David N. Cicilline (D-RI) 07/28/2017 Cosponsors: (23)	Attorney General	The removal of former Federal Bureau of Investigation Director James Comey	Judiciary Reported adversely (amended) 09/28/2017 H.Rept. 115-335	-
H.Res. 555 Rep. Raul M. Grijalva (D-AZ) 10/04/2017 Cosponsors: (23)	President Secretary of State	The Trump Administration executive order on the review of designations under the Antiquities Act	Natural Resources Reported adversely (amended) 10/23/2017 H.Rept. 115-364	-

Source: CRS analysis of data from the Legislative Information System of the U.S. Congress (LIS) and relevant issues of the *Journal of the United States House of Representatives.*

Notes: Reflects activity as of October 20, 2017. For purposes of clarity and consistency, House committee reports are cited in the table using the present convention: “Congress-report number,” although reports were not designated in this way during the entire period studied. Cosponsorship of measures in the House was not permitted prior to 1967. As is discussed in more detail the report above, regardless of how a committee reports a resolution of inquiry—adversely, favorably, or without recommendation—the act of reporting within the required timeframe means that only a Member designated by the committee can call the measure up on the floor. This has occasionally led to a seemingly counterintuitive situation where a resolution of inquiry is reported favorably, perhaps in an amended form, but is still not called up on the House floor by the committee that “favors” it. The committee’s primary goal in such cases was presumably to retain control of the legislation and, perhaps, to avoid certain difficult votes during the markup of the resolution.

INDEX

G

H

I

J

K

L

M

N

S

T

U

V

W

Civil Liberties: Overview, Issues and Trends

Author: Stefan Connell

Series: American Political, Economic, and Security Issues

Book Description: This book examines data privacy and protection in the EU and the US.

eBook ISBN: 978-1-53614-193-1
Retail Price: $82

Government Transparency and Secrecy: Measures, Access, and Policies

Editors: Grant Faulconer and Aiden Dashaw

Series: Government Procedures and Operations

Book Description: This book first assesses the meaning of transparency and subsequently examines the statutes, initiatives, requirements, and other actions that make information more available to the public or protect if from public release.

Hardcover ISBN: 978-1-62417-773-6
Retail Price: $145